TALES AND TRANSFORMATIONS

*Stories in Families
and
Family Therapy*

By the same author

Rituals in Families and Family Therapy
(edited with Evan Imber-Black and Richard Whiting)

Rituals for Our Times: Celebrating, Healing, and Changing Our Lives and Our Relationships
(with Evan Imber-Black)

A NORTON PROFESSIONAL BOOK

TALES AND TRANSFORMATIONS

Stories in Families
and
Family Therapy

Janine Roberts

W. W. NORTON & COMPANY • NEW YORK • LONDON

Copyright © 1994 by Janine Roberts

Printed in the United States of America

First Edition

Composition by Bytheway Typesetting Services, Inc.
Manufacturing by Haddon Craftsmen, Inc.

Library of Congress Cataloging in Publication Data

Roberts, Janine, 1947–
    Tales and transformations : stories in families and family therapy
/ Janine Roberts.
        p. cm.
    "A Norton professional book."
    Includes bibliographical references and index.
    ISBN 0-393-70174-3
    1. Family psychotherapy.   2. Storytelling—Therapeutic use.
I. Title.
RC488.5.R64   1994
616.89'156—dc20   94-13506   CIP

W. W. Norton & Company, Inc., 500 Fifth Avenue, New York, NY 10110
W. W. Norton & Company, Ltd., 10 Coptic Street, London WC1A 1PU

1 2 3 4 5 6 7 8 9 0

To the next generation, especially Natalya, Jesse,
Heather, Jill, and Davina:

May your stories, and the stories of all around the world,
be told, listened to, and heard.

CONTENTS

Acknowledgments   ix

Introduction: We All Have Stories to Tell   xiii

1   The Power of Stories   1
    Speaking with Stories   1
    Thinking in Stories   5
    Listening, Telling, and the Interaction Between   8
    Exploring Story Styles   11
    The Power of Stories in Therapy   21

2   In Their Own Words: The Use of Stories with
    Families in Therapy   23
    Stories and Family Therapy: A Brief History   23
    Family Stories: A Natural Resource   28
    Lore and Listening: Ways to Think About Stories in
      the Therapy Process   43
    Story Domains: Private, Public, and Some of Each   50
    Story Reserves   55

3   Meaning-Making and Stories: Voice, Time, Memory
    and Imagination   56
    Voice, Agency, and Possession   56
    Time: All Kinds of It   63
    Memory : Different Slices of It   67

Imagination: From the Singular to the Collective   71
Changing Stories: Voice, Time, Memory, and Imagination   71

4   Spoken Stories: Spontaneity and Immediacy   76
Allegations, Alligators, and Investigations   76
Three Story Forms: Spoken, Written, and Enacted   81
Spoken Stories: Tellers, Listeners, and In Between   84
Spoken Stories: Spontaneity and Immediacy   96

5   Written and Enacted Stories   98
Written Stories: The Power of the Word   98
Enacted Stories: Telling and Doing at the Same Time   115
Tales and Transformations   121

6   Cultural Stories: The Crucible for Personal Stories   123
Double-Sided Life   123
Interlacing Cultural and Personal Stories   129
Techniques for Accessing Cultural, Political, and
    Social Contexts   133
Back to Interlacing: How Personal Stories Inform
    Cultural Stories   144

7   Training Therapists: Listening to, Shaping,
and Elaborating Stories   147
The Sound of Silence: Exercises for Listening   150
Shaping and Elaborating Stories: Exercises for
    Story Facilitation   163
Tales of Others, Tales of One's Own: Working with
    Extended Story Frames   170
The Sagas Continue   181

8   Telling Tales Outside of the Therapy Room   183
Stories and Super Vision   185
Stories and Organizations: Telling It Like It Is   193
Communities and Stories: Braiding Individual, Family,
    and Community Tales   200
Interweaving Stories   209

Appendix: Selected List of Family Literature   213

References   217

Index   223

ACKNOWLEDGMENTS

THIS BOOK WOULD NOT have been possible without the ever-present support of my friend and mentor, Evan Imber-Black, Ph.D. Immeasurable thanks to Evan for her careful reading of each chapter—her feedback helped to sharpen and clarify my ideas and writing, and her enthusiasm gave me the energy and impetus to keep going. I am also grateful for the clinical work I have done with Richard Whiting, Ed.D., Georgi Lockerman, M.S., Judy Davis, Ed.D., Molly Scott, M.Ed., Deborah Marshall, M.S., Peg Giffels, M.Ed., and Audrey Tolman, M.S. Both doing the work and presenting on it gave me many opportunities to learn from them, try out ideas, and expand my own thinking. Alisa Beaver, M.Ed., Kumiko Ide, M.Ed., Pilar Hernandez, M.Ed., and Jennifer Iré, M.P.P.M., read and gave me thoughtful insights and comments on Chapters 4 and 5. I am most appreciative.

Research and vibrant writing on family stories by Elizabeth Stone, Ph.D. both inspired me in this work and helped me to understand the range of ways family stories connect us to our heritage while at the same time help us reach for new ways to be in the world. The ongoing work with stories by Joan Laird, M.S.W., with its emphasis on cultural perspective and with its deep awareness of gender themes, always informed me. Participants in the group I facilitated on stories, myths, and rituals at the International Women's Colloquium (Denmark, May, 1991) reaffirmed for me the power of stories to connect lives across time, place, and political boundaries, and to illuminate each person's distinct and unique experiences. Thank you. Special thanks to Juan Luis Linares, M.D., Yolanda Gomez Fontanil, Ph.D., and Esteban Coto Ezama, Ph.D., and their colleagues at CICOM in Oviedo, Spain, and to Helena Nikolaeva, Ph.D., Li Chieh, Ph.D., and the faculty and staff of Harmony Institute in St. Petersburg for their caring and collaborative work and friendship. To the many workshop participants, both here and overseas, who shared their stories, questions and ideas—deep thanks for all the ways you helped me articulate and better understand this work.

Susan Munro, from her first chronicling of stories about her own life, to her dream about me in which I told her I had an idea for a book, to her support and enthusiasm for this project from its inception, and to her meticulous and caring editing, has helped me develop in many ways as a writer. My heartfelt thanks. I feel very fortunate, too, to have worked with Regina Dahlgren Ardini. Her positive response to the final manuscript and thoughtful editing helped me greatly to focus and polish the last rewrites.

Thanks go to Jo Robinson for always being there ready to answer any questions about writing, editing, and publishing. Her advice was reliable, encouraging, and reassuring. Jerry Weinstein's computer expertise was invaluable and saved me at innumerable crucial moments. Doris and Lazlo Tikos, the Priest-Levy family, Arleen Thomson, and the Zeitlins, thank you for all the nurturance and sharing of family life.

The most sustaining support I have had over the last 12 years is from my daughter Natalya Zoë, who always asked me one more time to tell a story. Natalya stretched my mind with her requests— and helped me go deeper into memory and imagination. Jesse and Heather: Thank you for your openness and deep capacity to share your stories and create new ones together. My three children: Stories have shepherded us through myriad changes in our lives, and as you enter into your teenage years I hope they continue to do so. My sister, Tanya, with all her family history explores, has opened up a whole new trove of family stories. Uncle Paul's (better known as Dr. Photo or, more recently, as Dr. Click) photographs of historical family events as well as our current gatherings are incredible artifacts that help us remember and stimulate family storytelling. ¡Mil gracias to both of them! To my husband, David,

ACKNOWLEDGMENTS

I give deepest thanks for cheering me on, reading all the chapters, and committing so much of his time and energy to research, tell, and connect our family stories, both past and present.

None of the work in this book would have been possible without the generous and extensive recounting of their stories by clients, trainees, friends, workshop participants, family members, and colleagues. These stories moved me, kept me going when I was tired, and continuously reminded me of the capacity of stories to reclaim and make meaning of our lives. It is their voices, recollections, and hopes for the future that enabled this book to come to life.

INTRODUCTION:
WE ALL HAVE STORIES TO TELL

> Our meanings are almost always inseparable from stories, in
> all realms of life. And, once again family stories, invisible as
> air, weightless as dreams, are there for us. To make our own
> meanings out of our myriad stories is to achieve balance—at
> once a way to be part of and apart from our families, a way of
> holding on and letting go.
>
> —*Elizabeth Stone (1988, p. 244)*

FAMILY STORIES ARE A RICH RESOURCE in therapy that help us
understand who we are, and at the same time they can be used as
blueprints to rework and change who we are. This is a book about
bringing forth our tales, whether in spoken, written, or enacted
form, and helping people to possess them. As people tap into the
power of stories and restore the flow of meaning between past,
present, and future, they begin to access memory and imagination;
they find their own voice, break silenced stories, elaborate minimal stories, open rigid tales, and change vantage points from
which to tell and undertand stories. Thus, this is also a book
about the contexts in which our tales are told and how these
contexts support or suppress the telling of and listening to stories.

Lavinia Lockhart, mother of 22 children, was one of the first to
teach me about the possibilities of stories. I met her in 1965 in
Newark, New Jersey, through her nine-year-old twins, Kevin and
Keith. I was introduced to Kevin and Keith at their school where I

was working with the nurse as a VISTA Volunteer. Kevin came walking down the hall with his feet splayed out and his knees pressed together to try to give his legs enough support to hold him up. Beside him was Keith—almost a full head and a half shorter than Kevin. His legs had just not grown—they didn't fit the proportions of the rest of his body. His classmates called him "Little Man." It fit. Both boys had rickets and the nurse wanted me to work with their mother, Lavinia, to see if they could get treatment. The family had no phone, so the next day I walked over to their apartment.

After I explained who I was through the door, Lavinia undid the locks and let me in. "Come in, come in," she said. She cleared some clothing off a yellow vinyl chair. "Sit down. Just let me get my pocketbook." She snapped it open and out of a large black purse pulled out an old plastic sheet and handed it to me. It was cracked around the edges and had that dull overcast to it that plastic gets when it is handled a lot. Inside was a yellowed piece of newspaper. I took it out carefully.

"That's me holding Kevin and Keith when they were born." Lavinia pointed to the picture at the top of the clipping. "And it tells the story of how I had more children than anyone else in the city—22—including three sets of twins." She grinned at me. "You read it," she said. Lavinia stood next to me, watching me carefully as I read. Thus began my introduction to this woman who had been born in the South to a sharecropper's family and who had come north as a young woman looking for a better life. I found out later that Lavinia did not know how to read. As a child, she had worked in the cotton fields and had not been able to go to school. But she didn't tell me that now. She wanted me to read and see that her story was important—important enough for her to be interviewed and written up in the Newark Evening News. She never left her apartment without that clipping.

We all need to be seen and heard, to be known for our unique life experiences. We all carry our stories with us and when we tell them to others they have the power to link us together. Over the years that I have been an actress, teacher, then family therapist, the story of Lavinia and her children has stayed with me as a reminder of how central a role our stories play to pull together the events of our lives and connect us to others. As Lavinia watched and listened to see how I would hear and react to her story, and I in turn watched and listened to her response, we began to see what kind of relationship we could have together.

In family therapy, as clients tell, write, and read the texts of their lives, their stories become a wonderfully versatile tool that helps them reflect on where they have been, where they want to go to, as well as creates a collaborative therapeutic relationship. In this mobile society, regardless of the changes of locations and varieties of transitions in families, people always have their stories with them. Furthermore, work with stories can be done with any model of treatment and is a dynamic technique that can be used with a wide range of ages.

This book is about ways therapists can support clients in accessing their everyday stories. The focus is not on teaching therapists how to create and tell therapeutic stories, but rather it is on enhancing the clients' reflective and inventive capacities for making therapeutic use of their own tales. Therapists' stories as a rich resource for both therapy and training are explored as well. Particular attention is paid to the needs of today's unique configurations of families.

Chapter 1 explores the ways people think in stories, categorizes stories into six styles, and discusses their significance for clients—how they have access to time, are located in relation to events in their lives, and what possibilities for making meaning are opened up or closed down. Different ideas on how therapists can respond to stories, depending on the story style, are also presented. Chapters 2 and 3 delve into the history of the use of stories in family therapy, along with ways for using everyday stories as a resource in therapy. Also, the issues of control over one's story that can arise when stories move in and out of public and private domains are explored. Voice, time, memory, and imagination are scrutinized as key ingredients in the storying process.

Chapters 4 and 5 look at the distinctive contributions that spoken, written, and enacted stories make in treatment. The immediacy and rich vocal cues of oral stories are contrasted with the documentation and symbolic possibilities of written stories. The vibrancy of enacted stories, where the teller is both in the story and telling it at the same time, is investigated. Fifteen different techniques for eliciting and working with stories in different mediums are described and illustrated with case examples.

The last three chapters look at stories through a wider lens. Chapter 6 examines cultural stories, which provide the crucible for personal stories. A number of strategies for helping people understand how society frames and impacts their stories are described — strategies such as noting historical time lines, looking for migration and identity stories, and moving stories through time and telling them from different perspectives. Chapter 7 addresses the uses of stories in training. A range of exercises for looking at the complexities of listening in family therapy and developing listening skills are presented first. Then, many of the traditional training modalities, such as use of genograms, photos, and floor plans, are recast in a narrative frame. In addition, ways to use literature, analyses of trainees' personal stories, and hearing other's stories to make sense of one's own, are presented. As trainees experience the power of the story to reflect upon and understand their life and work and that of their colleagues, they are more likely to be drawn to and understand ways for using them in therapy. Chapter 8 moves out into the community to look at resources that support families' and therapists' telling stories beyond the therapy room. The ways stories can be used in supervision, oral history, theater, and in agencies and professional organizations are all examined. Looking at how tales are told outside of therapy can rejuvenate therapeutic work and give therapists other ways to understand and expand it.

I hope this book supports you in your work, as the stories I have heard and the people that have told them to me have supported me. And may it help you create the blueprints that will lead you to our own stories as well as to those of others.

Going home the longest way around,
we tell stories, build
from fragments of our lives
maps to guide us to each other.
  — Schneider (1993, p. 73)

Janine Roberts
Longview House
Leverett, Massachusetts

TALES AND TRANSFORMATIONS

Stories in Families
and
Family Therapy

1
THE POWER OF STORIES

Storytelling is a personal art that makes public what is private and makes private what is public.

— *Jane Yolen (1986, p. 13)*

I did not ask for the stories, but I was given them to tell, to retell and change and pass along. (Each one teach one, pass it on, pass it on.)

— *Lorene Carey (1991, p. 237)*

Speaking with Stories

EVERYONE CREATES, TELLS, listens to, changes, and retells stories. As stories are told, people name and shape the meaning of the daily events of their lives and communicate that meaning to others. Voice is given to their unique experience; then, through familial and community stories, voices are shared and joined. Stories allow for both continuity and change. Heritage is passed on, even as new tellers and listeners reshape and call forth different concerns, issues, and details.

Family stories also capture the particular events of a group of people as they live through the larger social, political, and economic changes of each era. They offer possibilities both to interpret and to make meaning of individual lives and family dynamics, while at the same time observing the influences of historical occurrences upon their lives. Take, for instance, several stories that are told about Julia Ward Howe, the Boston abolititionist and writer who lived from 1819 to 1910. One story tells how her husband took the considerable family wealth that she brought to the marriage out of her control and invested and handled it himself. Then, when he died in 1876, he did not leave the money and other financial resources of his estate to her. Ms. Howe became a well-known public speaker in part because she had to go on the road to support herself and her children. This story tells of her individual dilemma as well as women's problems regarding securing property rights and protection of their monetary resources. Another story about Julia Ward Howe tells how she became estranged from her brother because he supported the south in the Civil War while she supported the north and actively spoke out against slavery. The differences within her nuclear family mirrored divisions within families that were occurring all over the United States and reflected the political split in the nation.

Stories do not stay static over time. They continue to change as they are reworked in the context of other events, as they are told by new tellers, and as other interpretations become available to people. Shifts of meaning in a central family story are elegantly described by Lorene Carey in her autobiography *Black Ice*. In discussing the distance between men and women in her family, Ms. Carey recounts a central family story about Izzy, told by her great grandfather Pap.

> "There's a man whose daughter is standing at the top of some steps," he began, "and the child's name is Izzy. Now the father told the girl to jump down the steps, jump down to where he was. 'Jump, Izzy, jump,' he said. 'Papa's got you. Papa'll catch you.'
>
> "But she's scared. 'I'll fall, Papa,' she says.
>
> "But he answers her, his voice so gentle, so strong: 'Papa wouldn't let you fall. Don't be afraid. Come on now, jump, Izzy, jump.'
>
> "Finally the child gathers up her courage and jumps. She leaps towards her daddy's arms—and her father, he steps aside. The child falls, of course. She falls down on that hard ground, and it hurts. She's scraped herself, and it hurts. Her daddy helps her up and dries her tears, and she cries to him and cries and asks him, 'Papa, why didn't you catch me, Papa? Why did you let me fall? You said to jump, Papa, and I jumped.'

"'And he says to her, 'Listen to me, Izzy, and listen carefully. Learn this once and never forget: Trust no man.'"

Ms. Carey goes on to describe how she and other family members "learned the lesson and whispered it into each other's ears like poison. 'Jump, Izzy, jump,' we said when one of us fell short, and then we laughed the grim, hysterical laughter of caretakers whom no one took care of" (1991, p. 132).

In 1972, Ms. Carey, an African-American woman, left Philadelphia to attend the formerly all-white, all-male elite St. Paul's prep school in New Hampshire. For a while she used the image of Izzy to fashion a stance to protect herself at the school—to "trust no man." But over time, the story began to change.

> This time Izzy will jump of her own will when her legs have grown strong enough to absorb the shock; she will not lie on the ground, splayed out alone, crippled by distrust. She will learn how to jump through life, big, giant jumps. She'll fall, and get up again. Up, Izzy, up. Paint, dance, read, sing, skate, write, climb, fly. Remember it all, and come tell us about it. (1991, pp. 237–238)

Ms. Carey eloquently describes how her family stories located and gave her a sense of her history that was never taught at the New England boarding school, and at the same time helped her find her way out. She used the story of Izzy to understand family dynamics in the past, to interpret a stance that worked for her at St. Paul's, and finally to provide the main character and action for her new story. The story was reworked as she lived through the seventies and eighties and has developed into her own version of what is possible for women.

We do not always voice our stories as directly as Lorene Carey does, and we may not always be as aware of how we braid our individual stories with our family stories, but when we can do this, the power of stories to articulate multigenerational links over time is evident. They connect us with our history while providing us with vivid images, words, and scenarios to tell our own stories.

The story format also offers powerful possibilities to move between past, present, and future. Characters can be easily moved through time, new ideas introduced, and endings reworked and/or changed. We can locate ourselves in different positions in our stories in relation to how we appropriate and anticipate past, present, and future (Crites, 1986). There is a resonance, an echoing of themes and issues, that helps us to understand that in the present we are always carrying our past as well as imagining our future. The present is the pivot point linking past and future.

In stories we can express how we live with our past, present, and future simultaneously. When family members come to therapy and share central family stories, they quickly reveal key beliefs and themes, relationship dynamics, and how they make meaning of the events in their lives.

NO FOSTER CARE FOR MY CHILDREN.   Ten minutes into her first family therapy session (with her four children ranging in age from six months to fifteen years), Vera Moscone said, "I was a foster child. My dad disappeared, my mom turned me over to the state when I was six years old. I lived with a lot of different families—some good and some pretty bad. And one thing, I'll never let my children ever go into foster care, no matter what. I *know* what it's like." This was a key story in Vera's life, one that informed her view of herself in relation to her children, as well as her ideas about family. It helped explain how she managed to keep them all together through the death of her first husband, divorce from her second, and now a separation from her third.

To understand what kind of family story was being created, the therapist asked the older children how they had taken this story into their own lives. "How did it make you feel to hear about your mother's life before? When did you first hear this story? What did it mean to you? How did it or did it not connect to your own lives?" The eight-year-old daughter shared that she had always known this story, and that it made her feel sad. The oldest son, Zach, explained how the story made him feel safe: No matter what happened in the future, his mother would always be with them. But he also described how it made him feel like he needed to protect his mother, because she had been through a lot.

Vera was surprised at the different ways the children felt about the story. She used the story to remember her strengths, to get her through her hardest moments—to remind herself that, no matter what, she had to be there for the family.

Family members and the therapist started the process of looking at how they viewed themselves and/or each other through the various lenses of this story and wove together some of the meaning of their family life. With this story, they began to describe the different ways they linked the past, present, and future. The past story gave Vera a clear mandate for the future: She would never give her children up, no matter what happened. It reassured the children of their future with their mother, but also made them concerned about what she had gone through in the past.

Thinking in Stories

> This is what we do as we hear a storyteller speak: let our own imagination, our past experiences, our various passions and problems, help form images that accompany the words we're hearing.
>
> — *Robert Coles (1990, p. 334)*

Our minds retrieve, remember, and focus much of the information we take in each day in the form of stories. As Shank states, "Human memory is story-based" (1990, p. 12). We can access numerous complex experiences through the stories we tell. Because stories have many indices (such as place, central dilemma, resolution of a problem, sensory data), they help us with the central task of thinking called indexing. In order to work with new information, we need a place to connect it somewhere in our memory. As we think, we are constantly linking new ideas to previous experiences. Stories provide a wealth of indices with which to connect information on different levels or in different ways (Shank, 1990). Because each person carries a unique set of life experiences, stories provide multiple possibilities for each individual to make meaning of them. And hearing one story usually triggers another story. This is sometimes an unspoken process, where the individual scans the story in his or her mind but does not share it. Other times, it is shared immediately or later on.

When my daughter, Natalya, was ten, she was the tester of the new rope swing that had been hooked up in the top of a tree by her stepbrother. Shortly after she got on the swing, the rope slipped and sent her crashing eight feet to the ground. She bashed her mouth and left knee up pretty badly and broke her two front teeth. There was a lot of blood. In the following weeks, as we told the story of what had happened to her, we heard a multitude of previously untold broken-front-teeth stories, as well as stories about other accidents, tree-falls, and bloody traumas. The most intriguing story we heard was one about Natalya's godfather. Even though we have had contact with him two or three times a month since she was born, we had never heard this story before.

The Grey Goose and the Silver Tooth

In Hungary in 1942, in the city of Debrecen, Lazlo Tikos was a boy of ten. Because of World War II, there was no rubber available and he was out in the street playing kickball with a rock. The stone was kicked up and hit him square in the mouth, knocking out one of his front teeth. When he appeared at his doorstep, his mother said, "Oh my God, with the war on, we have no money for the dentist—what are we going to do?" Two days later found her and Lazlo walking down the street with a grey goose under her arm. In exchange for the goose, the dentist put a silver tooth in Lazlo. He had it for about twenty years until one day, after he had escaped to the United States (after the 1956 uprising), it fell out and he had it replaced with a regular white tooth.

Natalya's story triggered many other stories, reminding some people of things they had not thought of in years. Key indices in the story ("accident," "teeth," "tree," "falling," "blood") connected with many experiences in the minds of others. They responded to her story by telling their own stories—often saying things to connect with her, such as, "I couldn't bite with my front teeth either, that was so hard," or "I was in shock after I fell—were you?" As the stories were told, people demonstrated our shared human vulnerability to accidents and unpredictability. This had the effect of supporting Natalya and me through the trauma as well as "normalizing" the fall. We felt their empathy as they imagined Natalya's scenario. At the same time, here were our friends, family, and acquaintances all telling us their stories with only a few scars to show. Their teeth and other parts of their bodies were healed and they were fine. We were reassured that, over time, this would happen with Natalya as well.

Since it is impossible to talk about a problem without telling a story, stories are central to therapy. In the telling, the teller positions herself or himself in relation to the story themes, as well as to other people involved in the story, and what they think might change the story. People connect and make meaning of the events in their lives and express their values, beliefs, and visions through the stories they tell.

SAME EVENTS, TWO STORIES.   Nydia Mata-Rosario entered couples therapy telling the story of a marriage that involved moving year after year because of her husband's job. She felt as though she had followed him, torn up her roots for the family, and now she wanted him to do some particular things for her. It was, she said, "her turn." She also talked about how she found herself looking for more attention outside of the marriage when she did not find it within the relationship. Nydia presented moving as central to the problem of their marriage and positioned herself in relation to her husband by asking him to do something differently. And if he wouldn't, she implied she would.

Eduardo Rosario had a different version of the same story. He felt that he had never forced Nydia to move—that she had wanted the upward mobility that the job promotions guaranteed. Moreover, at this point in his career, during a national recession that had forced job lay-offs in his company, he was currently really working two jobs within the organization. Eduardo said to Nydia, "I'm very stressed by work right now. This is the worst possible time for you to put pressure on me. I need you to back off. And I get concerned that you are threatening me with an affair when you say you'll get attention elsewhere." He offered a different meaning for the moves in the marriage—that both wanted the upward mobility that the job changes made possible. There is not a lot he feels he has to give right now, and he feels threatened. He interpreted Nydia's statement that she will look for attention outside of the marriage as alluding to an affair.

Same events, two different stories, so what should a therapist do? Therapists need to let the multitude of perspectives that clients bring be told, hold them, and then help them construct new meanings that work better for them and in their relationships with others. Feedback from clients about what was useful in family therapy almost always includes comments like:

> It was a place where we could come and put out our different views and not get into a fight about it. You helped us really listen to each other.

> You didn't take sides.

> We needed someone like you who didn't already have a set version of the right story.

How the therapist positions herself or himself in relation to stories is crucial. She or he needs to help clients elaborate their stories, hear them out fully, and help them hear each other. Family members may then be able to begin the process of listening to themselves and each other differently, to perceive different facets of the stories, or to see where their stories have gotten stuck.

Listening, Telling, and the Interaction Between

By listening to a particularly individual pattern of words, catching a tell-tale emphasis, or recognizing that something is being said which the speaker may not ever have been able to say before, there is a recognition of the infinite possibilities and experiences lying just under the surface of things.

—*Ronald Blythe (1983, p. 38)*

The stupendous reality that is language cannot be understood unless we begin by observing that speech consists above all in silences. A being who could not renounce saying many things would be incapable of speaking. And each language represents a different equation between manifestations and silences. Each people leaves some things unsaid *in order* to be able to say others. Because *everything* would be unsayable. Hence the immense difficulty of translation: translation is a matter of saying in a language precisely what that language tends to pass over in silence.

—*Jose Ortega y Gasset,* Man and Nature
(cited in Becker, 1991, p. 226)

In the field of family therapy, with so much focus on directive interventions by the therapist (as in structural and strategic models), or on the kinds of questions the therapist asks (Milan model and solution-focused work), or on the role of the therapist in articulating multigenerational patterns (Bowenian), we have talked little about the elements of listening or witnessing in treatment. There has been even less discussion about what happens as people hear themselves speaking their story out loud, or on the sound of silence. Yet this is an essential part of the storytelling process since different stories are told depending on who is or is not listening and what can or cannot be said. Recounting a story out loud for people to hear is different from telling or writing it to oneself. There are important distinctions that need to be made between silence that invites talk and silence that pushes stories underground.

Laird (1993), one of the few family therapists writing about silence, makes distinctions between different ways in which stories, particularly women's stories, may have become unspeakable or silenced. There may be no language to describe events such as torture, genocide, or severe abuse and trauma. Words may misdescribe the events because they cannot capture the horror of them. Stories may have been silenced because of male privilege, control of media, print and other forms of communication. Abusers may threaten and/or hurt their victims to keep them silent about violence, sexual molestation, and incest. Out of fear for their own safety, victims may not speak. Laird highlights the importance of paying attention to the unspoken, for it is the continuous backdrop for that which can be told. A therapist needs to listen for the unsaid.

Listening in family therapy also presents unique challenges because usually more than one person is being listened to in the presence of others. As the therapist encourages one person to talk, other family members are listening as well as observing how the therapist hears the member who is talking. The therapist has to demonstrate a deep and respectful ability to listen to people of a wide range of ages, across a multitude of issues, and in a setting where they are always being "watched." People will choose what to share from their lives depending on how they feel they are being heard and how they see others being listened to.

Our minds are constantly involved in internal dialogues and visualizations. When we speak, we share only a small portion of our experiences. People talk about "thinking out loud"; there seems to be a way in which the mind often coheres and connects things it hears being spoken in a new way. The same story is never told twice; depending on the audience, the place, the responses of the listeners, and the questions, it will be modified and retold differently.

I first became intrigued with stories in the therapy process from the comments that families consistently made while they were in treatment. They would say, "This is the only place we have to sit and really tell our story—about what has happened to us," or "We don't do things in our daily life outside of here that help us piece these parts together." I began to see how therapy helped them to voice what was unique about their family—to tell their family story, especially when because of conflict or trauma or disagreement they had been unable to hear each other out.

The power of discovering one's own voice comes through dramatically in the book *The Courage to Heal* (Bass & Davis, 1988), a collection of stories by women survivors of child sexual abuse, most of which had been silenced for many years. Throughout the book, the authors describe the experience of being really listened to and believed as transformative. They are able to move beyond the isolation of shame and secrecy into a place where their feelings and experiences are authenticated—and where they are now connected with a courageous community of women who broke the silence.

There may be multiple levels to the telling. As Ella, a survivor who has told her story many times, described:

> For me, there were at least three different levels of telling. The first was telling the story and not feeling anything. Telling it as a third-party story. Saying "I" but not really meaning it happened to me. At that point I still didn't really believe it happened. And part of that telling was that I was really angry. It was a way to get back at them. Like "I'm going to tell on you." It's kind of like "I couldn't get anybody mad at you then, but watch this!"
>
> Then there was a really painful, scared level of telling. The tone of my voice changed and I looked like I was seven years old. My

language was more simple. And it hurt. That's the place I discovered my feelings. And usually people got sad when they heard it that way. They felt sorry for me. The people I told that way included my therapist, my close friend, people in caretaker positions, paid or unpaid. It included the people in my support group. I told not like a victim, but like a little kid that hurt.

The last way I've told has to do with stepping back and seeing the bigger picture. I looked at family dynamics and got the rest of the story. I saw what happened and why it happened. I put the abuse through a sieve and was able to see parts of it I couldn't see when I was only hurt or angry.

So I went from anger to pain to a fixing. In Hebrew there's a word, *tikun*, that means a fixing, a healing. That way of telling was a *tikun*. (p. 98)

The telling changes with different emotional states of the teller. The speaking itself takes people beyond their interior life, making it possible to hear *how* they tell the story as well as *what parts* of their experiences they choose as being the most salient. They are at the center of the storytelling, and as they thread the narrative together, their experience is distinguished from all others. As the story becomes situated, so does the teller.

The telling also changes with different listeners. Listeners provide confirmation of reality; they can also help the listener elaborate, expand, or tell the story from different perspectives. Tellers and listeners share both the spoken and the unspoken. Silence and pauses are an essential part of the rhythm of telling. Just as music cannot exist without rests, stories cannot exist without silence and the unsaid. The unspoken provides the backdrop for what is spoken.

Exploring Story Styles

The task of the storyteller is fashioning "the raw material of experience, his (sic) own and that of others, in a solid, useful, and unique way."

— *Walter Benjamin (1969, p. 108)*

How a therapist helps family members look at their stories can be quite different, depending on the role stories have or have not taken in their lives. As a way to make some distinctions between how the telling of stories occurs, it can be useful to think of six broad categories of story styles. The form of the story can be as revealing as the content. How stories are shared directly influences the meaning making possibilities of the tales.

Sometimes family members come in with very *intertwined* stories, so that events that occurred at one time are used to interpret other circumstances. Other families present with very isolated or *separated* stories, where they don't see the connections between parallel incidents. Story resources may not be readily available to families in one or more parts of their lives because they have been *minimized* or *interrupted*. Or the stories may have been *silenced* or kept hidden or secret. *Rigid* stories are told the same way over and over and may lead to a set meaning of key events. In other parts of people's lives, stories may have *evolved* and developed flexibly over time, giving them access to different ways to examine their experiences. Table 1 summarizes these six story styles.

It can be useful for a family therapist to think about what ways stories are or are not available to family members or others. When stories are fashioned and shared genuinely, we are intrigued and engaged. We often empathize with others' situations and in our imagination see them in different locales, at other times in their life, and in other situations.

Intertwined Stories

Yvette Crooms, the youngest of four children, told the story of how she was teased unmercifully by her older sister when she was growing up. Now, when she watches her oldest daughter tease her youngest child, Dennis, she wants to defend him against her. She finds herself jumping into the middle of their disagreements and upsets to "protect" Dennis. Watching their interaction triggers her memories of her own experience. Meanwhile, the children express that they have little space to settle their fights themselves. As the family examines these two stories, Yvette begins to see how she is responding to present interactions based on past needs.

With intertwined stories, the therapist needs to help clients respect the integrity of each story, to let each story stand on its own, while at the same time helping clients note the similarities and

Table 1. *Story Styles*

Intertwined
- One story resonates with another; time is not bounded
- Focus is on the parallels between situations/lives/life events or on making/defining the story as the *opposite* of a previous story
- Meaning is passed on unchanged from the first story in time to the second

Distinct/separated
- Similar dilemmas, issues not linked
- Focus is on each individual story
- No access to meaning-making across different contexts

Minimal/interrupted
- Little access to historical time
- Few details to flesh out the stories
- Hard to make meaning from multiple perspectives

Silenced/secret
- Hidden or subterranean text
- Story cannot be told
- Meaning is unclear, confusing; may contain hidden alliances or coalitions

Rigid
- Time is "frozen"
- Text is known—others can tell the story
- Set interpretation of the meaning

Evolving
- Recognition that the story is different at different times in life
- The details and points that are emphasized change
- Places provided to keep making new meaning

overlapping issues. This is especially important to do when there are strong parallels between story situations, such as people being in the same sibling order, experiencing similar events, or finding themselves facing a common issue.

A story may also be intertwined with another because it is formed *against* or *opposite* another story. Alexandra Nielsen, a single mother, came into treatment with her three teenagers; she was concerned about their behavior and how to set limits for them, especially with her middle daughter, aged fifteen. She was also feeling overwhelmed with all the responsibilities that go along with parenting three children alone. When asked to tell the story of her relationship with her mother when she was growing up, Alexandra said, "She was always monitoring my bodily functions, checking up on my friends to see what kind of kids they were, and insisted on knowing exactly where I was every minute. She would go through my things in my room and ask me about stuff that she found. I swore I wouldn't do that to my kids."

When asked how this story influenced her vision of her parenting with her children, Alexandra commented, "Well, I didn't want to be intrusive. I wanted them to make lots of their own choices and not feel like I was always looking over their shoulder." The therapist worked with her to help her see that the story of how she was mothered influenced the story she wanted told about her own mothering. And yet, her circumstances were quite different. Alexandra began to name how she wanted her children to take on more responsibilities around the house and how they needed to earn back her trust before they would be allowed more freedom to go off and do things. Her mothering was being done in a different time and place.

With intertwined stories people often experience time as collapsed—what is happening in the present is lived in some ways as if it were happening in the past. As one story resonates with another, meaning is passed between them, even though it may not fit the situation. When stories are too richly cross-joined, the first story seems to overwhelm the second story with interpretations of behavior and actions and with its own emotional field. People involved in the second story then find few possibilities of coming to their own meaning-making of the events in their lives. The meaning has already been passed on from the first story.

Some questions the therapist can ask to prompt the client to think about intertwined stories include:

- When you think of or tell this story about your life, what other stories are triggered in your mind?
- What is it about the story that makes you think of the other story(ies) (emotional content, place, certain words, people involved, way the story is told)?
- How do these stories influence or affect each other? Is this influence helpful or not?
- How would telling the story be different if it didn't trigger the other stories?

It can be helpful for people to see and name the links between events in their life and the meaning they ascribe to them. Then they can decide if the meaning that is spilling over between the stories has the significance that they want to pass on.

Distinct/Separated Stories

Distinct and separated stories represent the other side of the continuum from intertwined stories. Rather than stories being overly connected, they are not seen as linked. People then lack access to different levels of meaning and interpretation about their own lives.

When Stan Fujita was ten, his father abandoned the family after serving in Vietnam, and Stan never saw him again. When his own boys were ten and twelve, he found himself wanting to spend little time on family activities and experiencing powerful urges to go off on his own. It wasn't until a therapist asked him what was happening in his own life when he was the same age as his sons that Stan started to connect the two stories. Once he started to name some of the similar patterns, he began to understand more of his own emotional reactions. As he said, "I didn't have a father after age ten. What do I know about continuing to parent in a family?" This helped him become more aware that he could have different choices, that his father's story did not have to unintentionally become his story.

The therapist's role with distinct stories is to help people see how a story that seems quite separate may in fact be resonating with another. Linking needs to be done between different stories in time periods that are seen as quite distinct. People can then have the opportunity to tap meaning-making across different contexts.

Some questions that can help therapists and clients work with separated stories include:

- If you were to connect this story to another story in your life, what story(ies) might it be linked to?
- How would the first story be different if you made this connection (in emotional tone of the story, outcome, characters that people it, possibilities for the future)?
- What might the effect be on your life if the first story continues to stand alone?

With intertwined and separated/distinct stories, the therapist can help family members determine if there is too much or too little resonance between them. In the next category of story style, the process is quite different.

Minimal/Interrupted Stories

With minimal/interrupted stories, people may not initially have much access to their stories or stories from a particular part of their life. Rather than looking at the process of how meaning is or is not linked in beneficial ways, clients may first need help resurrecting and building the stories.

Sarah Johnson, thirty-seven and an only child, came to this country from England when she was four. Both parents were older and had died when she was in her early twenties. When she entered therapy for treatment of depression, she said that she had little to tell about her parents and her growing-up years. Wanting to understand more about her childhood and how feelings were expressed in her family, Sarah contacted a cousin of her father's who had been living here in the States when her parents first came over. This cousin in turn put her in touch with an elderly aunt back in England. Come to find out, this aunt had a whole packet of letters that Sarah's mother had written soon after they immigrated, which included stories about their trip across the ocean and Sarah's first reactions to the move here. Sarah also heard from her aunt a story that she did not know: Her parents were ecstatic when she was finally conceived because they had been trying for a number of years to have children. As Sarah started to collect family stories, she began to see her own parents' lives more richly and was able to envision a wider range of possibilities for her own stories.

Migrations, moves, losses, and/or cut-offs can sometimes mean that people lose contact with the locations, symbols, people, and activities that often generate stories. For instance, they may not have holiday gatherings or reunions with people where stories are passed down. Or, they aren't able to return to places or partake in events that remind people of what happened in previous years. When there are few stories available or when they have been interrupted, the therapist's role can be to help people expand their network of contact, or the kind of contact they have with extended family and friends, in order to help resurrect the stories that surround each person's life. Pictures, letters, and other artifacts all help stimulate the story-sharing process.

Questions that can help therapists and clients find resources to elaborate minimal and interrupted stories include:

- Who can you go to for information about your life around the time period of the story?
- What pictures, symbols, clothing, or other artifacts do you have from that period of your life that might stimulate story remembering?
- How do you imagine your life might be different if the story were more filled out and detailed?
- If the story had not been interrupted, how do you think it might have developed?

Stories can be fleshed out with "facts" gathered from other people and by retrieving old memories. They can also be filled out with "fiction." There may be situations where, because of trauma, war, and/or cut-offs, people do not have access to resources to embellish the story. If this is the case, the therapist can ask questions such as:

- If you were to fill out this story, how would you like it to be?
- What difference would it make in your life if you filled it out in this way?
- Who would you like to tell it to, when, and under what circumstances? How might this telling affect your life?

Silenced/Secret Stories

While the minimal/interrupted story style calls for retrieving and filling out stories, the silenced/secret story style presents complex issues of safety and disclosure because stories have been suppressed. Many families have stories that are hidden or secret. What is fascinating about these stories is that often, even though they are unspoken, their themes play central roles in family dramas.

In my family, my younger brother Mark disappeared for almost nine years. We had no idea where he was and thought there was a good chance he was dead, as he was very depressed when he took off from the alcohol treatment center where he had been staying. In the middle of the night in June 1990, I received a call from a man, asking me if this was his sister. It was Mark. We cried and laughed and talked, and he kept telling me how in battling his alcoholism he felt so alone and left out and isolated. He had been sober for six months and was ready and wanting to make contact with the family again, now that he was in better shape. I felt that he was ready to hear the family story that I had pieced together in the nine years in which we had no contact.

To Adopt Mark Out or Not

My mother was six months pregnant. My parents were in the midst of a very severe marital crisis — my father had moved out and was living with another woman. With three small children already, they had decided that they needed to give this baby up for adoption. The obstetrician had been told of the decision and they had asked not to see the baby after birth. He was quite upset with them and while the baby was neither named or brought to my mother while she was recuperating in the hospital, her doctor did keep my mother in a maternity room with three other nursing mothers whose babies were brought to them throughout the day. Finally, on her fourth day in the hospital, my parents decided to try to reconcile their differences and to bring the baby home. I remember the day he arrived (I was five at the time), when he was placed in my new navy blue baby carriage. I was thrilled to have a real baby sleep in it for several weeks rather than my dolls. It wasn't until years later that I realized there was no cradle and no baby furniture at home for Mark because they were not planning to bring him home from the hospital.

Over the years, the story of Mark's birth was intertwined with this marital crisis. Because of this, he took on a special role in the family. Strong dynamics came into play when my mother and father could not agree on how to parent him — dynamics that went far beyond the usual parental discord. It was hard for them to come together on many things regarding Mark. Mark did have a different place in the family.

As I told Mark the story, he kept saying things like, "Now it's starting to fit together," "No wonder I didn't feel like I belonged," and "That begins to make sense." On some level over the years of living in our family, he felt the story, even though he knew no details.

When there are secret stories in a family, people live with a subterranean text. Meaning is unclear, and there are often hidden alliances and coalitions.* A therapist can play a central role by helping people put the narrative together in a safe and protected way. This may need to be a slow and careful process depending on what has been hidden and for how long, and on what issues people still do not feel safe to disclose. Thoughtful work needs to be done on who can hear the story and when, and what support both the teller and the listeners might need. Questions to help with this intricate process include:

- In what ways has this story been silenced? By whom and why?
- What effect has this silencing had on you? On others in your family?
- What do you think the effects would be of continuing to *not* tell the story?
- What would happen if this story were to be told? What would need to happen to ensure safe disclosure?

Using such kinds of questions as a springboard, therapist and client can decide whether, when, where, and how secret stories can and/or should be shared with others. It is crucial that clients feel in control of this process because they have not necessarily been able to name and feel in control over what was happening in their lives.

Rigid Stories

With rigid stories, time is "frozen." Stories are told over and over in a similar way. The text is known and there are set interpre-

---

*See the novel *Family Linen* by Lee Smith for an example of the pervasive influence of a secret story on several generations. See also the book *Secrets in Families and Family Therapy* (edited by Evan Imber-Black) for a thorough explication of how to work with different kinds of secrets in treatment.

tations. A number of different people could tell the stories because they are well-known.

Tom's father grew up the youngest of five siblings. He felt that he had a rotten childhood and told Tom many times how no one came to his high school graduation to hear him play the trumpet, and how he worked like a servant in the family restaurant. When Tom would hear these stories, he already knew the affect, the punch lines, and the final outcome. He wondered what his father was trying to communicate to him about his own parenting. It was also hard for Tom to experience his dad in a fathering role because he seemed stuck back with all the things he felt he never received as a child.

The role of the therapist working with rigid stories is to try to get different perspectives incorporated into the stories, or to have them told from other vantage points. The therapist can also help clients rework them with other possible endings that they would have preferred. Dialogue about rigid stories can include questions such as:

- How long has this story been told in this way? Why do you think it took this form?
- For whom would it be hardest to change this story? Easiest?
- If this story were to change, what would the implications be for people in your family?
- How might you want to change the story? What would it take to do this?

The therapist can also help clients move rigid stories over to make space for other stories. For instance, the therapist coached Tom on ways to gently interrupt his father's stories of deprivation to ask him about times in his life when he felt more support from others.

Evolving Stories

Family stories need to be told and heard so that they can develop over time. For instance, the story that a child can hear and/or tell at age four about her parents' divorce is not the same one that she or he at age fourteen, or as a young adult of twenty-four, can comprehend. Key stories need to be told not once, but over the life cycle so they can be understood on different levels. As people develop, they are able to make meaning in different ways cognitively, they will have new sets of life experiences available to them to interpret events, and they may also have new information. This can help people to sense their movement through life over time, while simultaneously anchoring themselves in their history.

Therapists can help families explicate the meanings of their stories so that they do not feel as though they are reenacting the same stories, or see patterns that connect their life experiences that were previously unavailable to them. Stories are relatively simple formats that illuminate complex interactional patterns. They locate us in our lives. They tell us where we have come from and articulate central themes and values. At the same time, they can provide the foundation for new stories, new ideas, and beliefs to be shared. If we do not know the old stories, it is sometimes hard to move on to the new ones, because we are unsure of what it is we want to keep from our heritage and what it is we want to change. Understanding what has been given to us through the stories in our lives, while having an ongoing dialogue about the new stories that are being created, lets us both hold the past and move on with the present and future.

Questions therapists can ask to help identify an evolving story style include:

- How have stories changed over time?
- What in your family and/or community life supported this evolving process?
- If you were to tell central family stories five years from now, how do you think they would be told? Ten years from now?

Articulating processes that have helped stories evolve can give family members ways to think about intervening with other story styles.

The Power of Stories in Therapy

Stories are like a body. We can touch them and they touch the very heart of us.

—*Deena Metzger (1993, p. 82)*

A story can turn strangers into friends.

—*Anne Roiphe (1992, p. 28)*

Stories are a unique tool to use in therapy because they appeal to people of all ages. We all think in stories and they can give voice to people of widely disparate developmental levels. In treatment, when the age of people in the room may span four to eighty, stories offer a way to understand concerns and issues on different levels at the same time. They can hold the complexity of people's lives in a format all can understand. Great events and mundane details are interwoven in the tangled strings of our personal stories.

Stories can provide a resource and connecting focus for therapy. They offer a way to name our experiences without imposing a clinical language (which most often emphasizes pathology) upon people's lives. Also, we all have stories to tell: clients, therapists, people not in therapy, young, old, Black, white, Asian, Native American, Latina, Jewish, Moslem, Buddhist. Stories are a bridge across clinical and nonclinical populations, because in them we recognize our shared dilemmas. Moreover, the use of stories is not embedded in a particular model; no matter what the theoretical stance of the therapist, stories can be used.

A central part of therapy is helping people link and understand the relationship of their stories to their own life. As clients share stories with therapists, it is not just the content that is important, but the story styles as well. Exploring the kind of story-making with which they are familiar may help them to better see what resources they have or have not had available to them. Working with the story styles can open up new possibilities for making meaning out of their personal histories.

In the next chapter we look at some of the ways stories have traditionally been used in family therapy. Then a frame for stories that emphasizes clients' finding their own voices is proposed. Within this frame five different ways to work with stories in treatment are examined. In following the principle of always looking at the larger context of stories, we describe what happens to stories as they are told in primarily a public domain, the private domain, or cross from one to the other.

2

IN THEIR OWN WORDS: THE USE OF STORIES WITH FAMILIES IN THERAPY

Stories and Family Therapy: A Brief History

THERE IS A LONG TRADITION of using teaching tales in family therapy, arising primarily out of the work of the hypnotist and strategic therapist Milton Erickson. Erickson's stories, often from his life or experiences of his clients (as described by him), were chosen, told, and used first to model the world view of the client, so that rapport was established and the client felt understood. Then, Erickson proposed resolutions or solutions within the story (Erickson, Rossi, & Rossi, 1976). Rosen (1982) depicted this process as a way to present a "better design." The story was also a vehicle for the therapist to intersperse suggestions to help the client. For instance, with a terminally ill cancer patient, Erickson talked about growing tomato plants and with his voice gave special inflection to such phrases as "feel hope," "bring satisfaction," and "bring peace and comfort." Gordon explained this as an Ericksonian technique to help clients access certain "experiences and ways of thinking" (1982, p. 117).

Other hypnotherapists have elaborated on Erickson's use of stories. For example, Lankton and Lankton (1983, 1989) have focused on creating stories that contain multiple embedded metaphors to "seed the unconscious" of clients with suggestions for change. In this work, the therapist is seen as providing the resources of a "better story." Combs and Freedman (1990) write about ways to help the therapist create, find, and tell appropriate stories, whether to suggest ideas, to access emotional states and attitudes, or to embed suggestions. The focus of their book is on the inventive capacity of the therapist, not of the client. Rosen (1982), an analyst, has collected over 100 of Erickson's teaching tales and organized them into such categories as "teaching values and self discipline" and "learning by experience." Besides analyzing the meaning of the tales, Rosen comments on how reading or telling the stories can help therapists access more of their own unconscious associations.

There is a related tradition of teaching with tales in child psychiatry, best exemplified by the work of Richard Gardner (1969, 1971, 1976). Even though Gardner does not come out of a tradition of trance induction and suggestion, his technique of mutual storytelling has a focal point similar to the Ericksonian work—the better story is told by the therapist. First the child is asked to tell a story of his or her own creation—not one that he or she has seen, heard, or actually experienced. However, the child is encouraged to make it an adventurous story with some kind of plot. The story is audiotaped and often played back to the child and therapist. Clarifying questions are asked to help the child identify what can be learned from the story. Then the therapist tells a story that uses the child's characters and settings but introduces healthier resolutions and adaptations. The focus is on the dyadic interaction between the child and the therapist, and the clinician is seen as the person who can create the story that provides alternatives and solutions.

In family therapy we have recently witnessed the development of several narrative approaches to therapy. Linked to the so-called postmodern tradition in other disciplines, narrative therapies emphasize construction of reality through language and consensus; a collaborative view of treatment; and an awareness of the different political, social, and cultural realities of and constraints on of each of the participants. The text analogy is seen as quite distinct from the common analogy in family therapy that dysfunctional structures are what shape or create problems in people's lives (e.g., the classic structural family therapy description of the overinvolved mother, disengaged father, and symptomatic child). Rather, the focus is on the ways the problem is talked about and named, and how this "naming" subsequently locates family members in different positions in the social structure. For example, calling a young adult "schizophrenic" or "crazy" has deep implications for how family members and others outside of the family will treat him or her. A therapist's construction of the mother as too involved and the father as too distant could in fact become part of a problem. The meaning people give to the events of their lives as they talk about them is seen as central to understanding their interaction.

As a way of accessing this meaning-making, Anderson and Goolishian (Anderson, Goolishian, & Winderman, 1986; Anderson & Goolishian, 1988) have focused on the place of language in therapy. Calling therapy, "therapeutic conversations," they point out that communication is an ever evolving process of making sense of the world. There are no universal ways to describe structure and social organization: Different people have different ways to name and view them.

White and Epston (1990) have developed a narrative approach that is based on helping clients "reauthor" (Myerhoff, 1982) their stories. While sharing some of Goolishian and Anderson's focus on the importance of multiple voices and coconstruction of meaning, White and Epston show a decidedly more political bent in their work. For instance, they emphasize the societal context that allows certain stories to be told and silences others. They also stress that the term "therapeutic conversation" does not capture or delineate for them all the aspects of their restorying work. Their work is based on the idea that people's lives and relationships are shaped by

> the very knowledges and stories that [persons use] to give meaning to their experiences, and certain practices of self and of relationship that are associated with these knowledges and stories. A narrative therapy assists persons to resolve problems by: [1] enabling them to separate their lives and relationships from those knowledges/ stories that are impoverishing, [2] assisting them to challenge practices of self and of relationship that they find subjugating, and [3] encouraging persons to re-author their own lives according to alternative preferred knowledges/stories and preferred practices of self and of relationship that constitute preferred outcomes. (White, 1994)

White and Epston focus more on the actual stories of clients than do Goolishian and Anderson. They give careful consideration to the context in which the stories can and cannot be told, including power dynamics and repression and marginalization of stories. Drawing on Foucault, they link power and knowledge, making the assumption that therapy is always political, since it operates in an arena of who is seen as having knowledge about what. For instance, there is usually a hierarchy of experts in mental health systems, with psychiatrists having more power and "knowledge" than psychologists, or social workers, and clients having the least power. Therapists need to be keenly aware of who has access to speak and be heard and in what ways.

In *Narrative Means to Therapeutic Ends*, examples of White and Epston's work are primarily documents, letters, and certificates written by therapists. People's stories are told through the therapists' letters and documents, rather than through their own writing or speaking. Only a few of the numerous examples are in the words of family members.

In the therapy process, there is an emphasis on generating alternative stories "through a performance of meaning around unique outcomes" (White & Epston, 1990, p. 32). Novel questions and language introduced by the therapist are used to try to produce alternative descriptions of people's problems and stories about them. In this sense, the therapist is very interventive in the meaning-making process. This can be viewed in some detail in a videotape, "Escape from Bickering," made of Michael White working at the national AAMFT conference in 1989. White, with persistent questioning, tries to shape the story of eighteen-year-old Mike, a young man currently in a state hospital who has a history of setting fires, toward a new future story. He asks questions such as: What is the most pleasing development in your life? In your sister's life? What ways are you getting good at supervising your own life? What ways have you become an advisor to yourself? How are you doing things on your own suggestion? How are you taking charge of your future? In the end, a broader story evolves than just Mike as a firesetter. A frame is beginning to be built with Mike as a person who can take charge of more of his behaviors as well as challenge some of the inequities that are part of the institutional systems in which he is involved. But you can feel the tension as the therapist pushes his vocabulary, his line of questioning, and his language on Mike's story, and Mike and the other family members want to say what they have to say in their own words. Some of this is undoubtedly the pressure of doing a session in public and wanting the videotape to exemplify one's work. On the other hand, the video has some of the same focus of attention as *Narrative Means to Therapeutic Ends*—on the therapist's words.

Recently, other family therapists have focused more specifically on the story modality. Laird, with a strong background in anthropology, has done landmark work in looking at how women's personal stories can lack continuity and meaning if the issues and themes they deal with are not acknowledged in the larger culture. She articulates how the stories of women can be brought forth with what she names a "cointerpretive experience." Family stories are viewed in their historical context which includes "possibilities for men and for women, and of women's aspirations and disappointments" (1989, p. 447). In retelling their stories, clients are able to look at their levels of meaning in multiple arenas: the personal, public, work, and political. Laird also offers a series of questions to aid in this process of restorying, such as, "What does this story say about what you (or other women in the family) are supposed to be like? Loyal, self-sacrificing, independent? How does that differ from the stories that are told about men? What do the stories say about what men are supposed to be like? How do women get to be heroines in your family? Saintliness? Generosity?" (1989, p. 448) (See Chapter 7, pp. 168 for a training exercise inspired by Laird's questions.)

Rampage (1991), who has also examined women's narratives, focuses primarily on looking at ways to enhance the personal authority of women by looking at their "self-stories." She describes the importance of the therapist's being aware of the backdrop of these self-stories for women: the dominance of the marriage narrative "with its emphasis on passivity, selflessness, sacrifice, and dependency" (p. 122). Central tasks in therapy are to help clients look at how their interpretation of their story may reflect beliefs and structure of the dominant cultural stories, to help them question how the dominant stories may obscure or hide other themes in self-stories, and to search for new meaning that affirms their needs and sense of personal growth.

Family Stories: A Natural Resource

My own ideas about stories and therapy developed from my work with rituals and cultural diversity (Imber-Black, Roberts, & Whiting, 1988; Imber-Black & Roberts, 1992), collaborative training and treatment models (Roberts, 1982, 1983, 1986; Roberts et al., 1989), and years of training students from diverse backgrounds to be family therapists. The students, in their willingness to share their own lives, have taught me the power and depth of each person's story. In developing collaborative models, I have worked with various strategies to think about the "fit" between therapists' and clients' views of help and change, as well as a range of ways to access resources in many different parts of clients' and trainees' lives.

From Rituals to Stories

My work with rituals has evolved through three distinct stages that have a direct bearing on how I envision work with stories in therapy. My early work in the late seventies focused on the therapist's creating therapeutic rituals and prescribing to clients elements such as symbols and symbolic actions, and time and location of the ceremony, with the therapist orchestrating the ritual. This followed the early work of the Milan group (Selvini Palazzoli, Boscolo, Cecchin, & Prata, 1977). In the second phase, in the eighties, the focus was much more on creating rituals with clients. The therapist was seen as a coach rather than a conductor, helping people think about how they might meaningfully mark a transition, loss, or event that had gone unacknowledged in some important ways. The *process* of creating a ritual was as essential as any actual ceremony. In the planning, issues of inclusion, connection, distance, and significance of the life changes could all be addressed.

My current work with rituals emphasizes the resources that can be found in the ongoing ritual life of each family. Families in treatment, friends, family, and students have taught me the power of ritual to help us mark and make the ongoing transformations that life always requires. Daily meals, bedtime rituals, birthdays, anniversaries, vacations, life cycle rituals, cultural and religious holidays all reflect who is in the family, gender relationships, significant patterns of interaction, ethnic membership, and the values and beliefs of the family. This ritual life can be used in treatment to work through whatever issues are current for a family. Rather than acting as a conductor or a coach, the therapist helps the family access their own composing capabilities—capabilities that they already have available to them as they create rituals in their daily lives, even though they may not recognize them as such.

MORE THAN ONE PERSON'S BIRTHDAY.   The Diessners described distance between the stepmother, Maria, and her husband's teenage son, Rand, as a problem. When the therapist heard that it was Mr. Diessner's birthday in two weeks, she began to ask what they might do for the birthday that would both honor the father, Ellis, and connect Maria and Rand. Ellis decided that at his birthday party he would say a few words about these two special people in his life and the ways each were important to him. Rand and Maria agreed that they would work together on a small surprise for the party.

After a few false starts, Rand and Maria ended up making a photo board of Ellis's life. They first spent some time going through photo albums and loose photos together. They finally chose about twenty photos. Maria described this as a time to learn about her husband's life through his son's eyes. She said she was impressed with how much Rand knew about his father's life and how much the pictures of him and his father together when he was little meant to Rand. She had never really sat down and looked at the pictures before, because Ellis's first wife was in a lot of them. Rand, for his part, said he realized what a special relationship he had with his father—that he had known him a lot longer than his stepmother and that he therefore didn't need to be so worried about being left out. Both had a lot of fun choosing pictures, making up serious and silly captions, and sharing the board with others at the party. For instance, one photo showed Ellis mowing the lawn with a hand mower. Behind him was two-and-a-half-year-old Rand pushing the backs of his knees. Rand and Maria had written under the photo, "I can use all the help I can get!"

Ellis had described sometimes feeling as though he were in the middle in the family—pulled by Maria and Rand, both of whom wanted more time with him. In naming ways at the party that they were each special to him, he felt he was able to acknowledge both for himself and publicly a kind of comfortable balance between his parenting relationship with Rand and his connection with his wife.

The ritual life that was readily available to the family was brought into the treatment room as a resource. With some questions about what they might do differently around the ritual to work with some of the issues, the family members were able to start a very productive process outside of the session.

These three ways of working with rituals are not mutually exclusive, nor does one preclude the others. There is a place for therapeutic rituals primarily created by therapists, especially when individuals are under extreme stress and unable to organize themselves to mark or work through some key event. Rituals that are designed together are needed especially when there are few rituals available in the larger culture to deal with issues such as divorce, miscarriage, or the entrance of a foster child into a family (Imber-Black, 1989). Supporting already existing capacities in a family's life may require taking some time away from what family members initially present as problematic by asking them about daily rituals, family traditions, and life cycle celebrations, and asking them to think about whether their rituals feel rigid, minimal, or imbalanced. And, in fact, working with families and rituals may mean combining some aspects of each of these three ways. For example, after finding out about upcoming ritual events, the therapist may direct the family to do something quite specific for a mealtime or a ceremony.

However, these three different ways of conceptualizing rituals and therapy do represent distinct ways to think about therapeutic work, especially with regard to the relationship between therapist and client and how the therapist positions her- or himself in the therapist-client relationship, as well as the boundary between daily life and therapy. There is an evolution through the phases to greater emphasis on the collaborative nature of the therapeutic relationship, with a focus on what can be therapeutic about the daily life of clients. Each person's ritual life is seen as having healing possibilities. Ideas for change are embedded in processes in which clients are already involved.

As we think about stories and therapy, a parallel evolution can be noted. The work of Erickson and his followers and the work of Gardner are in the vein of the work of Selvini Palazzoli et al. (1977), with the therapist at the center creating therapeutic stories or rituals. The narrative approaches fall in the tradition of co-created stories, where the therapist and client work together to "restory" the client's life. *My focus here is on the therapeutic possibilities in stories that people already have in their daily life.*

The story format appeals to all ages and taps multiple levels of meaning simultaneously. This is particularly important in family therapy where participants have different developmental abilities and needs. Working with stories can draw upon the inventive capacity of clients and therapists of all ages. Moreover, stories provide an easy way for therapists and clients to make the bridge between the sessions and life outside of them.

To illustrate some of the benefits of working with family stories, let me share a family story that was written and illustrated by my daughter and two stepchildren several years ago. It helped the children and the adults in the family understand our experiences with divorce and remarriage, think about strategies to deal with the changes, and talk about them together in some new ways.

THE STORY OF THIS BOOK: LOSS AND CONNECTION.   A second marriage is always surrounded by a mix of emotions. While it celebrates a happy coming together of two adults, it gives a clear message to any children involved that their own mother and father are not getting back together. It marks the end of one phase in the children's lives and simultaneously announces a new phase.

We planned an engagement of a year to have time for everyone to talk and react to what it might be like to have the marriage of our two families, especially in the light of the previous losses. Naturally the children's feelings about the separation, divorce, and new relationship were all stirred up at the same time.

Donald Dragon's Divorce Book grew out of hearing and experiencing the mix of emotions of our three children when we talked of being engaged and married. They said they did not want us to get married because they were afraid of another divorce. They asked endless detailed questions about whom we liked better— their new soon-to-be stepparent or their own mother or father. A

Natalya, eight, Heather, eight and a half, and Jesse, eleven, wrote and illustrated this book at the beginning of the year in which we (their parents, David and Janine) were engaged. Natalya (Janine's daughter) and Heather and Jesse (David's children) had each been through a separation and divorce in the preceding years.

DONALD DRAGON'S DIVORCE BOOK

DONALD DRAGON'S DIVORCE BOOK

Written by Natalya Zoe Weinstein- Roberts (age 8) and illustrated by her and her *step* sister Heather Colman-McGill (8 & 1/2) and *step* brother, Jesse Colman-McGill (11).

INSPIRED BY THE BOOK DINOSAURS DIVORCE BY LAURENE AND MARC BROWN

CHAPTER ONE: SOME GOOD AND BAD THINGS ABOUT DIVORCE AND SOME ADVICE

ONCE THERE WAS A DRAGON NAMED DONALD. HE KNEW ALL ABOUT DIVORCE BECAUSE HE HAD BEEN THROUGH IT. SO IF YOU NEED TO KNOW ABOUT IT, TURN TO PAGE 2.

BY NATALYA Z.

2

FIRST WHEN YOUR PARENTS GET DIVORCED, IT IS HARD BECAUSE YOU DON'T
KNOW WHEN YOU ARE GOING TO SEE YOUR FATHER OR MOTHER OR WHEN
YOU ARE GOING TO DO WHAT OR WHATEVER. SO ONE THING THAT MIGHT
HELP YOU GET A LITTLE BETTER (IT WORKED FOR ME) IS IF YOU BRING A
SPECIAL STUFFED ANIMAL OR A SPECIAL SOMETHING WHEN YOU GO TO ONE
HOUSE OR THE OTHER HOUSE.

By Jesse

ANOTHER THING THAT MIGHT HELP IS IF WHEN YOU ARE AT YOUR MOM'S HOUSE, YOU KEEP A PICTURE OF YOUR DAD. AND WHEN YOU ARE AT YOUR DAD'S HOUSE, KEEP A PICTURE OF YOUR MOM.

By Heather

5

CHAPTER TWO: WHEN YOUR PARENTS MEET BOYFRIENDS AND GIRLFRIENDS

SOMETIMES YOUR PARENTS MIGHT START LIKING ANOTHER GROWNUP OTHER THAN YOUR MOTHER OR FATHER. THEN BE PREPARED TO BE JEALOUS. BUT, HOW DO YOU KNOW WHEN YOU ARE JEALOUS? TURN TO PAGE 6 AND FIND OUT.

6

FIRST, YOU KNOW YOU ARE JEALOUS WHEN YOU HANG AROUND YOUR MOTHER OR FATHER A LOT WHEN OTHER GROWNUPS ARE THERE.
SECOND IS WHEN YOU LAY IN YOUR BED AND YOU THINK THAT YOUR MOTHER OR FATHER LOVES THE OTHER GROWNUP BETTER THAN YOU.
THIRD IS WHEN YOU FEEL SICK A LITTLE WHEN YOU SEE YOUR PARENTS KISSING THEIR BOYFRIEND OR GIRLFRIEND. (AND ESPECIALLY WHEN THEY KISS THEM MORE THAN THEY KISS YOU !!!)

BY NATALYA Z.

7

HOW TO HANDLE JEALOUSY:
1. TRY TO IGNORE YOUR PARENTS.
2. (IF THE BOYFRIEND OR GIRLFRIEND HAS KIDS TOO), THEN TRY AND KEEP PLAYING WITH THE KIDS AND FORGET ABOUT YOUR PARENTS. THEN YOU GET ALL DISTRACTED AND TOO EXCITED TO REMEMBER ABOUT YOUR PARENTS.
3. TALK TO YOUR PARENTS ABOUT IT - DON'T KEEP IT ALL BOTTLED UP INSIDE.

8

CHAPTER THREE: STEPPARENTS

WHAT ARE STEPPARENTS?
STEP PARENTS ARE WHEN YOUR MOTHER OR FATHER GETS MARRIED TO
ANOTHER GROWNUP OTHER THAN YOUR MOTHER OR FATHER.
HOW ARE THEY DIFFERENT THAN YOUR FIRST PARENTS?
THEY ARE ONLY LIKE YOUR HALF MOTHERS OR FATHERS. THAT'S THE THING
WITH DIVORCE AND STEP FAMILIES. THERE ARE LOTS OF HALVES. LIKE
EVEN SOMETIMES KIDS FEEL SORT OF LIKE BEING CUT IN HALF. SAY ON
HOLIDAYS, YOU FEEL LIKE ALL PULLED APART LIKE IF ONE PARENT WANTS
YOU TO COME FOR HANUKKAH AND THE OTHER ONE WANTS YOU TO COME
FOR CHRISTMAS.
IMAGINE IF YOU KEPT ALL THESE FEELINGS TO YOURSELF. . . . . .

BY NATALYA

9

WHEN WILL I KNOW IF I AM GOING TO GET A STEPPARENT?
WHEN THEY GET ENGAGED, YOU SHOULD BE EXPECTING THEM TO GET
MARRIED.
WILL I LIKE MY STEPPARENT?
SOMETIMES YOU DON'T LIKE YOUR STEPPARENT BUT IF YOU DO LIKE THEM
THEN IT MAKES IT EASIER. ONE THING THAT HELPS GETTING USED TO THEM
IS DOING FUN THINGS WITH THEM LIKE GOING TO A FAIR WITH THEM OR
DOING A PUZZLE OR GAME.

AND IF YOU GET CONFUSED ABOUT THE DIVORCE AND WHAT IS HAPPENING,
JUST ASK YOUR PARENTS.

THE END

P.S. IF YOU WANT TO READ MORE, LOOK AT <u>DINOSAURS DIVORCE</u> BOOK (BY
LAURENE KRASNY BROWN AND MARC BROWN, ATLANTIC MONTHLY PRESS, 1986).

lot of jealousy about the new adult in their parent's life was expressed (as shown on pages 5, 6, and 7 of the book). There were also many questions about why the divorce had to happen and anger about their lack of say about whether there should be a divorce or not.

There was excitement, too, about the wedding as they made up songs to sing at it, picked out purple dresses to wear, and asked that the bride (age 43) have a long train on her dress so that there would be a need for both a train girl (Natalya) and a flower girl (Heather). Our children also seemed to be very comforted with the reemergence of a love story for each of us. When parents separate, it is sometimes difficult for children to know much of the love story of their own mother and father; the love story of earlier times in the relationship seems to be overshadowed by the divorce. With remarriage, children can see parents falling in love again and experience firsthand the love story.

THE CHILDREN: ACCESSING RESOURCES.   It was no accident that this story bridged the themes of divorce and engagement and remarriage. Time could be compressed in the story line so that the dual transitions of the children (divorce of their biological parents and new connections) could be acknowledged. The book also allowed them to tell the story from their own vantage point and in their own voice. For instance, children of divorce often need to live in two locations. Divorced parents can go on with their lives in one location, but children of divorce are always reminded of the split as they live with the physical representation of it: two houses and two different sets of routines. This is reflected in pages 2 and 3 of the book.

The children also voiced their own unique problem-solving strategies. These included self-comfort (page 2, taking a stuffed animal from one parent's house to the other's), emphasizing that there are some positive aspects to divorce (page 4, the candy store), and methods to hold both parents in their life at the same time (page 3). Children often experience a loss of sense of control when there is a divorce. This may be expressed by them with statements like, "I didn't choose to have the divorce Mommy, you chose!" or "Why do kids always have to do what their parents want them to do!" or "If you want me to be happy, get back together again!"

Or children may communicate this loss nonverbally with angry outbursts about other things in their life or by being overly quiet and carefully following the rules. Naming some of their problem-solving strategies in the story helped our children be more aware of the ways they do have influence over their lives. Their comment that there were "some good things about divorce," gave us a perspective that we had not had before.

Putting their "problems on a page," so to speak, also seemed to help the children. They could step back a little and listen and think about their experience. For instance, if you look on page 2, a picture drawn by Jesse, you see the baby dragon with a question mark over his head, the daddy dragon (wearing a bow tie) standing on one side of the baby, and the mommy dragon standing on the other side. In the baby dragon's hand is a stuffed bear. When we asked Jesse why the baby had a question mark above his head, he said, "Because he is thinking about which parent he should go to, his mommy or his daddy." This is a common feeling of children. As our daughter Natalya says, "When I'm at Daddy's house I miss you and want to see you, and when I'm at your house I miss Daddy."

It is one thing to be standing on the doorstep of one parent's home as you are being dropped off or picked up to go to your other parent's house—feeling that feeling. It is quite another to draw an illustration of the same situation and write words above it that describe a solution to cope with those feelings. The child can stand back and think about the experience as it is held by the picture and words on the page. Further, as people ask children what an illustration means, many possibilities for dialogue naturally emerge. After doing his picture, Jesse talked about a number of times he had felt torn about which parent to go to, especially when he went back and forth between his two houses every other day. This was new information to us.

Finally, creating the book helped the children begin to tell a common story of what it was like to move from divorce to remarriage. Each family goes through these transitions uniquely; when there is remarriage, some weaving of the stories enables the new family to begin to create its own family history.

Writing and sharing their story helped our children develop their own voice about what it was they had experienced. Strong emotional feelings had a structured place where they could be both expressed and managed. They found a way to make some common links between their past, present, and future. It was no accident that the story started out with loss and disconnection before it moved to connection. Themes emerged that had not been verbalized before, giving us a chance to discuss changes in new ways. The children also asked for extra copies of the book to share with friends and to take to school to show teachers and counselors; they experienced the power that comes when others outside of the family listen to them.

Lore and Listening: Ways to Think About Stories in the Therapy Process

Creating a story framework to contain and work through some of the events in one's life is only one of many ways to use stories as a resource. Clients can be asked about family stories they have heard or told to focus on a particular content area they have been exploring. If events have already been storied in a set way, the tale may need to be told differently. Invented stories may be called for as a way to bring some of the power of fantasy into the therapy process. Table 2 highlights different ways of working with stories in therapy.

Hearing Family Stories

Perhaps the simplest way to work with stories is to ask clients to share stories that help you begin to know them, to get inside some of their experiences. You can ask individuals to tell you their favorite story about themselves or someone else in the family, a story that most captures a sense of them, or a story about them that they wish were told differently. This is a good way to join with clients, and also often helps the therapist and the clients think about life beyond the problem that has brought them in for therapy. The process may lighten some of the heaviness that may be a part of current "stuck" dilemmas.

MOUNTAIN LIFE.   The Delano family reported a lot of turmoil with their thirteen-year-old daughter, Jenna. She was staying out all night, not eating with them and sometimes not going to school.

Table 2. *Different Ways of Working with Stories in Therapy*

Hearing family stories
- Getting to know people and their unique life experiences

Theme stories
- Asking for stories about particular content areas such as money, intimacy, betrayal, trust, and relationships between men and women, women and women, men and men, adults and children, children and children

Cohering a story
- Helping people pull together fragmented events and/or information

Restorying*
- Helping clients "reauthor" stories that have been told in ways that are not working for them (intertwined, rigid, distinct, silenced/secret, minimal/ interrupted)

Inventing stories
- Drawing upon the power of imagination to create future, hypothetical, metaphorical and/or fantasy stories that are representative of some of the issues clients are dealing with, but with animals, made-up people, in make-believe lands

---

*The meaning of restore is significant here; it means to put back in, to renew— to give back or return.

Gail and Roger Delano were in the midst of a very painful separation. In the room, the tension between Jenna and her parents was so palpable that it was hard to even have a civil conversation. Hoping to gain access to other parts of their relationship, the therapist asked them to bring in pictures of Jenna when she was little and share some stories of their life when she was young.

At the next session, Jenna at first refused to even look at the pictures. She kept the earphones to her Walkman on, and pretended not to be listening. As her parents showed wonderful pictures of them hiking, swimming, and exploring the mountains where they had lived a number of summers when her father was a forest ranger, the tone shifted in the room. Her parents described how creative and involved Jenna was in the world around her, how open she was to adventures and trying new things. They shared how delighted they were with her wonder about nature, how happy they were to be *her* parents. Jenna reached out for some of the pictures, the earphones slipped down, and she began to describe the tree house her parents were helping her to build in one picture, and the games they played in and around it. Telling and hearing these stories helped all three connect with a much greater range of family feelings than their present hurt and anger allowed. It also gave the message to Jenna that no matter what happened with her mother and father's relationship, they were always her parents. The atmosphere in the room softened and everyone was able to engage in a less heated discussion about current conflicts.

Theme Stories

It can be useful to ask clients to tell stories that center around the content of problems they have brought to therapy. These should be stories from other parts of their lives that help people understand what they have learned about these issues. As they see what messages and meanings they have taken in about sex, money, religion, intimacy, individuality, raising children, family, etc., they may be able to untangle their emotional reactions. In addition, when people tell and/or hear other family members' stories, they may gain understanding of the larger context of their reactions and a perspective outside their personalized frame.

MONEY THEN AND NOW.   Bernadette Thompson and Albert Nelson, an older couple, came in presenting a lot of disagreement around how to manage their finances, wills, and ownership of their house. This was the second marriage for both; they had been married for five years. They had moved into Albert's house and did not have any financial agreements worked out regarding how to share expenses for the house or how much to put into a shared checking account. The house was in only his name.

Discussion of money evoked very strong emotions. In trying to understand what meaning they each made of this issue, the therapist asked each of them to tell the story of what money had meant in the family growing up, including how it might have been different for men and women. Albert told the story of his immigrant father, who had literally worked his way over to the United States on a boat. Once here, he squirreled his money away, always afraid that he would not have enough. Albert's mother knew little about what was happening with money; Albert's father felt that the husband was supposed to take charge of it. Bernadette told a story of real insecurity around money. Her parents lost both their savings and their house in the Depression and never quite recouped. She felt that they were ambivalent about money; the message she learned was that in some ways having it just brought trouble down upon you. Her mother did not have any separate income, and Bernadette thought that was hard for her. She remembered her father doling out a certain amount of money each week for her mother to run the household.

Asking for stories around a particular theme helped illuminate what the spouses were carrying from their past into the current discussion. In hearing these two stories, the couple and the therapist were able to begin creating a larger frame in which to look at their present difficulties. The therapist helped Albert look at some of the reasons why it might be hard for him to be clear about what he had and to share that with Bernadette. Bernadette examined her own mixed feelings about money and why it was difficult to press Albert into a discussion about what money and assets they had and how they would distribute them. The therapist reflected on the very different availability of money to men and women in their families of origin and asked them to consider how that affected the power balance within their parents' marriages, and what implications that had for their marriage.

Cohering Stories

Sometimes clients are so much in the middle of a changing story that their story line is unclear to them. This is often the case when people go through major transitions and losses, such as the death of someone close to them, migrations, trauma, abuse, or several changes one right after the other. They do not have words or descriptions to locate where they are; they may feel as though there has been a break or rupture in how they make sense of the world.

"WHEN I FIRST REALLY LEARNED ABOUT DEATH." Eight-year-old Katie was very upset when a close family friend, Joe, died quickly from kidney cancer. She was very sad, found herself crying at all different times, and was also very worried about her father—not wanting him to be out of her sight. Her parents and therapist helped her begin to tell the story of what she was going through. They shared how it was common for people to feel weepy and sad at unexpected times after a death — that this was the body's way of trying to adjust to change. And they told her that it was normal to be afraid that something would happen to other people because the mind had to get used to something being very different. Katie's parents shared their sadness and told her that it was also normal to be emotional; they they would be concerned if she weren't. Her therapist and parents helped her name her experience. Katie called it "When I First Really Learned About Death," and told the following story: "This is the first time that anybody really close to me died. And I felt very sad and got worried that someone else was going to die, especially my Daddy because he was Joe's friend. And Joe was young and he died and I thought my Daddy could die too."

Restorying

Parts of people's lives may have already been storied in certain ways. As described in Chapter 1, people may find themselves with stories that are very intertwined with others, rigid stories, or stories that are kept very separate or distinct. Perhaps they have hidden, secret, or very sketchy stories. A new meaning-making process may need to be initiated to restory the events. It is essential not to impose upon clients the idea of the story style functioning in a particular way, but rather to let clients themselves come to some understanding about how they see their story life.

"YOU MAKE ME HIT YOU."   Gerda Denzler and Howard Wills had been married for eight years. They came into couples therapy asking for help with their distance from each other and lack of sexual and personal intimacy. In the fifth session, Gerda revealed that there was episodic violence in their relationship. Every six months or so, when they had an intense fight, Howard would hit, punch, or kick her. This story of his violence toward her had not been told to anyone, even though it had been going on for the last ten years. Gerda was ashamed to tell her family and friends; Howard did not share it with others. He justified his hitting Gerda by telling her that she made him so mad when they fought that, "You make me hit you."

Telling the story in therapy was a big step for both of them. The silence was broken on something that they were both struggling to understand and make sense of and that they knew was very problematic for their relationship. Ultimately the couple decided to separate. However, Gerda thought that it was essential that Howard take responsibility for his hitting in order for her to make sense of what had happened to them as a couple. This was very difficult for him to do, but in the last joint session Howard very angrily agreed that it was his fists and feet that had hurt her and that he was solely responsible for punching and kicking her.

Gerda continued in therapy, trying to understand what had happened with her life by incorporating the unspoken story into what had already been told. She had many questions about why she had stayed in the relationship, why she had married Howard (as the violence had also occurred before they were married), and what it meant to keep it hidden for so long. She felt she needed to go back and rework her own understanding of these events in her life. Gradually she build a different story of her life, her marriage, her time with Howard. It included a look at the power differentials between them in regard to money, status, and education, as well as their intense cycles of connection and distance. She looked at how she had convinced herself that the violence was an aberration, that each time it happened she had told herself it was the last time. Slowly, over time, she began to share with a close friend, a sister, and then her parents, a more complex story of what had been happening with her life.

Inventing Stories

Fantasy can be very appealing to families with children, as well as a good way to access some creative ideas that may not be available if people are bickering about the "truth" of a story. Clients may be able to imagine transformative changes in an invented story that are not conceivable within the "real" world. They can also talk about their own situation with a little distance from it, and with a sense of playfulness.

THE LAND OF IMPERFECT SPECIALNESS. Matthew and Rachel Cohen, a couple with two young boys, six and three years old, had concerns about their six-year-old. He was aggressive toward his younger brother and they were worried about how he was playing with other children. They were also concerned about his behavior at school.

Matthew and Rachel's parents had escaped to the United States because of the persecution of Jewish people in Europe during World War II, and had lost many relatives in the Holocaust. A strong theme in Matthew and Rachel's relationship was the desire to be better parents than their own parents "because no matter how perfect you are, and how overvigilant, terrible things can happen" (Roberts, 1988b, p. 93). As a way of looking at perfectness differently, I began a story about a king and queen who lived in a land of imperfect specialness and how, as they tried to raise a special prince, he became less and less special in the ways that they wanted. I then asked Rachel and Matthew to finish the story. They came back to the next session with the following fable.

In the Land of Imperfect Specialness

Anxiety about the children being perfect remained with the older Prince while the younger Prince seemed immune from such pressures. He was allowed to grow up as he pleased and was enjoyed while the elder Prince was watched carefully and every behavior examined. While the elder Prince was always praised, the anxiety over what he was not doing was always transmitted to him.

In the quest for the Prince to fit into his parents' perfect life, he became less and less perfect. His parents, grandparents, cousins worried about him as if his behaviors were a precursor of even more difficulties later. They wanted the Prince to be happy and saw him become more and more unhappy. The Queen, who was used to figuring things out, decided the Prince needed more structure and needed to learn not to hurt others and to share, for if he did not learn these skills he would be lonely and have difficulties making friends. The Queen set out to accomplish this task. She learned she needed to appreciate his imperfection as something that makes him unique and special. While he is not always well behaved, he has a zest for life and is very creative. He may not stay within the lines but he creates much nicer pictures with his own artsy style.

She needs to set appropriate limits and not worry about his every step along the way. The King needs to learn that he does not need to control everything, particularly his older son. He also needs to

let go of the image of the perfect child, the child who would please his parents, the child he was supposed to be.
The end.

Within the fable, the parents had embedded a number of ways to deal differently with their son. Although we had talked about some of these ideas in previous sessions, I had never made these suggestions directly. Matthew and Rachel were able to go on and implement their ideas and their six-year-old responded very positively to them. (See Roberts, 1988b, for a complete description of this case.) Within the invented story, they gave good sound advice to themselves about their current situation.

As we have seen, stories can be a resource in therapy in a range of ways. They can be a simple but meaningful method to join with people and bring other emotional states into the room. Theme stories can provide rich data to elucidate clients' dilemmas. The story frame can be used to help people bring coherence and understanding to major changes. Restorying can be used as a focus to rework people's relationship to their past and present. Invented stories offer creative possibilities of other ways to imagine one's life.

Story Domains: Private, Public, and Some of Each

Stories need to be considered within the larger frame of who knows the stories and if the individual or family feels in control of when and where the stories are shared. Stories of clients may be told primarily within the family (private domain). Or they may have entered the public domain as other people have become aware of a central family story. A school, social service agency, community center, or the court may have become involved. This is especially apt to be the case if outsiders have intervened because of violence, abuse, alcoholism, and/or addiction. Family stories told in therapy exist in both private and public arenas. Different strategies may need to be used depending on whether the story is primarily in the private or public domain.

The Private Domain

Some families seek help because they have been struggling in private with their story. In trying to understand their feelings and behaviors, they often describe themselves as not knowing whether their family dilemmas or their reactions to them are "normal." They want to hear other perspectives, other ideas. The therapist often connects them to others' stories—to the lives of other families. When it comes to the intricacies of human interaction in intimate relationships, families are the best teachers we have. The stories of the families that a therapist has worked with are essential teaching tools. Family members try to locate themselves and the issues they are confronting in relation to others; they will sometimes ask questions like: What do other families do in situations like this? Have you had other families come in to see you with similar problems? How do we compare with other families?

In their minds, clinicians often compare families they have worked with as a way to understand dilemmas at different life cycle stages, intricate patterns of interaction, and cultural, social, and economic issues. Teams that work together with the same families may describe a communication pattern in one family as a way to identify a different pattern in another. Sometimes you will hear therapists comment that they wish one family they were working with could see another family—this would help the family members understand their own issues.

When therapists share family stories with clients (carefully protecting confidentiality by not using real names and changing details), families in treatment get the rich benefits of others' experiences. And when these stories are told in a frame that places client concerns well within the "normal" range of behaviors, a palpable release of tension is often felt in the room. Family members breathe easier, and there is frequently an opening in their ability to deal with their dilemmas.

TWO FAMILIES—NOT ONE.   The Merker-Hamiltons are a remarried family who first began to live together a year and a half ago. The father, Wilmer, came to the marriage with one teenage son; his wife, Laurie, had two daughters, aged nine and eleven. They each shared joint custody with their former spouses, both of whom lived in town.

The three children were going back and forth between two different houses and both Laurie and Wilmer were stepparenting part-time in a situation where the children were in close proximity to their biological parents. Transitions as the three children went between their home with Laurie and Wilmer and their other parent's houses were very difficult. Both Laurie's older daughter and Wilmer's teenage son expressed a lot of resentment toward their stepparents.

Laurie and Wilmer had each imagined this family as a place to move beyond some of the problems they had experienced in their first marriages. Laurie's first husband was on the road a lot for his work and she had felt like a single parent much of the time. It was very important for her to do family activities together. She resented finding herself in the same situation: doing things with just the two girls because Wilmer's son wanted his dad all to himself. Wilmer had wanted more children, but his first wife had wanted only one. This second marriage was seen by Wilmer as a chance to enlarge his family and he was hurt when the girls pushed him away. Both parents saw their respective images of this ideal family crumbling as they had run-ins with the children. Instead of experiencing healing of wounds from their first marriages, they felt that events in the new marriage were triggering old issues.

When this family entered therapy, one of the first things the therapist did was to share stories about other cases, to communicate that building new relationships between parents and stepchildren often takes a number of years. She told the stories of the "Jens," "Wilsons," and "Anands"—all remarried families that she had worked with—and how initially the adults in each of these families had high expectations for the children to want to be in the family in the same way that the adults did. They found out that it was helpful to slow down expectations and to notice and build on small connections. In one story, the Wilsons were always sure to plan some fun activities between stepparent and child that were separate from the rest of the family. The Jens let each of the kids pick a favorite family activity to do one weekend a month; the parents went along with whatever they picked, even if it meant going down a water slide that they had had no prior interest in ever trying. The Anands tried a number of things to smooth over stepparent-stepchild relationships; they were only partially successful so one of the things the couple decided was to make sure that they had one or two special times a week just for themselves in order to balance out some of the negative times with their children.

The private story of the Merker-Hamiltons was connected to those of others, opening up new possibilities for different interpretations of their own story. Rather than seeing their lack of connection as aberrant and their "fault," they could view it as a normal phase in stepfamily development. They could incorporate some of the strategies of other families to help them get through this stage.

This is quite different from giving an educational lecture or advice about theories of stepfamily development. We are intrigued to hear about the lives of other people. Stories can create imaginative space where people can envision others and imagine themselves doing similar kinds of things. They can insert themselves into new situations.

The Public Domain

Other families come into therapy because their story has entered the public domain, often against their wishes, and with their having little control over what is told.

AIRED IN PUBLIC.   In a fight with her thirteen-year-old son, Leroy, Kristi Burdette pushed him out of her car. This was witnessed by someone living in their small town and she was subsequently investigated by the Department of Social Services (DSS). Her son was put into foster care and Kristi now had to convince the social service agencies and the court that she was a competent mother. She entered therapy with part of the family story having become a very public one.

Besides working with Ms. Burdette and Leroy to learn different ways to interact with each other when they had conflict, this therapy required careful attention to the fact that the family was involved in a public airing of their story. Central to the therapy process was helping them feel as though they had some input and control over how this story was being documented, shared with others, and told in court. The therapist helped Kristi request written DSS records and correct inaccuracies in them. The report that the therapist needed to make to the court was written with Kristi and Leroy so that they knew exactly what was shared and felt that they had some control over it (Imber-Black, 1988; Roberts, 1988a). The therapist did several separate sessions with Leroy around his sense of privacy being violated by being taken to the foster home by the DSS worker directly from school (without seeing his mother); having to meet weekly with the DSS worker and tell her how things were going in the foster home and in visits with his mother; and having to undergo psychological testing.

When a family story becomes public, the therapist needs to help family members gain access to what is being written and told about them, make sure it is accurate, and participate in any documenting of their story (Strategies for doing this are detailed in Chapter 5). Attention needs to be paid to the boundary between the public and the private story and to enabling family members to feel that they have some control over what is shared about their lives.

A Mixture of Private and Public Domains

Sometimes stories that are told in therapy inhabit both arenas, rather than being located in primarily the public domain or the private domain. The therapist may need to help clients look at the significance of a story in each of the domains, as well as decide where they would like the story to be primarily told.

CLOSING THE CASE OR KEEPING IT OPEN. A recently separated mother, Karina Abramson, had been investigated by DSS for a bruise on her five-year-old's arm that had been allegedly caused when she pinched him. The case was currently open and she was told by the worker that if she admitted to pinching him the case would be closed and the record destroyed, as it was not severe enough "abuse" to have a case worker assigned. However, if Karina did not admit to doing it, the case would stay open and on file for a year, so that if there were any other allegations made about abuse to her son, the workers could look at this file and use it as part of further investigations. Karina felt that she was really getting contradictory messages from DSS. The therapist had to work with Karina around her own view of what happened (private story) and what she might want to do differently as a parent, as well as what Karina felt like she could do to get control over the story in the public arena.

Karina told the therapist her view of what had happened with her son: She had grabbed him and shook him when he had been kicking his sister—she certainly had not meant to hurt him, but thought that she had probably held him hard enough to create the bruise. Given that she was in a protracted custody battle with the children's father, Karina ultimately decided to say to DSS that yes, she had grabbed him strongly enough to bruise him. She wanted the case closed, with the story out of the public domain, so that the children's father could not use it in some way in their custody dispute.

Distinguishing between public and private domains can help both therapists and clients look at the boundary between family stories and people outside of the family and determine what strategies may be needed to either loosen or tighten it. Some families need help controlling the family stories that are told about them in the public domain. Other families need a less private focus on their stories that allows them to learn from the stories of other families, as well as share their own.

Story Reserves

With remarkable efficiency, family stories communicate the essential values and beliefs of families and provide vivid ways to work with current dilemmas. They can be used in treatment to make strong connections between people, to delve into key themes, to play with "reality," or to reauthor individual and family lives. In the next chapter, we'll look at how stories can help us look at the imprint of our lives and repair what has been rent as we hear our voices and move though time with the restorative powers of memory and imagination.

3

MEANING-MAKING AND STORIES: VOICE, TIME, MEMORY, AND IMAGINATION

Voice, Agency, and Possession

It is 1965. My mother has died. My first book of poems has been published. My father, who, like my mother, has never been a reader of poems, reads my book. I am moved. The image of my father pondering what I have written fills me with unutterable joy. He wants to talk to me about the poems, but it is hard for him to begin. Finally, he starts. He finds some of the poems confusing and would like me to clarify them. He finds others perfectly clear and is eager to let me know how much they mean to him. The ones that mean most are those that speak for his sense of loss following my mother's death. They seem to tell him what he knows but cannot say. Their power is almost magical. They tell him in so many words what he is feeling. They put him in touch with himself. He can read my poems—and I should say that they might have been anyone's poems—and *possesses his loss instead of being possessed by it* [italics added].

—*Mark Strand (1991, pp. 36–37)*

MARK'S FATHER EXPERIENCED his son's giving voice to the loss of his mother as naming some of his own experience of bereavement and helping him to hold it. We cannot always control what happens to us in our lives, but we can control how we make meaning of it—by when, where, and how we tell the story and explain its significance. Whether we tell our story or others help us access the story, we can possess our experiences rather than being possessed by them.

In the last few years there has been a lot of interest in the development of voice and in how as people speak and feel heard they encounter a sense of personal agency. In particular, researchers have looked carefully at the ways familial and academic environments help or hinder the development of girls' and women's voices, minds, and senses of self. In Belenky, Clinchy, Goldberger, and Tarule's study (1986), 135 women from a range of cultural, racial, and socioeconomic backgrounds were interviewed about their family life growing up as well as their experiences in both formal and informal learning settings (such as schools, parenting centers, and children's health programs). Since families usually provide us with our first narrative experience, a series of questions about family history were included such as: What rules about speaking and listening can be inferred from a family story? Were children to be seen but not heard in the day-to-day life of the family? Or did both parents and children listen to one another with care?

In analyzing responses to these questions, the researchers began to see patterns among the families with regard to whether women felt heard. They described four different kinds of families. In *silent families*, children are not encouraged to tell of their experience, nor do parents share much of theirs. In a second type of family, children are encouraged to *listen to the voices of others*; but not to tell of their own experience. In other families, children are encouraged to speak but *in one voice*; they are not encouraged to speak of their own separate experience, but rather of the family line. In the fourth type, ongoing dialogue among all members is encouraged. Belenky et al. described this as *polyphonic voices*, where experiences of both reason and feeling are spoken and valued, and individuals feel that their inner voices are heard.

Family therapists need to consider the narrative experience their clients have had. Questions can be asked about the familial environments they grew up in, what they like about their "voice," what they think is unique or distinct about what they have to say, when they think their voice is the strongest, how they hear their own voice, and how they perceive their voice is heard by others.

For instance, Kay Odo, a woman in her forties, often seemed

unsure of what she wanted to talk about in family therapy sessions. She usually waited to follow someone else's lead and did not bring up issues of her own to discuss. When asked what her experiences were with being heard, she said, "At home I followed the party line. There were three of us girls. We were groomed for marriage, especially with helping our mom do all the things she did for our father. There was never any question about what I would do—I married young and had children right away. I was just following the script. There weren't any places to say what was happening to me." The therapist then asked her what she might have said if there had there been space for her to speak. Together, they began trying to build a different experience about being heard.

The conclusions of Belenky et al., while focused on women in academic settings, have other implications for thinking about voice in family therapy.

> We have argued . . . that educators can help women develop their own authentic voices if they emphasize connection over separation, understanding and acceptance over assessment, and collaboration over debate; if they accord respect to and allow time for the knowledge that emerges from firsthand experience; if instead of imposing their own expectations and arbitrary requirements, they encourage students to evolve their own patterns of work based on the problems they are pursuing. These are the lessons we have learned in listening to women's voices. (p. 229)

These findings raise questions about how to create collaborative and connecting therapy environments where people can have control and create their own meaning around issues they are exploring.

Therapists are perceived as "experts" who have had specialized training and who therefore possess valuable information that they will pass on to people; they are not necessarily seen as professionals who will help clients access their firsthand experiences or evolve their own patterns. It behooves therapists to be aware of their power and of how their clients perceive them. As Gale and Newfield noted in studying a session of Bill Hudson O'Hanlon (a solution-focused Ericksonian therapist), "This constructivistic perspective emphasizes how participants in interaction construct their own meaning. However, this study also tends to indicate that the therapeutic context sets up an unequal, hierarchical relationship between participants. The person with the greatest linguistic abilities (and the most perceived authority) is likely to have the greatest influence on the structure and sequence of talk" (1992, p. 163). The therapist's position gives him or her particular power to speak and to be listened to. If the therapy environment is to be one in which the authentic voices of all are heard, therapists need to take careful account of their unique role and power.

Adult voices may also be heard over children's. Family therapy videotapes often show children sitting for long periods of time without being really engaged. Unfortunately, there is a paucity of books on working with children in family therapy.* Story modalities linked with artistic and expressive activities like drawing, sculpting, and puppets can be a terrific resource to pull in children's ideas. Such active techniques are explored in Chapters 4 and 5.

Adults in therapy who as children sometimes experienced not being heard, who learned to speak what they thought others wanted them to say, or who learned that you get to be heard by growing up, may need particular help in regaining voice. Where one's voice has been silenced by trauma and/or secrecy, it may be necessary to slowly rebuild the trust that one's words are being heard by others.

THE CANCELLED BIRTHDAY PARTY. Mercedes Gonzalez, a Cuban woman in her mid-thirties who grew up in Costa Rica, entered therapy unable to concentrate on or finish her work or to stay involved with long-range projects. She was concerned about her own competence; she was unable to complete certification work required for her career in human services.

Mercedes had recently gotten in touch with an incident of sexual abuse by a man who worked in her elementary school when she was about to turn eleven. This had been a man she had known a long time and had trusted as a responsible adult. Mercedes felt

*Important exceptions are Joan Zilbach's *Young Children in Family Therapy* and the two edited books by Lee Combrinck-Graham, *Treating Young Children in Family Therapy* and *Children in Family Contexts: Perspectives on Treatment*.

that, when her parents found out what had happened, they blamed her because, among other things, they canceled her eleventh birthday party, to which a large number of friends and family had been invited. Once the party was canceled, Mercedes felt a deep sense of shame, convinced that others in the community knew what had happened to her and that they believed it was her fault. She felt they were talking about her behind her back. Mercedes never talked with her siblings and friends about what had occurred, and after the initial disclosure to her parents she never talked to them about it again. The story became secret and silenced.

Mercedes felt this event was a marker of her loss of innocence and trust in the world; she saw the world differently after the abuse. As she got in touch with this hidden story in therapy, she realized that she needed to do something different with it, that it was affecting her abilities to trust herself, to stay focused, as well as to trust others.

In therapy, she first needed to piece together and cohere the story. It had been unspoken for so long that it was fragmentary in her mind. What did her parents say to her about canceling the party? Her abuser left the school suddenly — was she told anything about that? How much did her siblings know? It seemed like her friends in the neighborhood pulled away from her after that — or did she pull away from them? As Mercedes patched the story together, she got in touch with her deep feelings of guilt about what had happened. She remembered her mother's crying and her father's anger and his words, "How could you let him do that to you!" No one comforted her. She imagined that people were saying horrible things about her.

The therapist reiterated to Mercedes in many different ways that she was a child when this happened, that she in no way was to blame for something wrong that an adult did — the abuser was responsible for his actions. The therapist also validated how hard it must have been for her not to have support during that time. She asked Mercedes about other emotions she felt during the incident and in its aftermath: fear, anger, sorrow, outrage, indignation. Together they talked about society at that time and the "liberties" men felt they could take with women's bodies, how almost no one spoke out against it, and how there was nowhere for individuals and families to turn when something like that happened.

As Mercedes started to incorporate these new ideas and emotions into her story without blaming herself, she wanted to tell it outside of the therapy room to see how others responded to it. She chose to share it with a few close friends—to hear how she was explaining it, as well as how they heard it. They sympathized, they cried with her, they cursed her abuser—and they told her she was not to blame.

With their support, she decided to next share the story with her family. First she wrote to her younger sister, the sibling to whom she was closest. She described both what had happened as she remembered it, and the effects she thought it had had on her. Her sister called her on the phone: She vaguely remembered the birthday party being canceled, but she never knew why. "I felt like you became more distant after that, Mercedes, but I attributed it to your getting older and wanting to separate yourself from the younger kids." Mercedes's sister was grateful that Mercedes had shared the story with her.

In the meantime, Mercedes and some of her friends decided that she needed to have that eleventh birthday party that she had missed. They put together a gala celebration that included foods, games, and presents that eleven-year-olds like, party hats, favors, and a big cake. Mercedes brought photographs of the party to therapy: pictures of the cake with big red letters that spelled HAPPY ELEVENTH! and pictures of her and her friends running three-legged races together. Mercedes laughed and cried, and explained in great detail how the party had taken her back to a time of playfulness and given her a sense of connection within the group that she had somewhat lost.

Then Mercedes wrote separately to each of her parents. First her mother responded, she had not realized how much Mercedes had thought about it—how much it had affected her. Then her father apologized for his anger, saying that at the time he was beside himself and didn't know what to do. Mercedes was able to begin a different kind of conversation with them; she was no longer left holding the story in pieces, alone.

Next Mercedes wrote to her abuser. She brought the letter into therapy to read: She voiced her anger, her hurt, her shame, her fury. Mercedes had no way to contact him—and she thought that, given his age, he might even be dead—but she wanted to articulate what she had been through as if communicating with him directly. Several weeks later she brought into therapy a letter she had written as if she were her abuser writing to her now. In it, she had her abuser saying, "I'm sorry for all the pain I caused you. I take full responsibility for what happened. You were a child who trusted me. I'm sorry I took away your innocence so profoundly."

The story was no longer fragmented and secret. Mercedes had given voice to it in numerous ways. With her friends she had created a different set of memories, beginning with her eleventh birthday, to launch her into her young adult years. She was with a community of people who believed her story, who did not judge her for what happened. With her family she had broken the silence and the story had now become part of a shared history that could be reviewed and told. Her story was no longer secret and shameful, but one over which she had taken control.

Subsequently, Mercedes was able to complete her certification course work. She had become more interested in the area of sexual abuse and had focused some of her study on it; she felt that she had some particular expertise that she could offer to others given what she had been through and the ways she had worked it out. She returned to Costa Rica to take up her profession.

Two years later, Mercedes was visiting in the United States. She called her therapist to share with her that in the province where she worked, she had been instrumental in organizing and training a network of people in schools and social service agencies that would offer treatment to young sexually abused children. This kind of support had never been available before. Her silenced story had been transformed into one in which she spoke out for others (Imber-Black & Roberts, 1992).

Other clients may not wish to or be able to give voice to a story in the range of ways that Mercedes did. But there are a variety of other techniques for evoking voice, as well as for invoking other ways of "speaking": for example, using symbols, having someone else write your story, using "mirror" stories and enactments. These are described in depth in Chapters 4 and 5.

Time is also a key element in reworking stories. Crucial to Mercedes's process was moving back and forth in time so that she could be a child of eleven, an adult, the abuser in present time, the adult now thinking about the child in the past. Stories give us the power to cut across what we perceive as boundaries of time.

Time: All Kinds of It

I began to talk about our western bias concerning the structure of time. I said that [we] think of time as linear, flowing from past, to present, to future like a river, whereas the [Pawtucket-Micmac Indian] Nompenekit thinks of it as a lake or pool in which all events are contained.

—John Hanson Mitchell (1984, p. 119)

Human beings inherit little History, but many histories. The past bequeaths a small nest egg of stable, undisputed facts and a thick portfolio of speculative issues—divergent, ever changing interpretations—because presents and futures alter pasts. . . . No one can predict the future of the past.

— "Notes and Comment," The New Yorker
(cited in Heat-Moon, 1991, p. 260)

He sees that time is what we live in, but that it is also what we carry within us. Time is then, but is is also our own perpetual now. We bear it in our heads and on our backs; it is our freight, our baggage, our Old Man of the Sea. It grinds us down and buoys us up. We cannot shuffle it off; we would be adrift without it. We both take it with us and leave ourselves behind within it—flies in amber, fossilized admonitions and exemplars.

—Penelope Lively (1991, p. 9)

The story modality offers opportunities to engage with the time frames of past, present, and future in some novel ways. A story is portable and contained—it can be easily picked up and relocated in time. The sensory aspects of story that help our imagination evoke place, smell, characters, mood, and movement can help people place a story in a new time frame. For instance, a person can be asked to tell a story as if it were five years from now, or five years earlier. Or, a person can be asked how she or he *would like* to be telling the story at some point in the future. Different perspectives can be brought to bear on stories as they are moved through different time frames.

People need to be in a comfortable relationship with their past, present, and future. Sometimes time frames become weighted in particular ways (Boscolo & Bertrando, 1993). People may be so immersed in the past that it is difficult to think about the present or the future. Others may be trying to obtain for the future what they were unable to have in the past. Or they may be wishing that what they have in the present, they had had in the past.

As discussed in Chapter 1, a story style may have a particular relationship to time. With rigid stories, time may feel like it is frozen. With separated stories, time periods may feel very distinct. Conversely, with intertwined stories, time may feel very collapsed. With minimal stories, there may be little access to historical time and details. With hidden and secret stories, time may be muddy, the teller unsure of what happened when. Evolving stories move fluidly through time; they are told at different times and places by different people with a recognition that stories change.

THE UNSPOKEN: LIKE FATHER, LIKE SON.   Angela Nelson brought her fourteen-year-old son Patrice into treatment because she was concerned about their relationship, his temper, and his school work. She told the therapist that her former husband and Patrice's father, Chris, had been incarcerated for the last seven years for breaking and entering. Later, in a session without Patrice, she disclosed that Chris was addicted to drugs and that is why he had been stealing. She also said that Patrice did not know this. As Patrice was growing older and looking more and more like his father, Angela feared that Patrice was going to turn out like Chris. She worried that Patrice might get into drugs. Meanwhile, he thought she was overly concerned and watchful of him, and he didn't know why.

A past story had become intertwined with a potential future story. But the main character in this future story didn't know a key detail of the past story. Because of this, neither of the stories could be discussed by mother and son, which left the mother alone with her own internal dialogue and the son without a context to understand and speak to his mother's concerns. Time was all bol-lixed up.

The therapist encouraged Angela to break the impasse, to tell her son the full story of his father. After a number of sessions she was finally able to. When she told Patrice that Chris had been a drug addict, he said, "Oh, I knew that." As is often the case, chil-dren are aware of more than their parents realize. Now they could openly acknowledge the weight of the past story and start working toward Patrice's own unique future story.

People's stories should contain a comfortable balance between the past, present, and future; they should also reflect people's movement through time. The same story is told and understood differently at age ten than at age thirty or seventy-five. New per-spectives are gained as people age and have distinctive experiences and different cognitive capacities.

It can be helpful to think about time relative to where people are in their life cycles. Children may be very involved in their here-and-now life. Connecting them to the past and future may require concrete, tangible examples. Adolescents are often leaning heavily toward the future, imagining their lives as they grow older. In middle age people have their feet in both the past and the future; they are also often in a unique position to help the older and younger generations connect time. Elders may be in a space where life review—reflecting as they look back over their lives—can be particularly helpful.

Questions That Can Help Therapists Think About Time

- In a particular story, where is a person placed in relation-ship to the past? The present? The future?
- From what other point in time might it be useful to tell this story?
- If this story continues to be told within the same time frame(s), what are the implications for the family? For the couple? For individuals in the family?
- How are people positioned in their life cycle in relation to time? What ways do you need to think about this in rela-tion to retelling a story?

For example, in the following case, past stories had become intertwined with a present story, keeping the parents locked into reactions that were not serving them well with their son.

"I REALIZE I RUN THE RISK . . . "   Tina and Gerald Jones described a lot of problems with their teenage son's neglecting his homework and other responsibilities (Whiting, 1988). Typically, after a lot of nagging, Jim would start something, but then go watch TV, go out with friends, or ride off on his bike, and not come back and follow through on what he was supposed to do. Neither parent experienced much success in being clear with him about what he needed to do and when he should do it. When the therapist asked Gerald to tell a theme story of what his relationship was like with his father when he was required to do things, he told a very poignant story of feeling obligated to do many things for his alcoholic father, a doctor, in order to keep the family together. For instance, when his father lost his driver's license due to drunk driving, he had to drive him everywhere on his house calls. Gerald stated that he never wanted his son to experience that kind of pressure and that it made it hard for him to set expectations for Jim. He also felt that, as a young person, no one had particularly supported or pushed him to do things that were important for himself, and that he had rarely pushed himself to achieve.

When Tina was asked to tell a theme story of what her relationship was like with her mother in regard to "requirements," Tina described an adolescence full of conflict because she felt her mother had set ways to do everything. Tina still did not have a good relationship with her mother, nor did Tina's son and daughter, and she was afraid to be too demanding with her son for fear that he would begin to dislike her as she disliked her own mother.

The "requirement" stories of both Gerald and Tina were intertwined with what it meant to require things of their son. Past time was the frame for present relationships. When asked what future story they would like their son Jim to tell about them, they agreed that it would be something like, "They were fair, they didn't ask me to do *too* much or tell me exactly how to do it—but they did support me in learning how to be disciplined about tasks." The therapist then suggested a way in which they could encapsulate the stories of the past and acknowledge their power, while highlighting the meaning of those stories in a different way. They tried to condense the message of their previous experiences into a phrase that could name their past fears or disappointments, rather than letting them remain unspoken but strongly there. Then, they linked this phrase with words that would outline clear expectations for their son in the present. Each parent would say the same sentence each time they asked their son to follow through on something. Tina would say, "I realize I am running the risk of your having a relationship with me like I have with my own mother; however, until you complete your homework (chores, etc.), you cannot go out, watch TV, etc." Gerald would say, "I realize that I am running the risk of pushing you in ways that I wish I had pushed myself; however, until you complete your homework (chores, etc.), you cannot go out, watch TV, etc."

Jim walked into the next session saying, "I realize I run the risk . . . " and the family cracked up. When the therapist asked, "What's going on?" Jim replied, "Well, that became the shorthand. After a couple of days they didn't have to say anything else. As soon as I heard, 'I realize I run the risk,' I knew there was something I had to do." Time was focused on the here and now, not on disappointments about past relationships and fears about the future.

Memory and imagination are what let us play with time. Our past is tugged along with us by memory. Imagination both expands memory and lets us move into future time, bringing into play the power of anticipation.

Memory: Different Slices of It

We need to tell someone else a story that describes our experiences because the process of creating the story also creates the memory structure that will contain the gist of the story for the rest of our lives. Talking is remembering.

—*Roger C. Shank (1990, p. 115)*

When people talk about their pasts, tell their own stories, they are culling anecdotes from their stacks of memories, tapping certain of the past days on the shoulder. Sometimes they choose not to speak, but you can see memory rising in their eyes like a tide. You can see older people wallowing, flounder-

ing a little as they make their way among teetering piles of
past moments. Proust thought of old people as walking on
stilts; I think of precarious piles of magazines in a house so
cluttered that little paths are necessary to get from one room
to another.

— *Rachel Hadas (1990, p. 76)*

The memories we access and the stories we then tell shape our
relationships and vice versa. Linda Weltner described how she
became painfully aware of this. She had just been playing with her
new granddaughter Jess. She commented to her daughter Laura:

'I love playing with babies,' I said. 'I'm having just as much fun
with Jess as I did with you when you were her age.'

'What do you mean, Mom?' Laura responded, puzzled. 'I didn't
know you had fun playing with me. All you ever say is how hard it was.'

I stared at her as if she were crazy. I felt accused, bewildered and
angry. I wanted to deny it, to insist she take such an unfair statement back. What kind of a mother did she think I'd been? But I
didn't defend myself. If I've learned anything in all these years, it's
that the most helpful response to any perceived attack is a question.

'What are you talking about?' I asked.

'Well, you always say how isolated you were, and how difficult
it was to make friends, and how overwhelmed you felt with Dad
away so much. I didn't know you ever had fun with me.'

I was silent all the way home, but that night I replayed the
stories I'd selected from my early experiences as a mother, trying
this time to see what messages they might have given my child.
(Weltner, 1991, p. 63)

And as Weltner did this, going over all the difficult stories she
had shared, she realized that she had created a particular version
for herself about her life, a version that emphasized the hardship
she had faced as a "displaced person," following her husband as
he pursued his career. She then asked herself the question, "OK, I
have this version, but at whose cost?" She decided it was time for
a serious rewrite. She sat down at the computer and went back 25
years to another string of memories.

. . . the thrill of holding a beautiful, but sticky, infant in my arms
immediately after delivery; the sight of her slipping peacefully into
sleep after breast-feeding; blowing noisily into her belly button

when I changed her diaper; my rush of joy when Laura stretched out her pudgy arms to be lifted; the songs her father and I made up and can still recall; the pleasure of watching her gentle ways with a doll; her face smeared with frosting and alive with pleasure at her first birthday party.

In offering up these stories, Weltner had a chance to share with her daughter a set of experiences that had been blocked in her memory—stories that communicated a fuller picture of her parenting of Laura.

Helping people recover and transmit different parts of their memories can be a central part of therapy. However, family members often come into therapy with a different agenda for memory: They want the therapist to tell them who remembered correctly—who has the "true" version of the story.

For example, Gary and Gregory, two brothers barely a year apart in age, had had a fight in the family basement in which they had come to blows. Each had a very different explanation of what had happened. Their parents were not able to corroborate anything they said because they were not home at the time. The therapist worked with them around the notion that they were probably never going to agree exactly on one story, but what was important was that they each had a chance to speak their version and to work through what kind of impact this incident was going to have on their relationship, what safety issues needed to be addressed, and what they wanted to do in the future when they became that angry with each other. The therapist shifted the focus from remembering and who was "right" to what kind of memory they would carry from the incident and how they had or had not worked it out.

Voice, memory, and imagination are linked in the sense that remembering and imagining provide the source material for each person's telling about past, present, or future. There is a powerful elucidation of how access to memory gives new voice in the Pulitzer prize winning novel by Jane Smiley, *A Thousand Acres*. The main protagonist, Ginny Cook, struggles to remember sexual abuse by her father that has long been hidden. As she and one of her sisters do finally recall it, Ginny, in a self-dialogue, says,

One benefit, which I have lost, of a life where many things go unsaid, is that you don't have to remember things about yourself that are too bizarre to imagine. What was never given utterance eventually becomes too nebulous to recall.

Before that night [when the sisters do speak to each other about the sexual abuse], I would have said that the state of mind I entered into afterward was beyond me. Since then, I might have declared that I was "not myself" or "out of my mind" or "beside myself," but the profoundest characteristic of my state of mind was not, in the end, what I did, but how palpably it felt like the real me. It was a state of mind in which I "knew" many things, in which "conviction" was not an abstract, rather dry term referring to moral values or conscious beliefs, but a feeling of being drenched with insight, swollen with it like a wet sponge. Rather than feeling "not myself," I felt intensely, newly, more myself than ever before.

The strongest feeling was that now I knew them all. That whereas for thirty-six years they had swum around me in complicated patterns that I had at best dimly perceived through murky water, now all was clear. (p. 305)

However, Ginny does not stay only with this clarity that came with remembering finally what had happened; she also tries to imagine her father and how he could have possibly crept into his daughters' rooms to abuse them. The book ends with Ginny stating:

I can't say that I forgive my father, but now I can imagine what he probably chose never to remember—the goad of an unthinkable urge, pricking him, pressing him, wrapping him in an impenetrable fog of self that must have seemed, when he wandered around the house late at night after working and drinking, like the very darkness. This is the gleaming obsidian shard I safeguard above all the others. (pp. 370–371)

Memory* lets her finally put the pieces together and imagination helps her see her father in all his terrible humanness.

*It is beyond the scope of this chapter to get into a lengthy analysis of the "false" memory-"true" memory debate that has recently emerged. (See the September/October 1993 issue of *The Family Therapy Networker* for a good introduction into the complexities of this issue.) What is clear is that in regard to remembering, therapists have enormous responsibility for using their power and social authority in a way that neither distorts memory nor silences or denies it.

Imagination: From the Singular to the Collective

We tend to believe that imagination is something private, but it is imagination that allows one to understand what people feel, who they are. It is the quality of that attention that is most important in any real imaginative act.

—*John Berger (1992, p. 11)*

. . . You know the mind, how it comes on the scene again and makes tiny histories of things, and the imagination how it wants everything back one more time. . . .

—*Richard Hugo* Letter to Matthews from Barton street flats
(cited in O'Connor, 1990, p. ii)

Imagination is what allows us to connect with other people because with it we can envision them in other times and places, in different situations. We can fill out the past, project a future; imagination is essential for moving stories through time, speaking in different voices, and elaborating memory.

Cases described earlier in this chapter illustrate the importance of imagination. Mercedes and her friends imagined themselves as children about to become teenagers. It enabled them to go back in time with Mercedes's story and enact a wonderful birthday party. Imagination helped Mercedes write a letter from the abuser's perspective—giving her an acknowledgment of his responsibility in words written as if he were speaking to her. Imagination helped her speak as an eleven-year-old, with all of the hurt and anger she experienced then. For Kay Odo, imagination let her and her therapist speculate about what she might have said when she was younger, if there had been space for her to speak. For Tina and Gerald Jones, it helped them project into the future and think what their son might want to say in regard to their guidance and life "requirements."

Changing Stories:
Voice, Time, Memory, and Imagination

Human beings are meaning-making creatures. Our minds have an incredible capacity to wonder, hypothesize, be curious, and connect disparate experiences. We are constantly trying to understand and link the many events of our lives, and stories are a central way in which we put information together and make sense of it. Each time we tell a story we position ourselves in relationship to it. Voice, time, memory, and imagination provide us with all kinds of possibilities to make new meanings and place ourselves differently in relationship to a story.

THE PRINCESS WHO LIKED TO SAY "NO!"   Lena and João Pineda came to therapy with their ten-year-old daughter, Teresa, complaining that she never accepted their saying "no" to her. They were having a lot of discipline problems with her, especially around how much time she could spend on the street corner hanging out with friends — they were worried about what would happen as she got older if they did not change the pattern now. When the therapist asked Teresa questions, she pretty much went along with what her parents were saying. The therapist did not think that much of her voice had been heard.

During the session, Teresa was doodling and writing things down and talked about some of the numerous stories she had written. Wanting to hear more from her, the therapist asked Teresa if she would like to make up a story about a princess who did not like to *hear* the word "No!" and invent it about a particular situation. Teresa said, "Sure, that sounds like something that would be fun."

At the next session, Teresa walked in carrying a green notebook. In it she had written a story entitled, "The princess that *liked to say* 'No!'" An interesting shift. In the story she wrote about how "no" was Princess Teresa's new word and to everything her parents said or asked her to do, she said, "NO!" The story also contained a detailed description of a time when Princess Teresa asked King João if she could talk on the phone with her friend who had just called, even though she was already in bed: King João passed the buck to Queen Lena and asked her if it was all right.

After Teresa read the story out loud, the therapist asked the family what they thought about it. They began an intriguing discussion where João said that in fact he often had a very hard time saying "no" and that he did turn to Lena many times for her to say it. Lena talked about how hard it was for her to say "yes" because of her own somewhat sheltered upbringing in Portugal and be-

cause she was always worried about what might happen to Teresa. She also said that she was tired of being the one who usually said "no"; she wanted to be the "yes" person in the family.

The fantasy story led to a story very different from the first problem story that the parents told. It moved from being a rigid story about Teresa's refusal to accept their saying "no" to a tale that recognized how yes and no are linked. Teresa moved into imaginary time with the fantasy story, which seemed to free her to name some of what she experienced around limit setting. As her voice got into the "problem" story, the picture became more complex: Joao remembered how he didn't often say no; Lena talked about her memories of her protected childhood in Portugal. People's positions were changing in relation to the story. It was no longer just about the parents' saying no and Teresa refusing to accept it; it was also about who had trouble saying yes, who had trouble saying no, and who turned to others to say no for them.

Voice, memory, time, and imagination all help us make meaning and create these kinds of evolving stories. However, they play themselves out differently in various story forms. Telling or writing a story for oneself is different from speaking it out loud. A spoken story will vary depending on the listeners and the setting in which it is told. Documenting and sharing a story, whether through illustrations, in written case reports, or with video, allows yet another kind of witnessing and listening. In the next two chapters, we will look at oral, written, and enacted story forms and see what they have to offer therapists and clients.

4

SPOKEN STORIES:
SPONTANEITY AND IMMEDIACY

Allegations, Alligators, and Investigations

SEVEN-YEAR-OLD SARABETH QUINLAN sat on the floor of the therapy room outlining, with a dark brown crayon, a large elephant with a long trunk reaching up to ensnare some delicate-looking leaves. She had already drawn a green alligator with clumpy round bumps, partially submerged in water. Her mother, Sonya, and their therapist, Lilith, were also on the floor with their own sheets of paper. Sonya was drawing square boxes, one after the other, filled with stick people, office chairs, and other furniture. Lilith's sheet was a giant flow chart with swirls, arrows, and different kinds of connecting lines between family members and various helping professionals. Each person was drawing her version of the story of the two-and-a-half year investigation of allegations of sexual abuse of Sarabeth.

It had all begun when Sonya, recently separated from Sarabeth's father, was reading Sarabeth (then age four) a story about good and bad touch. In the course of the story, Sonya asked Sarabeth if anyone had ever touched her around her vagina. Sarabeth said, "Yes, somebody named Bobby touched me there." It wasn't clear who Bobby might be, or if he was another child, or an adult. Sonya, wanting to make sure that her daughter was OK, took her to her pediatrician to be examined. The pediatrician did not find anything conclusive, but felt compelled to make a report to the

Department of Social Services (DSS). DSS did an investigation but did not find anything that either confirmed that something had happened or ruled it out.

Subsequently, Sonya went into individual therapy looking for help with the changes caused by the separation: For example, economic difficulties forced her and her daughter to move from place to place until they settled into their current apartment. She talked about the unresolved allegations of sexual abuse that still surrounded Sarabeth and with the help of the therapist asked DSS to open up the case again. DSS did, broadening the number of people they investigated as well as interviewing Sarabeth again. They then closed the case, again without reaching any clear conclusion. Sonya's therapist then arranged for Sarabeth to be taken to a medical center that had a special sexual abuse investigating team. Physicians gave Sarabeth an internal exam and measured her vagina to see if there had been any penetration; purportedly, this could provide some definitive answer. This procedure was very traumatic for Sarabeth. After it was over, the team told Sonya that the exam was inconclusive; they really did not have norms on the size of vaginas for girls that young, so there was no way to know for sure whether her daughter had been molested.

Six months later, Sonya and her daughter entered family therapy for help with difficulties Sarabeth was having in school: She was having trouble adapting from an informal kindergarten to a structured first grade. She did not follow group procedures and often wanted to go off on her own and do things—when she didn't get her own way, she threw tantrums. During the first few sessions, the therapist and the team working with the family became very aware that there had been no resolution around the allegations. The family was able neither to say it happened and hold the abuser responsible for his actions and do their own healing and move on; nor to say it did not happen. Day care and school personnel, who had been involved with the various investigations, seemed to see and treat Sarabeth as if she were an abuse victim. The trouble she was having in first grade was framed in terms of her being "a sexually abused child." There was little recognition of all the changes that had recently happened in Sarabeth's life (her parents' separation, her and her mother's move into a new apartment), changes that for many children trigger feelings of wanting to be more in control of their schedule and activities, since they cannot control larger events.

As the therapist, Lilith, discussed these observations with Sonya, Sonya shared that she felt that the interventions had become a problem in their own right; the interviews, and the questioning and physical exams of Sarabeth had affected the family. In retrospect, Sonya felt very guilty about proceeding with the investigations because they had been so difficult for Sarabeth and nothing definite had been determined. Sonya felt strongly that she and Sarabeth wanted to move forward in their lives without the label of "sexual abuse victim" inappropriately following Sarabeth around.

The resolution Sonya was able to reach about the allegations and investigations was that they would never know for sure if something had happened. However, what they did know for sure was that they had tried every possible way to find out. Now, she wanted some way to put that story behind them so that they could go on with their lives.

Over the first seven or eight therapy sessions, Sarabeth and Sonya had developed a close relationship with the team. Sarabeth knew most of them from having spent time with them in the playroom while Lilith was meeting with her mother for part of the session. Most sessions had ended with the team members voicing their reflections and telling some stories from their lives. Sonya had also taken to calling the team up on the phone in sessions when she wanted to know what they were thinking. Lilith had also introduced Eli the Elephant (a hand puppet). Eli had become like another participant in the therapy—especially as one who told stories, including stories about hard things in her own life. She helped other people tell their stories as well. Eli became symbolic of therapy as a place where all kinds of stories could be shared.

Back to the Therapy Room

As Sarabeth, Sonya, and Lilith finished drawing their stories, they taped them on a wall. Lilith also put a long blank sheet of paper up on another wall. Sonya then invited the team members to come into the room to witness the three of them telling their drawn stories. Sonya began. She explained the boxes on her sheet. Each represented an office visit to the pediatrician, DSS, therapists, the day care center, DSS again, the medical center. She told the names of the experts, described locations, and talked of her own pain and upset at each of the visits and the pain and hurt she thought Sarabeth felt as well. As she talked, Sarabeth listened intently and began making a little cave-house out of cushions and chairs—she seemed to be making a safe space for herself. When Sonya was done, Lilith asked Sarabeth if she would like to tell the story of her wonderful drawing. She did not want to. All she did was to acknowledge that yes, it was Eli the Elephant and the alligator—referring to one of the stories Eli told about how her trunk had become so long when the alligator had grabbed it and pulled it. This story was one of several that Eli had told about adapting to changes in one's life.

Lilith told her story next. She explained that her arrows and swirls represented all the helpers who had become involved with this family over the last couple of years. It seemed that having all these people in their lives made it harder for them to make the transition into their new family configuration of two. Lilith high-lighted the strengths they had demonstrated in sessions that appeared to help them through these times: their deep care for each other, their ability to share their feelings, their willingness to ask for help. Again, Lilith asked Sarabeth if she would tell her story.

Sarabeth, obviously exasperated, said, "You guys keep talking over and over to me about the same things."

Lilith responded, "Maybe you are saying you want to get on with your life." Sarabeth looked at her carefully. Sonya nodded her assent.

Lilith said, "Well, we have that whole sheet of paper over there on the wall for the new stories happening in your life, but before we think about that, what do you want to do with these copies of the old story?"

Sonya said, "I'd like to put them in the trash. Let's take them down." Sarabeth quickly came out of her cave-house.

"I want to save my story," she said, while tearing her mother's and the therapist's story down from the wall. She and her mother started to rip and crumple them. Then, Sarabeth threw them on the floor and started to jump up and down on top of them. Her mother joined her. They laughed and jumped harder. The team cheered. They stomped the two stories into two crumpled piles and as they shoved them into the trash Sonya said, "They'll make good compost for what I've brought to share." With that, she brought out a small bonsai tree that she had selected as a symbol of beginning a new story. (In two phone discussions with Lilith before the session, Sonya had shared several ideas of symbols that she wanted to bring in to represent their moving on with their life.) She also turned on a cassette tape that she had brought in a tape player.

Taking out scissors, wire, and a little booklet showing different bonsai tree shapes, Sonya said, "I'm going to cut off some of the old limbs and make a new shape. I chose the design 'Informal Upright.'" She called Sarabeth over and gave her the scissors. With the song, "I Feel So Different"* by Sinead O'Connor playing in the background, Sarabeth began to clip away branches and her mother started to wire and reshape the tree. There were a lot of tears in the room now.

This in-session drawing and telling of the story and then its symbolic transformation, provided a way for Sonya and Sarabeth to acknowledge their experience and to move beyond it. An interrupted story that had been told in bits and pieces in many public settings was brought together and finally given an end. Professionals were there not to investigate or ferret out other details, but to support the family. There was an opportunity to witness the story differently. The team listened, but did not intervene; they shared with Sonya and Sarabeth in some small way what they had gone through. The story was brought back within the control of the family. Sonya was able to openly acknowledge her mixed feelings about going through all of the investigations; Sarabeth had the opportunity to begin to understand how the different investigations were linked and how her mother felt about taking her to all those various places. The therapist, in trying to make sense of the impact of this story on their lives and others that were involved with them, gave them the opportunity to look back and try to understand their history.

It was fascinating to see how each chose to draw the story. Sonya drew each of the places that had come to signify more

---

*This song describes the singer's positive shift in feelings and views toward relationships and how she now "feels so different."

intrusion into their lives and no conclusions. Sarabeth drew Eli the Elephant—the symbol that many kinds of stories could be shared. Lilith, the therapist, tried to capture a sense of how all the contact with the outside systems had affected them as they moved from a family unit of three to two.

A range of techniques were used to facilitate this story-sharing. First, Eli the Elephant (introduced in the second therapy session) demonstrated the importance of being able to share stories. Then, the medium of drawing allowed each person to visually express her version of the story. These representations were then used as prompts to help tell the story verbally. The drawings also put the stories into a tangible form that could then be transformed. Finally, the old stories were tromped on and put into the trash to make compost for the bonsai tree. Incorporating the ritual reshaping of the tree with the story-sharing provided a powerful symbol of their new life: Things were not always perfect but they could be reshaped and continue to grow.

After this session, the family and therapist were able to address a range of issues. Lilith and Sonya met with school personnel to say "this is not a damaged child but a child who can be held responsible for her actions." They created a token system to acknowledge Sarabeth's good behaviors and she began to do much better in school. Sonya also made sure that any information on the investigations and the allegations of sexual abuse were taken out of Sarabeth's school records. And Sonya began to work out the divorce agreement with her husband.

Three Story Forms: Spoken, Written, and Enacted

How are decisions made in therapy about the kinds of techniques to use to facilitate stories? Whether stories are spoken, written, drawn, enacted, told in session or out of session, transformed from one medium to another, listened to by certain people and not by others, they will have different effects on clients, therapists, and the treatment. In order to think about these choices, story forms can be separated into three distinct categories: spoken, written, and enacted. While these three categories can easily overlap with each other (an oral story, for instance, can be written down), each of these forms offers unique resources to therapy.

Spoken Stories

Oral stories are often the most accessible: People naturally bring them to therapy. There is an immediacy with their telling, and the teller's emotional nuances are conveyed by voice, body movements, and pace of speech. Oral stories are not preserved (unless they are video- or audiotaped), but exist as "one of a kind" in the moment. Spoken stories are appropriate for any age: People do not need to be able to write or draw, nor do they need to be concerned about acting them out (as they might with enacted forms of a story).

Written Stories

The power of the printed word is accessed with written stories. They can be easily shared, disseminated, and passed on. On the other hand, when things are written down, they tend to become fixed—to be seen as "this is the way things are." In printed form, stories lose some of the potency of the impromptu, spoken word. However, the written form *does* offer rich opportunities for transformation: It can be specially preserved, put away for safe keeping, frozen, burned, cut in half, ripped, and/or shredded. Many symbolic possibilities are available, depending on where people want to move next with the story.

Enacted Stories

In enacted stories, tales are acted out in the therapy room with clients either playing the parts of themselves or others (as in role-playing and sculpting), or using puppets that represent either family members or fantasy characters. This is the most vivid form of storytelling. When stories are acted out, people are in the story and telling it at the same time. They are doing it with others and the participants have available to them the expressive capabilities of their bodies. Physical expression may be tapped in some new ways.

In the case described at the beginning of this chapter, it was important that the story of the allegation and subsequent investigations not only be "spoken" in therapy because the story had been documented in fragments over the years by DSS, medical doctors, and the previous therapist. Yet, the family did not have these reports and there was no denouement to the story. The therapist and family made their own documentation of the story which allowed them to pull the pieces together and set the stage for creating their own ending and moving on. This documentation also allowed the symbolic tearing down of the old story and its symbolism as compost for new growth.

In thinking about which story form to choose (oral, written, enacted, or some combination thereof), a key element to consider is how changing the medium might open up other interpretations, understandings, and/or new story opportunities. For instance, enacting a story that has only been rigidly told with flat affect may access more of the story's emotional meaning. Or, as a minimal story is elaborated verbally, writing it down may lead to a different appreciation of new information found, as well as a concrete awareness of where information is missing. In deciding which medium to use, each form's unique strengths should be kept in mind: the spoken story's simplicity and appeal to all ages, the written story's symbolic transformations and easy capacity to disseminate information, and the enacted story's tapping of emotional reactions.

Sometimes a story needs to be in a certain form, such as a written termination report. It behooves therapists to be cognizant of how the requirement of a particular medium may affect the meaning-making process. For example, the way termination reports are traditionally done (with no input from clients) moves the therapist out of the spoken dialogue with the client into an internal dialogue within the therapist which the therapist then puts down on paper. This is a large shift; there are no longer any feedback loops in place to check out ideas, meaning, and interpretations. (A number of ways to put these loops back in with written reports are described in the next chapter.)

In the rest of this chapter and in Chapter 5, techniques that can facilitate working with each of the three forms of story will be explored. These techniques can help clients give full voice to their stories as well as help clients and therapists think about ways in which the story can be worked with if it is told or shared in another form. The techniques that will be covered are listed in Table 3.

Table 3. *Story Techniques*

Spoken stories
- Telling one's story
- Story-go-rounds: One person starts the story, then each person in turn picks up from where the previous teller left off and adds to it
- Giving back stories: Another person tells what they hear of *someone else's* story
- Sharing mirror stories: Sharing stories that mirror issues in one's life or someone else's life
- Structuring the storytelling: Speaking as if writing a letter, creating unfinished fables, listening and telling from behind the one-way mirror

Written stories
- Mini stories: affirmations, appreciations, thanks notes
- Reading others' stories
- Writing a letter
- Writing one's story
- Co-writing case reports and documents

Enacted stories
- Acting out the story
- Sculpting
- Using puppets and other props

Spoken Stories: Tellers, Listeners, and In Between

Telling One's Story

Oral storytelling can include story-go-rounds, mirror stories, telling what you hear of another's story, and structured storytelling—using known formats (such as talking as if writing a letter) to help people tell their tales. In the first three chapters of this book, a number of examples were given of clients' telling six different types of stories: intertwined, distinct, minimal, silenced, rigid, and evolving. We looked at how these story styles enabled people to make meaning of the events of their lives.

However, it is not only clients' stories that can be an important resource in treatment; when thoughtfully shared, therapists' stories offer ways to link therapists and clients in exploratory, collaborative relationships. In asking clients what was most helpful/least helpful in treatment, many said that it was very supportive to hear stories from therapists' lives about issues that were similar to their dilemmas. Clients stated that this helped them feel that they were not crazy or so different from others, but rather that they were connected by common concerns. They felt less isolated with their problems. For some, the stories also suggested ideas for other ways of thinking about their problems and new ways of trying to resolve them. The boundary between what is public and what is private in therapy becomes more fluid when therapists share stories about their own lives. Usually, it is only the clients who "publicly" disclose in therapy. The lives of therapists have traditionally remained hidden in the therapeutic process.

Therapists in turn, describe that using this technique helps them empathize more closely with clients. As one team member stated, "When I listened to Zora tell her worries about whether her daughter was really sharing with her things that were happening to her or not, it touched my heart. It made me think about my own situation with my daughter and how I tried to work it through." When therapists tell their stories, they position themselves in closer proximity to clients. Solutions to dilemmas they share are not planned as embedded suggestions; rather, they are person-to-person sharings of ways people have found to cope with issues.

BACK TO ALLEGATIONS, ALLIGATORS, AND INVESTIGATIONS.   In the case described at the beginning of this chapter, Sarabeth's father had little contact with her. This was partly as a result of the sexual abuse investigations. He was never directly implicated, but he was questioned at one point in the process, and expressed fear about visiting with her alone—fear that other allegations would come up. As Sarabeth grew older, she had more and more questions about why she did not have much contact with her father, and started asking her mother to let her call or write to him. Sonya was hesitant to do this because she was afraid Sarabeth would be hurt if Sarabeth's father did not respond, or if he responded negatively.

At the end of the session where this had been discussed in detail, two members of the team asked if they could come into the room and tell their quite different stories about building relationships with their fathers after their parents divorced. One team member grew up in a small town in the South. Her parents divorced when she was young, and she lived with her mother. She was left on her own to take public transportation, get rides from relatives, and to figure out how to connect with her father. She described how hard this was—that she wished the adults had facilitated seeing her father more—but also how she felt like she had the space to work through how much or how little contact she wanted with her father. The other team member shared a different experience: She had felt caught in a loyalty bind between her mother and father after their divorce. If she spent time with her father, her mother was hurt. She was grilled by her mother about what she did with her father, what he was doing, and how she felt about him. She felt so trapped between them that it was hard to have a relationship with either of them. As she grew older, she was able to put some boundaries around her mother's intruding into her relationship with her father. She was able to talk to her mother about ways in which her questions and comments made her feel caught in the middle and how she wanted to be able to spend time with each of them, without feeling like she was hurting the other.

After hearing this, Sarabeth's mother thanked them for sharing their experiences and commented, "You know, hearing their stories made me aware that I have to trust that Sarabeth too will find her own way to have a relationship with each of her parents. Yes, she may be hurt along the way by her father, but I can't control that. All I can do is be there to comfort and support her if she is hurt." After this session, Sonya began to let Sarabeth call or write her father.

When hearing about a client's life evokes a story(ies) from a therapist's life, it is important that the therapist think clearly about whether or not the story that comes to mind is appropriate to share with the client. There are a number of key issues that therapists need to consider.*

First, the therapist may be more in touch with his or her own emotional reactions when recalling a story from his or her life. These emotions need to be taken care of responsibly by the therapist and a boundary kept between them and the client's emotional responses. The therapist must keep in mind that telling a story from his or her life is not being done for the benefit of emotional discharge; the story is being told to help the client and the therapy process. The therapist cannot have an emotional investment in

*Thanks to Georgi Lockerman for help in talking through and thinking about many of these issues.

needing the story to be listened to or reacted to in a particular way. If the therapist is self-disclosing, it should be done in the spirit of letting the client choose when/where/how to react and/or use (if at all) the story. The telling of the story should usually be brief and to the point; the client can always ask further questions.

Second, the therapist needs to decide which pieces of the story to share. For example, sharing any solutions to dilemmas only makes sense when the therapist recognizes that the client is "with her" in the telling of a problem. The therapist also needs to decide what level of disclosure is comfortable for him or her.

Before sessions, team members and supervisors can help therapists think through some of these issues by asking questions like: What would it be like for you to share that story with the family? For the family? For the team members watching? Why do you want to share it? Has the family seemed interested in hearing your stories, or would they seem irrelevant and/or intrusive? These kinds of questions can guide postsession analysis as well.

Story-Go-Rounds

Family members often come in prepared to tell *their* sides of the story. For some time, they may have been creating their versions of who the key players are, who is at fault, and who needs to do something differently. One way to intervene in these competing stories is to ask people to do a story-go-round. Rather than asking for each person's individual view of what has been happening, ask them if they would be willing as a family group to tell you the story. This can be especially helpful to do if, as people start to share their views, others start to challenge them, argue with them, or get very upset.

In a story-go-round, the family members sit in a circle and one person begins the story with three or four sentences. The next person picks up the story from there and adds some thoughts, and so on around the circle. This can be done in a playful and inventive manner, and people can be encouraged to use some of the traditional markers that indicate a story mode that fits their social and cultural context. For instance, a family with children might feel comfortable beginning with "once upon a time" or "in the land of," or ending with "skit, skat, scout, the tale's all told out."

DIFFERENCE IN THE FAMILY. The O'Callahans, an Irish Catholic family with four children ranging in age from 13 to 23, came in with concerns about their oldest child, Eileen. She had moved out of the house and was living with her boyfriend. Her father was furious and would hardly speak to her, and her mother felt caught in the middle between her daughter and her husband. Family members came into the first session very tense, and immediately began interrupting each other as they tried to speak. The therapist asked if they would agree to do a story-go-round as a way to slow things down a little but still hear from everyone. The 13-year-old daughter, Meg, started. She said, "Once upon a time I used to be really close to Eileen and now she's not there anymore and I'm lonely and Mom and Dad are fighting a lot about it and I'm really confused because they keep telling me, 'don't copy your sister, don't be like her' and I don't know what to do."

Her older brother Robert picked up the story next. "The older kids are confused, too. We think Eileen should be able to make some of her own decisions and we want to be able to make some of our own decisions, but she's doing things that we were taught in our family never to do."

Then William, age 18, said, "We're all mixed up about what it means as we get ready to go out on our own more. I mean some of the things Eileen is doing are not that bad and some of our other friends are doing them."

Mr. O'Callahan went next. "Well, if they are, then I don't know about them and I wonder if they are really people you should be friends with anyway. We taught all of you to do right and if she can't follow the rules of the family, she's not in the family. It's as simple as that."

Mrs. O'Callahan followed her husband. "In a way it is as simple as that, especially when the kids were younger. But, I don't know what to do now. Eileen is 23 and starting to make her own life."

Amazingly, Eileen was able to end the story with a bit of humor. She said, "And they came to family therapy and didn't live happily ever after—that would be boring—but they did sort through some of their anger and confusion with each other."

This story-go-round gave the therapist a sense of the different positions family members were in, but without the presentation of

five or six intense competing stories. Themes other than just the
"badness" of Eileen had a chance to emerge. Other family members could voice some of their confusion as they experienced the
conflict between Eileen and her parents. The theme of what it
means to be a family with children growing older and making
decisions began to emerge.

Before beginning a story-go-round with clients, it is important
to give them a few simple ground rules. Encourage them to use
the story format. Ask each person to speak a few sentences and
try to connect them to what the previous person said. Support
them in telling their own ideas rather than reacting to previous
sections of the story with "that's right" and/or "that's wrong."*

Giving Back Stories

Often what is central to the telling of a story is the teller's sense
that he or she is being heard. If he or she does not feel heard, he
or she may tell the story over and over, or be unable to move on
to other stories. When a story is told back to someone, there is a
chance to hear how others have taken it in.

TWO BEDS, TWO HOUSES, OR BEAR-BEAR'S LOCATIONS.   When I
separated from my daughter's father, she was just turning six.
Bedtime was the place in her daily routine where she focused on
her loss of her parents' being together. At night, she would say
how much she missed her dad and how hard it was to sleep in two
different beds and how we both used to say good night to her.
"And what is the matter with this house anyway—it has a lot of
spiders in it and the other house didn't and I'm not going to sleep
until you go around the room and get that piece of spider web,
and that spider, and that looks like another part of a web over
there." All this from a child who had never been afraid of any kind
of insect or bug.
It was hard for me to listen to Natalya's complaints about how

*A good way to practice doing a story-go-round is to ask your own family at the
dinner table to tell a story (make-believe or real) in this fashion. Or try it out with
colleagues you work with by asking them to create a training or work group story
in this format.

different things were and how hurt she was. I felt responsible for her upset. I tried to minimize it, to stay focused on what was working well for us. And of course the more I minimized it, the more she wanted to talk about it. Along with a nightly litany of how hard it was to have two beds in two houses, it got to the point that I was now being asked to pick up not only spider web pieces and spiders, but also any dark specks or pieces of fluff in the room that could possibly be anything to do with spiders.

She didn't feel heard. I needed to do something different. I started by just listening to all the complaints at night, no matter how tired I was or how late it was. I asked questions to make sure I really understood. I kept notes about what was difficult. And then I began to tell her the story of "Two Beds, Two Houses, or Bear-Bear's Locations." (Bear-Bear was the stuffed animal that she had slept with since she was six weeks old.) I described how one bedroom was more cave-like with a sloping roof and low skylight and the other more boxy and light; how different it was getting hugs from only one parent at night; and how hard it was to know that any time she was going to see one parent, it automatically meant that she was not going to be seeing the other parent. I talked about Bear-Bear, who also went back and forth between the two houses, and what he found easy and hard about it. I tried to let Natalya know that I was hearing her story. (This eventually became a written book that she and her stepsister and stepbrother illustrated. For a look at how she drew the spiders, see page 91.) After the telling of this story several times, the nightly routine of hearing how hard things were and picking up all the "spider" pieces stopped.

In therapy, it can be important for therapists to give people back their stories by letting them know that the details as well as the emotional significance have been heard. Pulling together information with phrases such as "I hear you saying . . . " or "You describe . . . " or "It seems that . . . " and then as much as possible using their own language to tell what you have heard, can be a good way to communicate that you have been listening. When therapists can hold the particular way a person has constructed a story, this often can then free the client to work with the story in some new ways.

4

At Mommy's house before the bunk bed's came, I got to sleep with
Mommy in her bed. I liked that, to be right next to her but she says I move
around a lot and snore so mostly I sleep on my top bunk. (You should hear
my Mommy snore - she can't hear it so she doesn't know.) Sometimes Peter
Panda sleeps with Bear-Bear and me. He's a new step-brother panda to
Bear-bear that Abby just gave me for my 8th birthday.

It's light up on top of my bunk bed and I like being able to see down
over all my animals and books and toys. But, there are spiders. My
Mommy's house is in the woods under a lot of trees so the spiders just drop
down on it. At first at night I used to ask her to come in and clean out all
the spiders before I would go to sleep. I told her I wanted her to be back
with me at Daddy's house where we all used to sleep and there weren't any
spiders.

Sharing Mirror Stories

Telling stories from one's own experience that mirror someone else's concerns or problems can be an important way for people to feel supported, and for them to get other perspectives on their dilemmas. When mirror stories are told between family members, they can help rebuild empathy and an understanding of the different positions in which they find themselves. It is important that the stories be told with the aim of supporting someone else's concerns and not to compete with them or to minimize them. Mirror stories are distinct from therapist or team stories because they are shared between family members with the intent of shifting their experience through the story-sharing process.

I FELT LIKE THAT TOO.   The Cohen family described in Chapter 2 (see pp. 48–50) came in for therapy describing difficulties parenting their six-year-old son, Able. Matthew, the father, reported being particularly aggravated with Able when he asked him to do things. He felt Able purposely dawdled and procrastinated, and the more he tried to get him to get ready to go or clean up or finish something, the more he slowed down. When asked why this upset him so much Matthew said, "Well, I guess I'm reminded that I did the same things with my dad. I didn't feel like I could be openly resistant, so I dragged my feet on everything."

The therapist asked Matthew if he had ever shared these stories with Able. Matthew said, "No, I hadn't thought of doing that."

The therapist then asked, "What was going on inside of you when you felt like resisting?"

Matthew replied, "Well, part of me wanted to be good and do what my father asked. I knew he would praise me and I liked that. But another part of me really wanted to do what I wanted to do — it was a little more exciting and fun. It was like there was the 'good' part and the 'naughty' part competing inside me."

"What do you think would happen if you shared some of your stories with Able and explained to him some of your own mixed feelings?"

"I'm willing to try it," Matthew answered.

When a parent shares with a child stories of similar dilemmas, it can do a number of things. It can help the child see that adults were once children who struggled with similar things. In going back to his or her childhood, a parent can sometimes empathize more with the child's position as feelings are reexperienced. Vocabulary and ways to think about, understand, and describe emotional reactions are shared in the stories, giving children tools with which to describe their own experience.

In the video "Just a House, Not a Home" (Minuchin, 1982), after the father and stepmother tell stories at home about the trouble they used to get into in high school, the teenage son (whom they were arguing and fighting with a great deal) says, "It's like they are real people who were my age once."

This same strategy can work in other situations, not just parent-child relationships. Older and younger sibs, or peers that have experienced similar concerns or problems can share their stories. When working with mirror stories, it is important to remember that no one set of experiences is ever completely the same as another. It is up to the listener to find what resonates with his or her own observations. The point of telling the mirror story is to make openings for different kinds of conversations as two or more people connect their stories and find ways to name and understand their experiences.

Structuring the Storytelling

Sometimes a story is in a very chaotic form or is very hard for others close to the teller to hear because it is so painful or because it stirs up so much turbulence in the relationship with the teller. It can be necessary to use formats that structure the telling for each person as well as for the listener. These can be known formats such as letter writing, shaping a story by providing an unfinished fable, or using some of the technology of the therapy process to set up a structure. For example, a person can go behind the one-way mirror to hear another person's side of the story that he or she finds very hard to listen to, and then use the phone to tell his or her version.

SPEAKING A LETTER. Emma and Edward Droke were in the middle of a very painful separation after a 15-year marriage. They had a history of intense fighting that occasionally erupted into swearing and hitting, and at times they found it very difficult to be in the therapy room together. The volatility of the situation was heightened by the fact that they had both become romantically involved with the same person. Ms. Droke had moved out and the therapist was trying to get visiting arrangements worked out for their four children. As she asked Edward and Emma to go over their typical day, now that they had separated, and what their current needs were in regard to parenting, they kept interrupting each other and arguing about what each had to say. At one point Mr. Droke started swearing at his wife. After the therapist stopped him, she asked the couple if they needed a more structured format to feel safe. They both agreed that they did. The therapist adapted the psychodramatic technique of verbal letter writing (Sacks, 1974). She asked the couple to sit back-to-back in their chairs, and for one person to talk to the other about their schedules and where the children were when, as if he or she were writing a letter to the other one. The letter "sayer" was to start out with the date, address, and name of the other person (for example, "Dear Emma") and continue as if writing the letter. The therapist stayed with the letter writer, listened to what was said, and added a postscript at the end that stated some of the unspoken in the letter (as in psychodramatic "doubling"). For instance, after Emma spoke her letter, the therapist said, "PS, I really hope you can hear how much I mean it that we will always have to be parents to the kids no matter how we feel about each other, and that we have to find some ways to be parents together no matter how upset we are with each other about other things."

UNFINISHED FABLES.   Unfinished fables are another way to provide structure. A version of the invented story (described in Chapter 2), the unfinished fable offers a way of thinking about a situation outside of the boundaries of ordinary description. Fables can be particularly helpful when the therapy is feeling stuck and the same kinds of scenarios are repeated again and again, as they offer ways of introducing other characters, time frames, and content. They can also quickly tap into a more playful part of a person's experience.

A fairly long unfinished fable was described in Chapter 2 (see p. 49). However, they can be much less involved. For example, Greg, age nine, was brought to therapy by his parents because they were concerned about his social skills. The parents, especially his father, Roy, seemed more concerned about it than Greg. Roy, a very gregarious man, found it hard to believe that his son did not want to spend more time with other boys or join team sports and groups like the Boy Scouts—things he had always enjoyed. The therapist asked Greg if he would finish a story that he told him. Greg said, "Sure." Here is the therapist's beginning:

> Once upon a time I knew a Beaver named Benny. Now he lived with his mother, father, and two brothers. But Benny, quieter than his two brothers, was always being questioned by his mother and father about why he didn't play more with friends. Benny's dad, Bucky, was a great dam builder and he was always out helping other people with their dams and he'd ask Benny to come with him and he didn't understand it when Benny said, "No, I think I'll enjoy myself at home." Benny felt that his dad was always questioning and watching him. And the more he did it, the more nervous Benny felt. So Benny thought, "Hmmm . . . what are some ways I can let him know I'm working on this—to get him to keep from flapping his tail around in my business?"

Greg came back to session with a finished story telling how Benny could talk about the friends he played with in Beaver school, share more about why he liked doing some things alone, and ask Bucky Beaver if there were any times he liked being alone and what he liked to do then. This provided a jumping off point in therapy for some different interchanges between Greg and his father.

THE ONE-WAY MIRROR AND OTHER STRUCTURED TELLINGS.   Other ways to do structured tellings can involve asking people to listen for particular things such as what they think is hardest for a person to share, most painful, most difficult. This can get the listener invested in the process of listening in a different way. Rather than listen for how they are going to refute what the person is saying, they will think about the emotional experience of the teller.

The technique of doubling (taken from psychodrama) can also be used to flesh out a story. A therapist or team member sits next to someone telling his story and adds thoughts that may not have been voiced by that person but that the doubler intuits from voice tone and quality and/or affect that is expressed. The teller always has the chance to comment on whether what the doubler says feels accurate or not. This can be especially useful when the story is told with primarily one affect, such as anger, to help the person get to other emotions, such as hurt or sadness.

The technology of family therapy can also be put in the service of structured storytelling. For instance, a person can go behind the one-way mirror to listen to something that is hard for him or her to hear (Coppersmith, 1980a). Mr. and Mrs. Paulsen came into treatment with their 17-year-old son, Robert, who was hardly speaking to them. Robert and his mother had gotten into a fight the week before about use of the phone, and in their fight the phone was ripped off the wall. In the therapy room, Robert was unwilling to share his story of what had happened. However, he was willing to go behind the one-way mirror and listen to his mother's version and phone in when he disagreed and then tell his side. Robert had a lot to say on the phone and gradually two versions of the same event emerged. Watching through the mirror can buffer some of the emotional intensity that may exist in the room. It marks a boundary between each of the tellers, each of the stories. It also separates clients from nonverbal feedback so they are free to clarify their own perspectives, rather than being concerned and/or upset about how other family members are reacting.

Spoken Stories: Spontaneity and Immediacy

Various techniques can help people to tell their stories and, just as important, to know that they have been heard. Stories shared between therapists, team members, and clients can create connections and a sense of "normalness" about problems families bring to sessions. Story-go-rounds can help cut into the process of competing stories. Giving back stories can help bring together disparate information as well as let others know the ways in which they have been listened to. Mirror stories can help people put themselves in different positions in relation to each other—children can imagine their parents as young once, parents can remember when they were in similar situations to their children. Structured storytelling may be needed as a support to help tell very emotional or chaotic stories or stories that are very painful for others to hear.

There is more to telling one's story than being invited to speak it. The web of stories that we weave can create an environment where people feel validated, seen, and honored for their unique life events. Oral stories proffer immediacy and simplicity. They can quickly bring numerous vantage points into the treatment room or outside of it.

5
WRITTEN AND
ENACTED STORIES

Written Stories: The Power of the Word

WORKING WITH WRITTEN TEXTS can include a range of activities, from the simple writing of affirmation notes and thank-yous, to reading the stories of others, to using letter writing both in and out of session, to the more elaborate writing of one's own story or creating a family book. These techniques sometimes require more time than working with oral stories; they also draw upon the use of reading and writing skills.

The concreteness of words on paper can help hold intense emotions and let people see various ways to express them. Writers and/or recipients can also read the words at different times and places and then integrate the ideas put forth into their lives in some new ways. The written format also means that the text can be transformed with word changes and symbolic actions such as preserving the document, putting it in a safe deposit box, freezing it, and burning it (Whiting, 1988; Imber-Black & Roberts, 1992). There is also flexibility in who reads it, and how and when it is read.

The therapist can facilitate the writing process by transcribing stories as people dictate them. Using a computer can be a wonderful way to work with text as changes can be quickly made and copies easily printed for everyone. If a family has a computer at home, these same kinds of things can be done there. Adults and older siblings can help people write. A particular benefit of having certain people write down the stories of others is that the tellers can then sometimes feel like their story has really been heard by the writer. For other people, using a clear format like letter writing can help organize the process. Most people know the letter format and can easily work within it.

The technology that is often used in family therapy sessions to facilitate supervision can be put into service for the family. A story can be audio- or videotaped. Younger members of the family or members who cannot read can take the audio- or videotape home and thus be able to "read" the story. Family members can also tell stories on audiotapes, then give them to the therapist to transcribe.

Mini Stories

Affirmations, appreciation notes, and thank-you cards all fall into the category of "mini" stories. They are quick, condensed, positive expressions that speak to central interactions between people, but focus on only one key part of the story. Therapy often calls attention to what is problematic—mini stories can be good ways to bring out other aspects of relationships.

EMPHASIZING THE POSITIVE.   Marissa, a single mother, sought help with the intense struggles she and her 12-year-old son got into around chores and regarding limits on what he could and could not do outside of the house. Marissa had raised Doug pretty much on her own. When Doug was a year-and-a-half old, she had divorced his father, who had been recently convicted on charges of breaking and entering and sent to jail. Marissa often worked two jobs; money was tight and no monetary or emotional support was forthcoming from Doug's father, who was in and out of jail. She depended on her parents for help in watching Doug, especially when he was younger. Marissa felt very unsupported for her parenting. She saw her mother, in particular, as very critical of how she had brought up Doug. Marissa also felt that Doug did not really understand all she had sacrificed to run their household.

Single mothers often get little confirmation from outside the family. In the media, there are few good role models of women raising children alone. Society sends many messages that if children do not have a father active in their lives, they will somehow grow up damaged. Marissa had picked up some of these messages: For instance, she first requested that a male therapist see Doug alone because "he needed a man in his life."

Work in therapy included, among other things, supporting the strengths of this dyad and helping them see what they did for each other. Doug was behind the one-way mirror watching the therapist work with the pattern of criticalness that Marissa felt she was passing down the generations and that she wanted to change. In the discussion, it was clear that Marissa was not only very critical of Doug and his father, but of herself as well. A team member with Doug behind the mirror asked him what he usually did for his mother on Mother's Day, which was coming up. Doug said he usually gave her a card. The team member then asked Doug if he would consider making her a long scroll-kind of card with specific messages on it about what he appreciated about his mom. She said, "You know Doug, your mom doesn't get much appreciation from others in her life and its hard for her to appreciate herself. You might have the best chance of helping her hear it."

Doug agreed to make the large card and the team member began to write for Doug. Doug came up with a long, articulate list that spoke to the range of challenges this family faced:

> I appreciate that you take me places even when you are tired and don't really want to take me.

> I appreciate that it's not always easy for you to get along with your mom but you still try.

> I appreciate that you work two jobs to make enough money for us.

> I appreciate that we have a good time together most of the times that we do things.

> I appreciate that you have to do the parenting all the time, that you don't have someone that can help you.

Doug rolled up this list, took it home, and presented it to his mother on Mother's Day. She hung it up in the kitchen, not quite believing that he had in fact said those things. When she came back to the next therapy session, she needed to be reassured that those were really his words. However, because they were written down and something that she could look at each day, they became a consistent reminder of what Doug did appreciate.

In another case, where there was a lot of conflict between a 15-year-old girl and her mother, the therapist asked the daughter, Amanda, to do a variation of this appreciation list. She asked Amanda to affirm what she respected about her mother, Tanya, by writing it out. While Tanya watched in session, Amanda wrote out a number of things that she particularly felt good about in regard to her mother. These included things such as, "You taught me to speak up for myself; you showed me that women can be strong." The therapist used the generation of this list as an occasion to validate Tanya, commenting on how her good parenting had obviously given Amanda a lot of skills to carefully observe, note, and express herself. Tanya was then asked to hang the list at home in a central place, and to read it through at least three or four times each day, paying attention to how she felt as she read it. She was also asked to note when she had similar feelings during other parts of the day and to share these at the next session.

This intervention helped this dyad begin to break the cycle of negative interactions they had found themselves caught in, where one difficult interaction led to another. Small structured ways to highlight some of the things that worked between them were now in place. As Tanya put it, "Amanda's writing the list made me begin to trust again that we did have positive things between us. Reading the list reminded me of that, even when we had some kind of a scrap. Having to search for other times when I had some of those feelings opened me up to other things that did happen between us but that often got lost in the bickering."

The writing down of affirmations and appreciations is very different from hearing something verbally. Writing enables meaning to be taken in different ways; writing gives the chance for the ideas to be mulled over, rolled around in one's mind, and considered in various moods and situations. These affirmations can hold the kernel of central themes and stories between people.

THANKS FOR THE THANKS CARDS!   In a midsize urban school setting, the school counselors and psychologists were spread out over about 20 different schools. They did not have a lot of consistent contact with each other. Their roles within each of their respective schools (most worked at two or more buildings) had some built-in tensions: They were often seen by the teachers as having an easier job because they did not have the responsibility of a classroom of students; each principal was always vying for their time, trying to have them spend more time in *their* building. As a result, some of the counselors did not have much support within their schools and really needed support from their professional network. However, this was hard to provide for each other because they had to cover so many work sites.

Two of the counselors designed a thanks card and printed a number of blank copies. They distributed these cards through the school mail to each of the counselors and psychologists, so that they could write personal affirmations to other coworkers. People used them to write thanks for reports done particularly well, presentations at team meetings, and helpful workshops and counseling sessions that students and parents told them about. As one counselor wrote to the two counselors who started it, "Thanks for the Thanks Cards! They gave me a way to acknowledge how much my work depends on the work of others. I've hung up the ones I've gotten myself—on an overcrowded day when everyone wants some of my time, it helps to read them and remember why I'm doing this."

A remarried family, the Sterling-Isaacsons, does something similar. When children enter the household for their week with their mother and stepfather, at their first meal together each writes down one thing they appreciate about having the family together; these are then read aloud and commented upon. This invites everyone to be attentive to the change in structure and starts their time together on a positive note.

Reading Others' Stories

At times, what is most helpful for clients trying to understand their own story is to read about aspects of someone else's life that resonate with their experience (Tsempoukis, 1968; Weiner &

Stein, 1985). This can give them ideas on how to pull together disparate parts of their own life and help them feel less alone and isolated. Clues and strategies about how to think about concerns or solve problems are often more available to people when they are embedded in a text that is somewhat removed from the emotional field that surrounds their own history.

Having clients read what others have written is sometimes easier than asking them to write some part of their story. There is a variety of materials available for both adults and children, ranging from published books to your own compilations of client stories (with the clients' identities protected as well as with their permission). Published books may include things like autobiographies, biographies, story vignettes (as in books like *The Courage to Heal*, see Chapter 1, p. 10), or novels and storybooks. Self-help literature often includes clients' stories. When asked, clients will tell you whether they prefer novelists' renditions of human dilemmas, allegories, dramas, or true-to-life versions. They may have particular books that they already feel have been especially helpful to them.

Some children's authors, such as Jill Krementz, have focused on the stories of children under stressful conditions (see, for instance, her books on parental death, adoption, divorce, chronic illness). Told in the children's own words and accompanied by photos of the children, the stories offer an intimate mode of learning about the diverse ways children of different ages have coped with various issues. The benefit of these kinds of collections is that readers will find echoes of their questions and concerns somewhere in them. For instance, when a young teenage girl Deana was adjusting to her adoptive family, Deana found that she particularly related to one of the stories in Krementz's book *How It Feels to be Adopted* (1982) told by Melinda, as she too was adopted when she was older. Melinda described how she worried about her first mother at times, and how she found it hard to go back to the agency for follow-up visits because she was afraid she would see her there and she would want to take her home with her again. (Melinda and her mother used to have monthly visits at the agency when Melinda was in foster care.) Melinda also described wanting one of her adoptive parents around at all times so she could feel secure. As Deana said, "It was as if she had written about my mix of feelings when she said she wondered and was concerned about her mom, but really wanted to stay settled and close to home with her adoptive parents."

Mental health groups have started to publish some clients' stories. For instance, the Child Welfare League of America published three books on adoption written and illustrated by three adopted children in the Herbert family of the Washington, DC, area. *Being Adopted*, *I Miss My Foster Parents*, and *The Visit* each tells some part of their own story. Seven-year-old Latisha described going to visit her birth siblings who were in other adoptive homes. She wrote, "When it is time to leave we feel sad because we will not see each other for a long time. We hug and say goodbye."

The appeal of books of this type to other children can be great because the drawings and storylines help them directly imagine another child in a similar situation. With color xeroxing so inexpensive now and with computers often readily available, therapists can publish their clients' stories quite easily. These can then be made available (with clients' names changed and permissions given) for other clients to read if they wish. For instance, in the Robeson family, four-year-old Alicia had lots of excitement, questions, and worries about the upcoming birth of her new sibling. Using a simple text put together by adults, her parents helped her fill in the blanks and "write" down some of her concerns, as well as illustrate her story, which is shown on the next two pages.

Other children who read this (or have it read to them) are given some handles that it is OK to talk about both the good things and the bad things that might be happening with this change. Also, seeing the range of emotional reactions described by Alicia—from feeling sad and angry because the baby is playing with her toys to feeling good that a baby will be in the house—can help them name their own feelings.

The danger in having clients read the stories of others is the possibility that the story may not fit in some ways. For instance, Donald Dragon's Divorce Book (see pp. 32–40) was shown to two boys whose parents had recently divorced. The boys still very much wanted their parents to get back together and were doing everything in their power to try to make it happen. It was hard for them to accept the pace of Donald Dragon's Divorce Book, which moves quickly from divorce, to dating, and then to the possibility of stepparents entering the children's lives.

Some of the good things about having a new baby in our family
might be that

it's nice to have a baby in the house. Sometimes, with a grownup, it doesn't cry.

Pictures of The baby.

Good changes are sometimes hard too. One thing that might be
hard is

that the baby will cry. when it starts to crawl, it might sneak under the bed.

Here's a picture of something that I and my new brother or sister might do together. I'm giving the baby a bottle. I'm feeling sad and angry because the baby is playing with my toys.

Baby

Alicia

It is essential that stories be presented as a catalyst for people to name their own story, rather than as a prescription for "the way your story should be." Resonance needs to come from their experience and articulation of what it means to read and hear another's story.

Letter Writing

Writing letters offers some of the same benefits as structured storytelling described in the last section of Chapter 4 in that it is a known form and is not usually seen as a task as large as writing a story. Yet, letters can capture core events and themes of someone's story. They can be a very useful adjunct in treatment when clients do not have direct access to someone or they do not feel comfortable saying something directly to them.

Deciding whether to actually send letters needs to be worked out with clients. People need to talk through what kind of response (if any) they are looking for to the letters (Carter & Mc-

Goldrick Orfanidis, 1976). Expectations need to be clear that the letter writing is more for them than someone else, in that a person receiving a letter may have a whole wide range of reactions. Letter writers need to feel secure about what they have written and what it does for them, no matter how someone else reacts to it.

TWO SCARS—ONE FOR OTHERS TO SEE, ONE FOR HIM TO SEE. Two sisters, Clara, 17, and Connie, 15, had a stepfather, Ethan, in their lives for about nine years. They had little contact with their biological father and considered Ethan their father. In fact, when he first married their mother, Ethan said that he wanted to adopt them. However, as the years went by, it did not happen. In fact, Ethan developed a severe drinking problem and eventually became involved with another woman and left their mother. She became quite depressed with his sudden leaving, and the mother and daughters went through quite a difficult time, including a lot of conflict between the oldest daughter and the mother. As mother and daughters pulled themselves back together, they entered family therapy to look at their relationships with each other, particularly in light of another upcoming change, as the oldest daughter prepared to leave for college.

During therapy, both daughters expressed that they felt a lot of hurt and anger toward their stepfather for what they saw as his desertion of the family. Clara said that for months after his leaving she wanted to "scar him in two places: on his face so everyone could see it, and on his arm so *he* could always see it." In talking it over with their mother, they decided they wanted several sessions alone with their family therapist to work some of this through. Their mother supported them in this decision because she felt that they had often acted out her anger and upset at her second husband during the separation and subsequent divorce; she saw them as being very protective of her and her emotional state. She wanted them to have a chance to express their own reactions without feeling like they needed in some way to help her.

In their first session alone, the two daughters considered whether they wanted their stepfather to come meet with them. They decided that they did not want him there, but that they each wanted to communicate to him their story of the impact of his leaving the family, and what they currently felt about it. They each decided to write him a letter. They were not sure if they were going to send their letters, but they felt the structure would give them a way to work through what they wanted to say to him. In their third session, they read aloud the letters they had written. As the supervisor of the case wrote,

> The session during which the girls read out loud the letters they had each written was unforgettable. Everyone behind the one-way mirror was in tears. Listening to the strong, clear, articulate voices of these two young women felt like an honor. It was as if we were witnessing their growing up before our eyes. With both feeling and control they were each poignantly able to tell the man whom they loved as father, how much he had hurt them, and how much he was losing by having deceived and abandoned them. The endings of their letters speak worlds:
>
> (Connie, age 15) I don't want to reconcile with you, just explain myself in hopes for an end to all my anger. I would appreciate a response, but if it will be a kiss up, phony I didn't know or let's put it all behind us, don't bother. I no longer hate you as a person, but I do despise your past and present actions.
>
> (Clara, age 17) This letter is not to get you back into my life because there is no place for you here now. I have grown older and much wiser since you left. I have accomplished many things and I wish I could thank you for helping me but I can't. It's too bad that you had to leave. You are missing out on the best parts of my life. I have a wonderful boyfriend, I got my license, I'm attending Rutgers in the fall and I will be on the soccer and basketball team. If only you could have shared in all this but I guess your priorities are different than mine. Thanks for the first five years. (Davis, 1992)

After sharing their letters, the sisters discussed the experience of writing them. Clara talked about being surprised to realize all that she had accomplished on her own without her stepfather. She also said that she no longer had the feeling of wanting to scar him. Connie told of her relief of having the anger off her chest. Both girls also talked about the usefulness of letter writing: "Even if you don't send it, you get to say it, and sometimes writing makes it easier to say hard things out loud since you already 'said' it on paper."

Writing One's Own Story and Family Books

The writing down of one's story and illustrating it, rereading it, and sharing it with others offers a *documented* way to work. The process of writing allows people time for introspection and rethinking of their experience. The written form also lends itself to editing, changing parts, and deciding on other ways to frame, begin, add to, or end the story. Stories can be written by one person or by a group. The therapist can help by supplying materials, and offering ideas for how to do it, as well as with the production and copying of stories.

Junge (1992) describes writing the family story of a father's suicide with a mother (called Ms. F) and her two young sons, Jimmy, age four, and Mark, seven. The father had a history of depression and had been hospitalized for a month shortly before his death. Three days after he was released from the psychiatric hospital, he overdosed on some medication. Ms. F became very depressed and experienced intense anger at the mental health professionals who had been treating her husband. The two boys were unable to focus on their schoolwork and were very sad. A psychologist met with the family for four sessions. However, the psychologist felt the sessions were of little help because Ms. F could do little more than weep during them and seemed very detached from the two boys because of her guilt, anger, and grief. With the help of an art therapist, the psychologist decided with the family to make a book about their deceased father and husband. It was to include photos of him, their memories and feelings about him, events before his death, as well as their questions and answers about his death. They began to work on this book each week in the session. The art therapist wrote, "During our work, Ms. F became increasingly capable of concentrating and helping her sons to do so, resuming her nurturance of them. The distancing device of making the book and the focus on its pages seemed to dam up the previous overflow of the mother's feelings, giving her more control and more comfort and allowing more room for her son's feelings" (pp. 288–289).

The book was created over six sessions to talk and work through the family's concerns, questions, and issues about the father's life. When it was finished, the therapists bound it and asked the family to place the book in a safe place at home so anyone could read it whenever they wished. They also asked the family to read it to-gether at least once a week.

A year later, Ms. F called the clinic at the insistence of the younger son, who had said, "The book is falling apart and needs to go back to the clinic" (p. 289). It was indeed falling apart; Ms. F and her two sons had read the book together almost every night. "Ms. F stated that the book had given the family an avenue for communicating about Mr. F and a vehicle whereby they could continue to express feelings of all kinds. Each family member individually had read the book as needed in her or his own way and it was the only thing in the house consistently returned to its 'safe place' on the shelf" (p. 289). The therapists put the book back together with the family's help and also created a new section about what had happened in the family since Mr. F's death. During the second year, the family still read the book together, but less often.

A book like this can work on several levels. First, it can provide a structure for telling a very complex story. Second, it can be a holding place for a wide range of memories, feelings, and reac-tions. It can help people acknowledge what they have gone through, as well as help them move beyond it. For this family, the book became a central organizing tool that helped them communi-cate and share their experience.

A simpler version of writing one's story can be done by having people write down descriptive chapter heads of their story. This too can help a person cohere and make sense of events and their emotional reactions. For instance, Eric, in his mid-forties, wrote the following chapter titles:

Vietnam: All I Could Think of was Getting Home to my Sweet-heart

Honeymoon: She'd Won a Honeymoon Trip while I was in 'Nam—But We Had to Use it by the End of the Year!

No Time to Decompress: Home a Month and We Got Married

Same Time Next Year: Now We Were Parents—Hard to Look Back

Descriptive chapter titles can capture central tenets of a story. They can be combined with photos, letters, and quotes to flesh out the story.

People may also have parts of their story already written down or documented in some way. They may have written poems, short stories, or essays, or put together picture albums with captions. It can be important to find out how their experiences have already been storied.

For example, one woman had written an extensive and thoughtful story about being one of the early women ministers in her faith. I asked her if she was willing to share it with me. She brought a copy of it to the next session.

> The Philadelphia church basement out of which I directed the hunger project contained a pantry, storage room, and scant office space. I had just unlocked the three rooms when Lenore and her daughter arrived. Catherine looked to be about ten; she was alert, absorbing everything in sight. As her mother and I began to talk I realized that Catherine's eyes were fastening on my clerical collar. I tried to continue my conversation but was distracted by the inquisitive one, who looked as though she would burst if she didn't speak.
>
> "Would you like to ask me something?" I said to Catherine. She nodded and opened her mouth several times before the question popped out. "Are you the Pope?"
>
> What a delightful conversation followed! Catherine was Roman Catholic—she knew that women could not be priests. The only other label she had for a person wearing a symbol of religious vocation was pope. We talked at length about the church and about God, about what I thought and what she thought about women being barred from choosing to be priests. She wanted to know why I did choose, and what it was like for me. Catherine saw possibilities she had not seen before. Women of the cloth can create space for new visions. (Judith Mulllins, personal communication, 1991)

As I read her story, it helped me understand ways she had struggled with previous adversities and how she saw herself as a woman in the context of the larger culture. I was able to experience her great sense of empathy, care, and humor. I had a much fuller picture of her life and it helped me tap her considerable resources; if I had just asked her questions in session, I think it would have taken me much longer to find out about them.

Case Reports and Documents: The Therapy Story

Traditionally, the therapist or case worker has been the author of assessment and psychosocial reports, treatment plans, and/or termination reports. Clients' lives are storied through the eyes of these professionals, and clients typically are not shown or given these documents. This process seems inevitably to lead to inaccuracies as well as distortion of information and reinforcement of a hierarchy that the "professionals" best know the stories of clients. For example, when Alexandra gathered together 20 years of psychiatric reports on her that she had never seen (Roberts, 1988a), she found many errors, including no acknowledgment of the intense allergic reaction she had had to drug treatment in one hospital, and statements that her father had attempted suicide, when in fact he had only threatened it.

This process may be particularly problematic for families who have had extensive long-term involvement with helping systems — for instance, families with developmentally disabled offspring, foster children, and children in other need of services. Psychosocial reports may be following these families around from agency to agency. As Cohen (1992) notes in working with families with a member with cerebral palsy, "The main focus of such histories usually has been on deficits. These reports are generally written by professionals with little input from the family, and they often rely on information from previous reports, which were in turn derived from still earlier reports" (p. 52). He shares the story of a family whose history stated that the son needed dental work done because the parents had neglected his teeth; in fact, when the son had been in residential treatment, another resident had beaten him and kicked some of his teeth out.

As Imber-Black has noted (1988), this process just reinforces the rigid helper-helpee complementarity that is often found in family–larger system relationships. This can further disempower families, making them feel that they are in a one-down position. If an essential component of treatment is to help clients find their voice and share their stories, then it is imperative that they have collaborative input into the written documents that tell their story.

There are a number of different ways that the story may be written down: through co-creating treatment plans, having clients read and comment on all documents, and/or having clients read and write up any case descriptions that are to be published. In most clinical settings, some kind of assessment is usually required after the first couple of sessions. This can be done in conjuction with clients by giving them a draft of the therapist's thoughts and asking them to critique it and offer their comments. For instance, the Baldridge family was given a copy of an assessment report that began like this:

LOOKING TOGETHER AT WHERE WE ARE AT IN THERAPY AFTER THE FIRST FEW SESSIONS

This is a first draft. <u>Please underline what you particularly agree with. Put question marks by what you have questions about??</u> Write in your own ideas or changes, so they can be added.

The rest of the report was divided up into five sections: (1) Who has Gathered Together; (2) Brief History; (3) Things Working on in Therapy; (4) Musings About What has Worked and Not Worked in Therapy; and (5) Wonderings About Where to Go From Here. Every section had questions directed to different family members as well as blank lines for additions/changes.

Each family member was given a copy of the report and asked for their input. The 14-year-old daughter wrote TRUE in big letters across the section that stated, "Tension between son and daughter leads to mother moving in to protect the son and more conflict between mother and daughter." Mrs. Baldridge chose to underline the last part of a sentence: "The son and daughter are fine drawers, very thoughtful observers of their family, quite attentive to feelings passing between people, <u>as well as adept at finding loopholes or openings when things are unclear.</u>" Next to her underline she wrote, "Right on." Mr. Baldridge chose to add to the last section (Wonderings About Where to Go from Here), "I believe in the process of talking together about problems (anger, disappointment, resentment as applied to relationships) — negotiation is the hope that I have of finding a way in which we can listen to each other and accept our individuality. Just accept each other. Not necessarily agree, but try."

These comments were then used to put together the final report. The family was given a copy, and one was filed in the clinic.

Another family, going through a very difficult separation, was given the option of choosing the standard intake report (which the therapist had written up), or a letter written to the family, including subsections of comments to different individuals (but which all could read). The family members took both copies home, read them, and decided on the letter format because to them it seemed a more human way to describe their family.

Co-writing final reports can serve as termination rituals (Imber-Black, 1988; Roberts, 1988a) that can be especially important when the family has a history of hidden and secret information being passed on about them. With Alexandra and Julius, the couple where the wife had a 20-year psychiatric history, redocumenting that history was a central part of treatment. It gave them a chance to correct misinformation and name their own resources for coping with life's stresses, as well as to recast their story in a nonblaming systemic frame that gathered together the complexities of their experiences. They were named as the experts who knew best how to come together and solve problems, rather than sending Alexandra out to larger systems for help. Later, when I decided to write up the case for publication, I found I could not write the case alone — we collaboratively wrote the chapter that describes our work (see Roberts, 1988a).

Clients may or may not wish or have enough time to get this involved with case reports. A simpler way to include them is to ask them to read and comment on cases you will be publishing and to include and name their contributions (see Roberts, 1988b for an example).

Agency or private practice issues may require more time-limited variations of writing the story of therapy. In one large community mental health center, clinicians would write the contact notes at the end of each session, and then share these with families during the next session to get their feedback and input (Alexander Blount, personal communication, 1989). The information generated by this process was then used to write any treatment plans and assessment and termination reports. Other therapists take a few minutes at the end of each session for both the therapist and client to write brief notes about it. The therapist then takes responsibility for putting these notes together for the following session.

Some clients may need or prefer to have clinicians read their case notes to them. Other clients may not want to get involved in the details of what their therapist is writing.

In some agencies, there may be issues around clients' having access to this information—traditionally it may have been kept secret from them. The therapy case report is one of the concluding written stories in treatment; clients need to have ownership of this document, for at the core of any assessment/treatment plan is their life story. They need to have input in some way into what is written about them, and they should keep a copy of it.

Written Stories: Transformations and Reflective Distance

Written stories can run the gamut from simple thanks and appreciation notes, to structured forms like letter writing, to elaborate storybooks, to the concluding therapy case report. Stories in written form lend themselves to being shared among people. They are a durable representation that can hold both time and complexity on the page, and can offer some reflective distance to both the author and the reader.

Enacted Stories: Telling and Doing at the Same Time

With enacted stories, participants in therapy do not just describe interactions or talk about changes in behavior, they actually do them. Enacted stories allow people to tell the story and be in the story at the same time. As people create and put themselves into scenarios, movement, action, touch, and other sensory elements are brought directly into the treatment room. Enacted stories can provide powerful access into emotional states as well as help people experience the possibility that something really can be different.

Of the various techniques for evoking voice that have been described, enacted stories can take the most time with clients. Time is needed both to set up the enactment in a manner that gives a sense of safety and exploration for participants, and, when they are completed, to process and link what happens with them to issues being worked on in therapy. Time may also be needed to do various versions of enactments. Members of the family may want to exchange different roles or take over directing the scene so that various points of view can be demonstrated. Enacted stories usually cannot be described in sessions and then done for the first time outside of the therapy time. People need a supportive environment for getting up and doing something that is probably out of the ordinary for them, as well as for the reactions that can be strongly evoked by the enactments.

Stories can be enacted through role plays, family sculpting and choreography, and with puppets.

Acting Out the Story: Role Playing

Role plays require no preplanning or use of props. They can be a vivid way to access interactional patterns in all dimensions, including the emotional. Gloria, 36, lived with her 59-year-old mother, Norma. Norma was widowed some 10 years earlier and Gloria had lived in the family home off and on throughout her adult life. The two of them sought counseling because of intense conflict between them as well as for Norma's concerns about Gloria's health and her weight. Gloria was about 150 pounds overweight and was experiencing a variety of health problems because of this. Norma and Gloria described a pattern of getting into escalating fights two or three times a day around a variety of issues, including food, how the home was or was not taken care of, and the fact that Gloria was not working or actively looking for work. (Norma worked as an administrative assistant in a small firm that made brushes.)

As they described their situation to their therapist, Jim, he sensed that, while most of the time the disagreements ended up in a lot of conflict, with threats hurled that one or the other should move out of the house, once in a while their disagreements did not escalate to this level and they reached some closure on the issue. He asked Gloria and Norma if they would be willing to act out two scenarios: a time when they had disagreed about something and had been able to settle it without an intense fight, and a time when it had really escalated. As they enacted these times, he asked them to mentally note, with as much detail as possible, what happened when things did take off—what led to its getting out of hand, as well as what allowed them to disagree and work things out more calmly.

After a little apprehension and checking to see if Jim really wanted to hear what they got into with each other, they did the role plays. They found out that during the times that did not become so intense they stayed focused on the topic they were disagreeing about, and they each took responsibility for their part in the hassle and talked about their own behavior, rather than what the other person should be doing. This gave them a basis to begin transferring to some of their more intense struggles what worked with regard to slowing things down between them. Interestingly they also found that in the role play of the escalating fight, they could not get into it as intensely. As Gloria remarked, "Because I was supposed to be watching what happened in order to explain it, my emotions didn't take off in the same way."

Enacted stories can be done where one person takes the role of the other, one person directs it, then someone else directs it. People can be asked to freeze at key choice points and then choose options — clarifying that they can move in different directions during interactions.

Ways to carry some of the learnings from acting out scenarios into life at home can include prompt cards written out to remind people of key actions they want to be sure to do, phrase cards to help them access helpful phrases; and props, such as a red scarf or cloth (the red flag), to put out as a signal that things are progressing along a familiar path and other actions need to be initiated.

Sculpting

Sculpting can be a way to create a tableau of family interactions that can hold and communicate a sense of the way each person in the family sees and experiences it (Duhl, Duhl, & Kantor, 1973; Papp, Silverstein, & Carter, 1975; Simon, 1972). The focus is not so much on showing how a particular scenario goes (as in role playing), but rather on letting each person in the family place members in position to each other to show what they think is the essence of the relationships. The person who is creating the sculpture shapes people's bodies and facial expressions, and in family choreography (Papp, 1976) gives them key words to say, and/or adds a movement for them.

Sculpting can be a vivid way to communicate various versions of how people see the family, especially when there are perspectives that people are not aware of. It can also be a good way to help people envision what they are working toward and how they would like things to be in the family.

For instance, with the Harris-Morgan family (with three children, including one teenaged adopted daughter, Theresa), each of the family members sculpted the family as they currently experienced it. All of the sculptures showed Theresa separated from the family in some way. In one, she was standing on a chair, hands on her hips, and mouthing words at her siblings. In another, she had her back to her parents, arms folded, and her head hung down. There was a deep sense of isolation and pain in the sculptures. Then, the eight-year-old daughter was asked to sculpt how she would like the family to be in the future. She put the family inside a teepee, holding hands out over the fire, but touching each other shoulder-to-shoulder. This broke some of the wariness they had with each other, and gave them a chance to begin talking about how they would like things to be different.

With the Giardina family, the therapist had gone to the family home, eaten with them and done a session there, as well as gone to school to observe the seven-year-old son. She felt she had a good sense of current interactions. Mr. Giardina, in particular, voiced that he did not see how people could feel good about themselves in the family, given the way people were treating each other. The therapist did not ask them to sculpt how they currently saw the family but, rather, how they would like to see it in the future. Kristin, the oldest teenage daughter, put her sister out in the backyard pushing their two brothers on the swing and herself in the kitchen with her dad, making Sunday brunch and setting the table (her father was flipping pancakes); her mother, who had recently moved out of the house, was off to the side calmly watching.

When asked how it felt to be in this scene, Kristin said that it felt good to be doing things together, to be helping without being nagged. After each of them had sculpted how they wanted it to be in the future, they then set some goals for how to do things in their daily life, based on what they liked in the sculptures. These included things like helping with chores, not swearing at each other or using putdowns, finding more things to do together as a family, and being able to ask each other for help.

In order to help people feel secure with these more active techniques, people can be told that the "pass rule" is in effect at all times (Chasin, Roth, & Bograd, 1989). That is, they can choose to pass on either participating in or directing a sculpture or role play. People also need to know that they will have a chance to comment on, or redo a role play or sculpture that someone else directs that they have different ideas about. People need the safety of knowing that their voice is not going to be silenced by someone else's interpretation and also that they will not be left with raw feelings. Rather, they will have the chance to re-form and work through painful situations.

Using Puppets

Using puppets can be a more impromptu, sometimes easier, way to get at a central family story than telling it directly or writing it (Irwin & Malloy, 1975). Puppets work especially well with families where there are children in the age range of 3 to around 14. Using puppets as props to speak through and creating a puppet show often help people get into story creation.

WE'RE FRESH OUT OF THAT. The Devereux family had four young children between the ages of five and ten. Mr. Devereux worked days teaching high school shop and his wife worked nights at a clothing factory. The parents did not see much of each other. Mrs. Devereux got the children off to school in the morning and then went to sleep. Mr. Devereux was there when they came home from school, fed them dinner and then put them to bed. The parents brought the family in because of concerns they had with their five-year-old son, Ariel. He was not doing particularly well in a full-day kindergarten and his teacher was recommending that he repeat kindergarten the following year. Mr. and Mrs. Devereux were trying to decide whether to hold him back or ask that he be put in first grade.

In the second session, the therapist asked them to make up a puppet show. They created a family of animals playing and having a picnic in the forest. Ariel, who had chosen to be a lion, was quite wild. He kept grabbing the food from the other puppets and chasing them. The father chose the dragon puppet and was creating elaborate picnic sandwiches for each of the animals being acted out by the children. After making a long grinder with five different types of fillings in it for the horse puppet held by his oldest daughter, he said, "We have everything, we have all kinds of food on this picnic."

Then, Mrs. Devereux, holding a giraffe puppet, emerged out of the forest asking for a tuna salad. "Nope," said Mr. Devereux as the dragon puppet, "We're fresh out of that." So then she asked for chicken salad. "Don't seem to have that either," was the reply. She finally had to settle for a peanut butter and jelly sandwich.

When asked how this puppet show was like things at home, Mrs. Devereux said, "Well, it was like it in two ways. First, Ariel was noisy and moving around a lot; he's like that at home. Then, it's sort of like the cobbler's wife who goes without shoes. When everyone else asks for things they want — the kids, the neighbors, our friends — they usually get it from my husband. He's Mr. Nice Guy doing things for them. But when I ask . . . it's a different story."

Mr. Devereux sheepishly agreed that yes, this was usually the way it was. The therapist went on to engage them in a discussion of ways in which they might want to change this. "Remember the peanut butter and jelly sandwich" became a humorous code phrase to alert them when this pattern was occurring.

Enacted Stories: Re-acting and Re-telling

Enacted stories, simple role plays, more elaborate sculptures, or stories told through the medium of puppets, allow tellers to both be in the action of the story and name the interactions at the same time. Experiencing both of these positions simultaneously seems to deeply engage the tellers as well as lead to strong emotional experiences. They can feel themselves in the story as they step back and look at it.

Of the different story forms discussed, enacted stories probably require the highest comfort level on the part of the therapist as well as the most training. Oral and written stories are more commonly found in people's everyday lives. The therapist needs to communicate to clients ease with using enactments as well as a belief that they will open new possibilities for them.

Tales and Transformations

Working with both the content of stories and the form in which they are shared allows clients and therapists a rich variety of ways to connect across different ages and diverse experiences, as well as mark what is unique for each person. Clinicians need to be aware of what processes are involved when a story is spoken, told, and/ or enacted. Elements to consider in choosing a story form as well as a technique within that form include identifying what form(s) the story is already in, as well as what other mediums the client and therapist are familiar with and are attracted to. Therapists can ask themselves and family members: What will happen if this story is told in another form? How might it be heard differently, be expanded upon, or made available to us and to others in new ways? In what ways would a shift in form or the trying out of a particular technique support a sense of agency and possession for the teller? For the listener(s)? In another medium how might memory and imagination be tapped in some provocative ways? Will other possibilities for nonverbal expression and/or verbal expression be opened up? How might the responses of tellers, listeners, and witnesses change with a different story form or the use of another technique?

The style of the story may also highlight the need for one form over another. A story that has been secret for many years most likely will not lend itself to an emotional enactment as it is first being disclosed. On the other hand, a story that has been told over and over verbally in a rigid format may benefit from an enactment as a way to enter into exploring other emotions and understandings of the tale. The timing of where the person is at in regard to the story may also have implications for which story form to pursue. Is this story just emerging—or is a person in the middle of it—or is it a story with a long life but still no end? For instance, in the opening case of Chapter 4, Sonya and Sarabeth had an overt-old story with no denouement that was being shared in bits and pieces, here and there, over a long period of time. By drawing this story out, then telling it to professionals in an arena where there were no elements of social control and judgment of the story, the family had a chance to bring together all of its pieces, and to shape their own resolution of it.

There may be constraints on a form to take into consideration as well. The story form may need to be written in order to be shared with significant others who are not living in close proximity. Or perhaps a story needs to stay in an oral form because the therapist is not able to write the story in the first language of the clients—the language which may be the most comfortable and meaningful to them. One form of the story or technique within the form may also be more culturally syntonic for the clients.

Stories can be spoken, written, and enacted in a multitude of ways. However they are shared, it is essential that clients feel that they are in control of their own voice. Nowhere is this more important than in how their story is passed on to others (others who are often unknown to the clients) in the form of assessments and treatment and termination reports; clients need the opportunity to be involved in the telling of their story in these documents.

The content and form of stories also need to be examined within the larger frame of the cultural context in which they are embedded. In the next chapter we'll look at our cultural stories and how they inform and interact with our personal and familial stories.

6

CULTURAL STORIES: THE CRUCIBLE FOR PERSONAL STORIES

Double-Sided Life

Glasnost comes from the Russian word *glas* or voice. So it
literally means voiceness, or speaking out.

— *Vladimir Pozner (cited in Smith, 1991, p. 94)*

WHEN WORKING WITH Russian psychologists in St. Petersburg in
1993, I was struck by how they described their existence as double-sided in relation to the stories they could share about their
lives in the last several decades. They grew up hearing and reading
the official stories about life in the former Soviet Union — these
stories highlighted the political and economic successes of the re-
gime but left untold the stories of repression (such as the 4–8
million people killed during the time Stalin was in power), disas-
ters (such as Chernobyl and the world's worst nuclear accident in
1957 in the Ural Mountains), and ethnic differences and/or tensions (the former Soviet Union has over 100 different ethnic
groups). Moreover, the official stories did not convey the difficulties of the day-to-day life of many of the people.

During these same decades, there existed personal stories that
the people of the former Soviet Union told a few trusted family
members and friends. These stories described an existence different from the party line. They told of six to eight families sharing a
kitchen and bathroom in a six-room cold-water flat, and of di-

vorced couples having to stay together in the same room because neither one of them could get another apartment. They described the networks of support that had been created to help each other: during a factory lunch break one woman shopped for milk for all; another looked for fresh fruits; a third tried to find durable goods stamped as being made in the first two weeks of the month before factories rushed to fill monthly quotas and shoddy workmanship took over. They told of women and children waiting downstream from a forced labor logging camp, checking log booms as they floated by for the initials of their husbands and loved ones carved in the wood; if the initials were there, it meant they were still alive. (Tengiz Abuladze of Soviet Georgia showed this in his 1986 movie, "Repentance.")

As the Russian psychologists depicted this double-sided life, they said it was hard to have a sense of coherence about what was really going on. They were always trying to piece together the stories—to read between the lines of the official stories, to interpret them, and to see where their own experiences fit in. It was impossible to speak openly of the contradictions they saw, to name the untruths that were being promulgated. A political anecdote told by Vladimir Pozner, a Soviet television commentator, captured a sense of this dual life: "A man goes to a local health clinic and demands to see 'the eye-ear doctor.' The nurse explains there is no such thing—there is either a doctor who examines your eyes or a doctor who examines your ears and throat, but not one eye-ear doctor. But the patient is insistent. They argue and finally the nurse says, 'Well, there isn't one but if there were one, why would you want to see him?' The man replies, 'Because I keep hearing one thing and seeing something very different'" (Smith, 1991, pp. 95–96).

Stories that could be shared in the larger culture did not provide a broad-based arena to support a variety of personal stories. Rather, the cultural stories propagated a set political line that cut people off from their personal stories. Cultural stories are narratives about events and issues that cut across the lives of individuals and affect groups of people and families. They often offer particular constructions of historical events and societal issues and are silent about others, and have embedded within them strong messages and expectations about values, beliefs, and norms.

In the United States, many groups that are outside of the majority culture have had a similar experience to the Russian psychologists. As John Edgar Wideman, the African-American writer, said, "Everyone has to create legitimate myths and stories about their culture. These help us understand our right to be here, why this is *our* city. I didn't hear enough of those stories about African-Americans when I was growing up, so I have a real stake in telling stories, in legitimizing the culture. We know if we don't tell them, somebody else will, and they won't be positive" (Watson, 1990, p. 21).

James R. Kincaid, in a review of 17 important recent works by and about Native Americans, raises a series of questions about the context of stories: "Who gets to tell their stories? How do our stories of what is past, passing, or to come get to be manufactured, circulated, and understood? Whose stories are they? Who gets to make and tell them? Who is listening—and how well?" (1992, p. 1). He notes how infrequently the stories of Native Americans have been told, especially from their perspective. As Joe S. Sando, director of the Pueblo Indian Study and Research Center in Albuquerque, New Mexico, stated, "The American educational system is successful only in teaching dominant society values, methods, and superiority. We read only of *their* successes and *their* heroes. Perhaps this is because non-Indians write the books." (Kincaid, 1992, p. 29)

Which cultural stories are allowed and told in the larger societal context has deep implications for the family story process and family relationships.

FROM KULAKS TO THE KOMSOMOL TO QUESTIONING THE COMMUNIST PARTY. In the late 1920s, Natasha's paternal grandparents were accused of being kulaks, or the so-called "rich" farmers. They owned about 30 acres of land and 11 cows. As Lenin pressed for collectivization, the kulaks had their land and animals taken away from them to create collective farms. Natasha's grandparents and their seven children, ranging in age from 3 to 17, were forced to travel over 1,000 miles and relocate in a more isolated part of the country on a newly created group farm. Boris, the youngest child, was Natasha's father.

Boris grew up when the focus was very much on fervently embracing communism. He joined the Young Pioneers, then the Komsomol. He learned not to speak about the kulak past of his parents, as kulaks were described as enemies of the people. He lived through the Great Patriotic War (World War II) when Stalin was seen as the savior of his country. In his twenties, Boris rose quickly in the communist party and was given a very responsible job as an assistant to the director of a new sugar factory in southern Siberia. Shortly after, he married Irina, also a communist party member. Their first daughter was Natasha.

Many of the people who worked under Boris in creating the sugar factory were individuals who were sentenced to forced labor. They were sent to work for specified periods of time for so-called crimes against the state. When Natasha was growing up, this was not spoken of openly or acknowledged; she figured this out in her adult life when she learned more about the realities of Stalin's activities.

Today, Natasha, in her forties, is a biogeneticist and no longer a member of the communist party. As Russian society has opened up, she has tried to piece together and understand the effects of this double-sided storying in her family's life. She knows few stories about her paternal grandparents and feels that the denigration of them as "kulaks" forced her father and aunts and uncles to distance themselves from that side of the family. Her parents are still committed party members and when she tries to talk to her father about the workers on whose backs his plant was built he justifies what happened to them as an essential part of building the former Soviet Union — the individuals needed to be sacrificed for the larger good of the state.

On her mother's side, Natasha has discovered a great-grandmother who she thinks was Jewish, but her mother will not acknowledge this. Her maternal grandfather probably had some Gypsy heritage, but Natasha knows very little about him.

Which cultural stories were allowed to be told in the lifetime of Natasha's family directly impinges on the quality and kind of personal stories that could be passed down among them. Natasha feels that she has little history about her forbears because there were so many parts of their identities that could not be spoken about. She also finds it hard to talk with her parents about their lives because the communist party and the ideas that it felt people should embrace are now ones that she is questioning. But her parents, now in their late sixties, struggled and worked hard all their lives for communism. In their young adult years, there was primarily one story about what it meant to be a good citizen of the former Soviet Union. Now, they are being asked to consider that it was not only the *only* way to live their lives, but also the wrong way. Yet, to change their view of their lives means to question many of their values, as well as decisions they made. As Merle Goldman wrote about Sidney Rittenberg's life (the American who lived in China from 1942 until 1980 and was the highest ranking foreigner of the Chinese Communist Party), "[Rittenberg] still does not acknowledge that Mao's utopian Great Leap Forward caused the death of more than 30 million peasants, or that the Cultural Revolution, in which millions of people suffered persecution, brought anarchy to China. Obviously it is still necessary for him to find some good in a movement for which he gave the best years of his life" (1993, p. 11). Natasha feels that her parents find themselves in a similar dilemma.

For Natasha, many family stories are just not available. She finds herself cut off from basic information about her family. It is hard to communicate directly with her parents about some of the contradictions of their lives, given the official story line they were forced to buy into and the new stories that are now emerging. Natasha thinks her situation is common for people of her generation, that many of them don't have information about their grandparents. Also, her generation, in the middle of their lives, are being given the chance to reconfigure their personal stories within the political and historical events of their times in a manner that lets them begin to integrate them and to speak to the lies and coverups that occurred. However, this seems to be a very painful process for numerous people in the older generation because the new stories call into question many of the deep-seated beliefs that governed their life choices.

FROM JAPAN TO THE WEST COAST TO IMPRISONMENT IN A JAPANESE INTERNMENT CAMP. In the United States an example of a story that was silenced for many years was the imprisonment of Japanese-Americans during World War II. Karen Suyemoto, a psychologist, describes the effects this had on her family. In 1942, Karen's father, then age 12, was forced out of his small home on the west coast along with his parents and eight siblings. They were imprisoned at an internment camp, Topaz, in a barren desert near Delta, Utah. Her father lived there until he was 15½. For many years, Karen knew little about the family's experience there. It was not spoken of in the larger culture, nor was it talked about at home. As Karen wrote, "My sister and I have grown to realize that this is an important part of our identity that has been missing, this link to our father and his family past: the understanding of the camp experience and the impact it had on my father and his family. . . . This event [the internment camps] is just beginning to be acknowledged and publicized" (Suyemoto, 1992, pp. 24–25). One of the ways this has happened is that the United States government finally made reparations and gave a public apology to those who were imprisoned. Karen went on to write that this acknowledgment has supported her in exploring the "huge impact it had on myself and my family." The public documenting of another family's experience, by Yoshiko Uchida, in the book *Desert Exile: The Uprooting of a Japanese-American Family* (1982), also provided her with information about the camp and opened up the possibility of inquiring about and elaborating her understanding of her father's and grandparents' experience. Her family also embarked on a journey to visit the camp. Karen described it as follows:

> The year my sister and I graduated from college, my father, step-mother and I went on a tour of the canyons in Utah and Nevada. While there, we drove to Delta and visited the site of Topaz. This ritual return gave me a much deeper understanding of the experience than I had had before, not only in being at the site myself, but also in being able to share this experience with my father. He later said that, even more than receiving the reparation money from the government, this journey allowed him to feel some closure and come to terms with the experience. (Suyemoto, 1992, p. 24)

The opening up and telling of the cultural story supported the family's accessing of their own story. With the reparations and apology there was a recognition by the political leaders of what had happened. The documented account of someone else's experience in Topaz helped Karen imagine and ask her father about his time in that same camp. Visiting the camp together helped them directly connect around this family story.

Interlacing Cultural and Personal Stories

How, when, where, to whom, and the type of cultural stories that are told have profound implications for what happens with the telling, listening, and witnessing of personal stories. It may not be safe to tell central stories. For example, in Russia, during certain time periods, people could not admit their background (Tartar, Gypsy, aristocratic, Jewish, kulak). In the United States at various times, people have not been able to openly acknowledge that they were gay or lesbian, Jewish, Irish, or from other immigrant groups. The stories of African-Americans, Native Americans, recent immigrants, and women have often been silenced. Pat Griffin, in describing her work interviewing gay and lesbian teachers, captured a sense of their need to constantly monitor what parts of their stories to tell in an environment where they felt things were not open and/or safe. "The stories the participants shared during these interviews present a picture of a professional life filled with daily decisions about how much of one's self to reveal or conceal, driven by an underlying tension between fear of accusation and a quest for integrity and integration" (Griffin, 1992, p. 183).

But it is not just a matter of whether there is danger in sharing stories. It is important to have the possibility of resonation between personal stories and cultural stories — resonation that allows people to see how their particular experience is intertwined with the political and social history of their society. If, in the larger community, certain cultural stories predominate and others are not told, individuals may not have support to acknowledge and see these reverberations. Billingsley (1992) talks about the idea that slavery broke most of the ties of African Americans to the African culture, which meant that African Americans did not have support for looking at how their heritage was passed on. In order to help articulate one's story, cultural stories need to represent many aspects of a people's life—they should be broad-stroked, yet acknowledge all of the individual variations that will be found.

Cultural stories also have profound implications for how the past can be explained as well as the future imagined. For example, there have been two predominant strands of stories told about Native Americans in the United States. The first centers around the theme of the "Noble Savage," which is enacted in anthropological museums across the world where their way of life, customs, and rituals are portrayed as if they occurred only in the past.* The other predominant strand is the theme of the "Fierce Savage": historically, Native Americans were depicted as people who needed to be civilized, which justified the killings and policies that destroyed "probably 90 percent of the American Indian population within the first century after the European arrival in America" (Weatherford, 1988, p. 195) and allowed the settlers to confiscate their land.

The cultural stories told in either of these veins do not begin to communicate the tremendous diversity of Native Peoples (over 700 tribes in the United States alone), the ongoing richness of the lives that many Native Americans are currently living, nor the role the Europeans played in destroying cultures. Also, the hard realities of many of their current lives and the damage done to Native Americans is not contextualized. For example, the image of the "drunken Indian" does not carry with it an awareness of the Whites' systematic and deliberate bringing of alcohol onto the reservations.

It is hard to link past, present, and future in one's life when the cultural stories that frame one's experience are storied in stereotypical, inaccurate, narrow, and rigid ways. For instance, it is difficult for young Native Americans to imagine a multidimensional future when their present life is not seen and their past life has been storied in a banal manner. As Annie Mae Mills, with Sioux heritage, said, "What I was learning from the media and books and museums about my past neither helped me with what I

*For example, at the Ethnographic Museum in St. Petersburg, Russia, the major Native American groups of North America are shown as they might have lived 100 or 200 years ago. There is nothing to suggest anything about the richness of the native heritage today.

was currently trying to put into place in my life—nor picture a fuller future" (personal communication, December, 1991).

The National Museum of the American Indian being planned as part of the Smithsonian Institution in Washington, DC, has as its central focus the current life of Native Americans. With this museum, a different kind of environment is being created to elicit cultural stories. It is conceptualized as an interactive setting where exhibits will incorporate storytelling, song, and performance. History will be presented from the Native American's perspective. It is also envisioned as a meeting place where members of many different tribes can gather, share, and plan for the future.

The Holocaust museum, recently opened in Washington, DC, is an example of an attempt to tell the full story of what happened in Europe during World War II. The organization of the museum and the design of the building give visitors some experience of what the death camps were like. Each visitor entering the main museum is given the biography of a person who was sent to the concentration camps whose life he or she can then follow throughout the exhibit. In the part of the museum that is for younger children (ages 8 to 11), the story of Daniel is told, with stage sets of his house, community, ghetto room, and the camp where his family died. The building itself is constructed to remind people of the death camps. Paul Richard, a writer for the *Washington Post*, described the museum: "James I. Freed's architecture is masterful. Though it owes its debts to art museums—its spiral downward pathway to the Guggenheim, its bridges-under-skylights to I. M. Pei's East Building—Freed's architecture is aimed specifically at the Holocaust. The best thing about it is the way it somehow pulls you, through your admiration, back to the black truths of Auschwitz and Treblinka. Freed's towers suggest guard towers. His dull brick walls evoke industrial efficiency. His I-beams and glass roof make you think, appropriately, of train stations and tracks and voyages toward death" (1993, p. G-l).

Almost every day a visitor presents to the museum staff an artifact from that time, an artifact that represents his or her story or the story of someone close to them. When this first happened, the staff was surprised, but now it has come to be accepted as a part of the exhibit.

Anna Goldstein, of Harrisburg, Illinois was one of the first. She brought a card than once saved her life. As a young woman, Anna used a Polish girl's birth certificate to create a *kennkarte*, an ID card that enabled her to avoid imprisonment and death in the Warsaw Ghetto.

"Mrs. Goldstein was hesitant at first to let it go [said an assistant curator at the museum, Susan Goldstein—no relation]. She cried. It was very painful. 'Is it suitable for the museum,' she asked. I said, 'Oh yes. It's very suitable.'

"We never promise to exhibit a donation. We say it will go in the archives. It will never go on loan. It will be available to scholars. It will always be here. If we have the object, the real thing, not copies," Goldstein (assistant curator) says, "we have the story." (Grossman, 1993, p. 2D)

The public forum of the museum stimulates the telling and holding of the individual stories. People see that their story has a place.

Besides cultural stories being repressed, silenced, or told stereotypically, they may also be lost because of migration, loss, and/or dislocation. For example, my daughter's paternal grandparents, both of whom migrated here from the Ukraine to escape the pogroms in the early decades of this century, did not have any sustained contact with family members they left behind. There was no crucible that encouraged the telling of cultural stories—no letters, artifacts, photos, or memories stimulated by being in the same environment where the events occurred.

Therapists have the responsibility to be aware of what the privileged and dominant cultural stories are, as well as to ask their clients about the unheard cultural stories. For instance, some of the editorial boards of feminist journals have not had significant representation of women of color. Structurally, this gives a message that their voice is not of central concern to feminism. Therapists need to be aware of the larger frame that encompasses both their clients and their own personal stories.

Allen and Laird (1990) offer a way to think about this in relation to men's stories and therapy. They describe the kinds of public stories of manhood that are often available to men: "Very powerful myths of masculinity exist. Men are expected to be independent, autonomous, logical, and powerful. Men are strong and silent. They should be able to lead, to confront crises and to solve problems, without leaning on anyone else, to protect and defend their wives, children, and property. And they are to be courageous, unafraid in the face of threat" (p. 85). Allen and Laird note that stories of men's domestic life have been hidden and that little is known of their private thoughts. They also highlight how in the media and TV men are often presented as incompetent with familial matters such as parenting or understanding their spouses. "If women's public stories have been limited and distorted and if women lack the 'proper' language for public discourse, men's domestic stories are virtually unknown, and men are often at a loss for words in the intimate environs of family life" (p. 82).

To illustrate their ideas about men's stories, Allen and Laird present the case of "Bob." In working with him, he was asked to look at what he learned about masculinity and how he had taken it in and chosen to live his life. This was done by looking at the larger cultural messages as well as the story of his father's life and his relationship with his dad. This helped him look at the ways that it was hard for him to show his vulnerabilities and to ask for support, as well as how his style of wanting to be in charge led him to discount others. As he started to ask for help and backed off from trying to order others around, a different story began to emerge for him of what it means to be masculine.

Techniques for Accessing Cultural, Political, and Social Contexts

When working with personal stories, it is essential that the therapist be aware of the larger context for what could and could not be shared about people's lives. This does not mean knowing all the details and spending hours in therapy reconstructing the large-scale political and historical events that have affected clients. Rather, it means being cognizant of some of the general cultural themes to be able to help clients examine the interweaving of cultural and personal stories. Ways to do this include working with time lines of historical periods; overlaying them with particular themes that are relevant to clients (such as racism, sexism, class, homophobia); moving personal stories through time into different societal contexts; and looking at particular personal stories that are very intertwined with ethnic and racial heritage (such as migration and identity stories).

It is important at the outset to say that the ways in which any of these techniques are done is essential to their usefulness. Whenever one tries to do some fitting between an individual's experience and larger external occurrences, there is the risk of overgeneralizing and/or stereotyping. For instance, to say that all Japanese-Americans felt that they were in a tenuous position in this country in World War II because so many Japanese-Americans on the West Coast were moved into internment camps may or may not be true for a particular individual or family. On the other hand, if the larger picture is not brought into the treatment room, a disservice is done to ourselves and to our clients by focusing on their particular concerns and not tying them to larger societal pressures and issues. It can be very healing for people to see that the dilemmas they are caught in are not unique to their experience, but rather are embedded in larger societal problems and societal change. This can help them move out of stances of self-blame to positions that recognize how the social context affects individual lives. Sometimes this also leads to political action or advocacy work.

In general, I would recommend not using any of the techniques discussed in this section until the therapist feels that he or she has a very solid understanding of any key stories that a client is telling. Also essential is a sense that the understanding has been communicated to the client and that the client experiences the therapist as having some empathy and connection with the story. These techniques should also be presented in an exploratory frame as something that might help the client think differently about his or her story and experience. The client should not be presented with an implication that the story should be different, but rather that these techniques offer possibilities for a different entrance into the story. Space in therapy for a client's meaning-making of the story also needs to be protected—the focus is not on the therapist's interpretation of cultural and personal events. Together, the client and therapist need to find ways to appreciate the complexity and diversity that individual stories have in relation to larger societal events. The therapist can help the client respect the integrity of his or her individual experience, while seeing commonalities in issues in the larger society that affected his or her story—and that may have affected others' as well.

As Glenn Loury, a professor of economics at Boston University, wrote, "My sons will be black men of the 21st century, but not by their singing of racial anthems peculiar to our time. Theirs will be a blackness constructed yet again, out of the external givens of their lives, not mine" (1993, p. 12).

Historical Time Lines

Time lines of major historical and social events can help locate the personal stories of both clients and therapists. For instance, the psychologists that I worked with in Russia constructed this sequence of large scale occurrences that many of their clients have lived through:

World War I: 1914–1918
1917 Revolution
Civil War: 1918–1921
1920s: Lenin and New Economic Programs
1930s: Collectivization—Stalin and repressions
Great Patriotic War (World War II): 1941–1945
Death of Stalin: 1953
Khrushchev: 1956–1964
Brezhnev era: 1964–1982
Afghanistan War: 1979–1989
Gorbachev era: 1985–1992
Yeltsin and the 1992 Revolution

Certainly many more microevents could be added to this, and in other parts of the former Soviet Union a different time line could be constructed. However, this broad outline was a frame in which to think about individual stories. The psychologists looked at their own families of origin and thought about which of these events most affected them. It also gave them a skeletal structure that enabled them to peruse the kinds of family stories they had or did not have that related to these events, and to think about how they were shaped in form or in their telling by the official stories that were told. In explicating Natasha's story ("From Kulaks to the Komsomol to Questioning the Communist Party"), the scope of the time line seemed to let her move back and locate her family story in a larger frame than just the familial dynamics. As someone coming from outside the culture, this time line also assisted me in identifying areas for questions.

To amplify the usefulness of these kinds of time lines, they can be overlaid with descriptions of different possible experiences people might have had historically depending on whether they were rural, urban, rich, poor, female, male, etc. This can help prevent overgeneralizing. For example, if information regarding the experiences of women is added to the Russian time line above, a more complex picture emerges. In the former Soviet Union during the 1930s and 1940s, large numbers of women entered the paid work force and contributed greatly to the increased gross national product. Also, due to the high percentage of men killed in World War II, the generation of elders that is now found in the former Soviet Union is predominantly female. The addition of this knowledge about women could provide cues to ask about changing work roles for women coming of age during the '30s and '40s, as well as to inquire about how extended family relationships may be different for this generation because so many of the elders are women.

Telling Stories in Different Societal Contexts

Moving stories through time, or telling them from the perspective of a person from in a different position in the culture, or assuming other listeners can often make it easier to see the impact of the larger societal context. This context often surrounds people so intensely, that its influence remains unnamed.

CHANGING TO A DIFFERENT TELLING POSITION. Earl Shorris, a Latino author, talks about moving beyond multiculturalism to pluralism and not only accepting others who are different from oneself but imagining the other as well—that is, trying to move inside of the lives of people who are different from oneself in order to understand something of their experience (1993). This does not mean that a person then knows another's experience; there is a danger in saying, "I know how you feel." But by imagining oneself in another's position and telling his or her story from that perspective, a person can sometimes move more deeply into the context that surrounded and influenced that story.

While Sara was growing up, she experienced her mother, Jean, as very intrusive in her life. It seemed that her mother always wanted to know what was going on with Sara and was very concerned about anything she kept private or secret from her. Jean was always buying her extra little things and asking her if she would like this or that; Sara felt in some ways like she was trying to buy her love. It was not until Sara was asked to write the story of her mother in the first person (as if her mother were writing it) that Sara began to understand her mother's behavior differently.

Sara's Mother's Story

We were poor. That was shameful. And then there was my older brother's suicide when I was nine. My parents felt that with his death, they had failed as parents. My mother especially felt responsible and she withdrew from the family into her own private grief.

I got married young. It was the fifties—what did anyone know from marriage? It was supposed to be a big honor to help your husband, and to raise your children. That was your life—you weren't supposed to go out and have a life of your own. I was there, watching my children carefully—trying to give them what I didn't get. Now women are supposed to do different things with their lives. You can't win.

Sara moved herself to the inside of one aspect of her mother's story. After Sara wrote this, she had a number of different perspectives from which to understand her mother's behavior and a context that included thinking about class and gender. Sara described how she saw Jean growing up and marrying in a time when women were supposed to center their life around their children, and that the additional legacy of growing up in a family that was both poor and deeply affected by suicide contributed to her mother's need to watch over her. Sara began to verbalize how Jean was trying to make sure that her daughter was all right, that Sara had the things that she herself was deprived of, and that she was being a good mother. Other words were being used now, instead of "intrusive."

MOVING THROUGH TIME.   Picking a story up and moving it forward or backward over the years can help the societal environment stand out. People can be asked to imagine telling the same story 30 — or even 100 — years from now, or 30 or 100 years ago. How would the different contexts inform or influence the story? Would some part of the story stand out in more relief, or stay in the background more? How does a changed setting shape the story?

Noelle Guttman and Aroldo Sneh, a remarried couple, came into treatment with a lot of disagreements on how to parent the four children they had brought into the marriage. When asked to tell the story of how they were becoming a remarried family, they said that they perceived themselves as having two quite different styles of creating family. Aroldo saw himself as pretty laid back and really open to "going with the flow" with his 12-year-old son and 14-year-old daughter. Noelle felt the children really needed limits and clear boundaries, and that with her very busy schedule she needed structure and clarity about who was doing what each day. Both of them had somewhat conflictual relationships with their former spouses and when the kids went back and forth between their house and their other biological parent's house, they experienced tense transitions, especially in trying to settle into the expectations of their new house.

As Aroldo said, "No one ever told us it would be like this."

"Yeah," said Noelle, "If they had, I don't know . . . "

The therapist asked them to imagine how they might tell this story of two families coming together to a therapist 20 years in the future when hopefully there were more models about how to do it.

"Well," said Noelle, "The first thing is we wouldn't be telling it to a therapist, we'd be getting together with other remarried parents in a community group of some sort."

"And our former spouses would be there sometimes too," added Aroldo.

"Hmmm, okay," said Noelle, "And there would be novels and TV shows that told it like it was and we'd be sharing how the schools supported us by always having copies of things for two households and our friends would be very sensitive to how complicated holidays were for us and we wouldn't feel pushed up against the wall like there's something wrong with us."

"Sounds good," said the therapist. "So, how can you get some of that kind of support for yourselves now? Is there one other couple that you know that you can begin to create a network with? Who can you enlist as an ally at the school?" The therapist used their view of how it would work in the future to launch a discussion of how they might start to bring some of these elements into their life now.

Asking clients to imagine a future story is related to the technique of future-oriented questions in that family members are given a different perspective from which to view themselves and their dilemmas (Penn, 1985). However, there are some differences between therapists' asking future questions and clients' "picking up" one of their stories and moving it forward or backward in time. First, with future-oriented questions, it is primarily the therapist who is framing the questions and shaping the direction of the discourse. The focus is often on the family unit, not the societal surroundings (Penn, 1985). When clients move the story in the context of a societal future or past, they are the ones who more directly shape the course of the conversation. Also, asking them to envision the story within the frame of a changing social and political environment will hopefully support them so that they see the ways in which their personal stories are intertwined with the cultural stories.

IMAGINING A DIFFERENT BACKGROUND.   Another way to access different vantage points that can highlight the larger context of stories and their embedded messages is to think about how the story might be different if the person whose story it is came from a different class, cultural, and/or racial background, or was a different gender or of different sexual orientation. It is probably not necessary to retell the story with this changed perspective, and in fact it may feel disqualifying to some people to do that. But it can be a useful way to think about how the meaning of the story changes when the teller changes in some way.

For instance, Evelyn Suong came into treatment with her husband wanting very much to feel more competent in speaking up: both to him and at work. She felt that her husband Bill frequently took her for granted, and that she was passed over for job promotions because she was not assertive enough.

When asked to tell a theme story about what she had learned about herself with regard to assertiveness, she told a tale of being the third daughter out of five children and how she felt she had been taught very well to help others and not to brag about herself—that was not considered ladylike. Evelyn described watching women do a lot of the work behind the scenes in her family and how painful it was when, with recent state budget cuts at her agency, one of her coworkers had said to her, "Oh, you're not going to get cut; after all, you're Asian-American." Evelyn said, "When I hear things like that, I really don't feel like I can speak up for what I do—it's like my work has nothing to do with my competence."

Later in therapy, when Evelyn was asked how her theme story about assertiveness might have been different if she had been an Anglo-American male, Evelyn said, "I imagine that I would have been encouraged to show off my accomplishments—to share them with others. No one would have dared say to me, 'Oh you won't get cut because you're a white male.' They would have talked about what I do well." Imagining the teller with a different background can provide a way for therapists and clients to begin to tease out how the story is impacted by gender, cultural, sexual, and racial identifications and discrimination. This is not done in a frame of putting down other groups or encouraging people to see themselves as victims—rather, the emphasis is on understanding the context for one's own story.

CHANGING THE LISTENER. Another variation of this kind of technique is to imagine different listeners hearing the story. For instance, how might the story be heard if it were to have an audience of all males, or all teenage girls, or all women of color? Stories are calibrated and changed depending on who is listening. "Changing" the listener can help people recognize the interactive nature of storytelling and listening and how the situation influences how the story is told. It may help therapists, other family members, and clients think about how they are listening. Tellers may realize that they are assuming certain details with some listeners, or that they are protecting other listeners by saying things indirectly or not filling in all of the details. Therapists may become aware that in their listening they are locating themselves in a particular way in relation to the story.

For example, Chin Savin had come to the United States from Cambodia with her brother 10 years ago. Her sponsor had encouraged her to seek out therapy for nightmares and flashbacks that she was continuing to have. After doing some work around the trauma of her perilous escape and her journey here, her therapist asked her how she might tell her story differently if the listeners were other Cambodians who had also fled to the Thai border and lived in the refugee camps before coming. Chin said, "Certain things they would understand: that would be the difference. I would not have to speak it all out—they would know what I was telling about. I would not have to be reminded so much of each thing."

The therapist realized that perhaps Chin was being restimulated more than necessary, and that the telling was more painful in some ways because the therapist needed the details to flesh out the story. The therapist chose to do less probing and did more reading about Cambodia, especially the stories of other Cambodians who had come here. She looked at some of the movies out about Cambodia and talked to a Vietnamese social worker about his work with refugees. Imagining different listeners led the therapist to learn more information in order to make herself a different kind of listener.

In other situations, the client may want a therapist with special experiences, or to be of a certain age, or male or female, because they think having experienced life from that vantage point will help the therapist listen in a particular way. One way to handle this is to ask clients to imagine that the therapist has the experience, or is of the gender or age that they were expecting, and then to explain how they think things might be different. Allen, a recovering alcoholic, was surprised to find out that his therapist was not a sober alcoholic, as were most of the other therapists at the treatment center. His therapist asked him to imagine that he was a person who had had drinking problems in the past. He then asked how, if this were the case, things would be different between them. Allen said, "Well, you'd be harder on me—you wouldn't let me fool you. You'd understand more the traps of drinking and the lousy cycles you can get into." Doing this from time to time kept them both aware of particular things each needed to be listening carefully to.

Imagining different listeners can be an important technique for people who have lived through traumatic situations, such as sexual abuse and violence, especially when secrecy and denial have been part of the experience. In working through the story of what happened to them, there may be family members and friends who they wish had acted or responded in a different manner. Or there may be people close to them with whom they have never discussed it. In sorting out who to tell what and who might be brought into the therapy, imagining different people hearing various parts of the story and their reactions and responses can help the client decide how to proceed.

For example, Barbara, who was sexually abused by her father some 20 years before, had not talked with her mother about it in over 18 years and had never discussed it with her sisters. For years, Barbara herself had not remembered the details, but upon reading Katherine Brady's book, *Father's Day: A True Story of Incest* (1979), a flood of memories came back to her and she sought out therapy.

In treatment, after working on some of the issues surrounding her father and the abuse (he had died five years earlier), Barbara looked at her relationship with her mother and sisters. She felt that the denial and secrecy of what had happened to her had built a wedge between them. Her relationship with her mother was particularly conflictual—in part, she thought, because her mother had made her tell an investigating social worker that her father was not abusing her, because the family so desperately needed his income. Barbara wanted to bring them into the therapy process in some way but she was not sure how. By imagining that she was breaking the silence and telling the story of what had happened to her, and thinking about what their responses might be, she began to formulate a plan. First, she brought in the sister closest in age to her that she thought would most likely believe her. Then, she brought in her other sisters. After they had made some new connections with each other, Barbara asked her mother to come in.

Looking for Migration, Identity, and Other Cultural Stories

While all stories have cultural elements within them, certain kinds of stories may tap more deeply into people's ethnic and racial heritage and how this heritage is passed down through the generations as well as how it is or is not embraced by the larger culture. Migration stories, which share how family members came to be where they are, have embedded within them people's connections to their background. When, why, and how people came — what they had to overcome, what was left behind, what they were able to bring with them — have deep implications for how people can hold their ethnic heritage as well as adapt to a new setting. The way they were welcomed — or not — by their new home community and or/country also has a strong effect on how people see their own heritage.*

Besides migration stories, families and individuals may also have identity stories that give messages about who they are, how they relate to other groups, and how to conduct themselves in the world. Stone (1988) talks about the ways in which these stories, as a first language, a private language, define who is in and out of the family, norms, key beliefs and values, and actions. "[They] fasten the identity in place and keep if from floating off, slithering away, or losing its shape" (p. 7).

Therapists can scan the information they have from clients to see if they have relevant stories about how clients came to be where they are and how they see their identity in relation to their background. This can be done by working with genograms to look for migration stories, and asking people when they first became aware of their similarities or differences to others and how they felt in relation to their home communities.

Jamila Sands, an African-American woman, originally came into treatment with concerns she had about her son who was failing his last year of high school. As the problems with him lessened, she decided to work on her own issues: about who she was and the life choices she was making. When asked when she first became aware of how she was like and different from others,

---

*Lost in Translation by Eva Hoffman beautifully explicates many of these issues as she shares the story of her migration from Poland to Canada and then to the United States.

she talked about how when in upper elementary school she went to one of the first integrated schools in South Carolina. "That's when I became aware of differentness. Before then I hadn't run into prejudice much—I was mostly just with Black folks. We had to be escorted in by the police—parents were spitting at us, calling us names. And you know, when I got into my teenage years, we were into Black is Beautiful and we didn't call ourselves Negroes any more—we were Black and Afro-Americans. Now, we have to say African-American. It seems like our identity is always changing, as we try to find some way around these white people. No wonder I wonder sometimes just who I am."

Getting in touch with this helped Jamila and her therapist look at some of the unique issues of identity development when a person is also confronting racism. Looking at how messages from the outside impacted her supported Jamila in sorting out who she wanted to be and how her identity was influenced by the larger culture.

Back to Interlacing: How Personal Stories Inform Cultural Stories

Part of the great power of Alex Haley's book *Roots* (one man's story about his heritage) and of the subsequent television special was how it established for African-Americans that there were ongoing cultural patterns and links to West African culture. The larger society had been trying to diminish these connections for years, saying that the West African culture had been destroyed with the institution of slavery. As people read, heard, and saw *Roots*, they realized the connections between the language, music, foods, and social organization of Haley's ancestors and later generations. The heritage of African-Americans was affirmed. Personal stories can enlarge the cultural stories. They can provide the impetus for looking differently at the cultural stories that are told.

Another example of this is the story of Anne Frank. The publication of her diary and the telling of how she died in Bergen-Belsen shortly before the end of the war forced the world to acknowledge the Holocaust and what had really happened in World War II. Throughout the world people of all ages were able to deeply connect to her story of unfulfilled promise. The museum that has been made of the place where she and her family hid has provided an ongoing way to name what occurred.

The culture may "speak itself" through each individual's story (Rosenwald & Ochberg, 1992, p. 7), but individual stories also build the cultural stories. Therapists have a unique role to play in supporting the interweaving of these stories.

Therapists' Responsibilities to Tell Tales Outside of Therapy

Joan Laird (1993b) has talked about the responsibility of therapists to go beyond the role of ethnographer of the individual lives of clients and share clients' experiences with the larger society, especially those stories that have been silenced.* By sharing these personal stories, therapists can help foster a vibrant development of the cultural stories of our times. As our ways of life change, the personal stories are needed to elaborate, fill out, embellish, and change our family therapy theories and the ways sociologists and others look at families. Our family constructs have often not kept up with the complex societal shifts that have occurred; whole new dimensions now have to be considered. For example, with the increased number of lesbian couples choosing either to have or adopt children, different questions and issues are raised when both parents can potentially become pregnant. How do you decide who will become impregnated and by whom? What will the role of the father be? Is adoption a more viable option? Can both parents legally adopt? How will parenting roles be defined? Unique pleasures and dilemmas confront lesbian couples who have decided to raise a child; therapists who work with these clients have a lot to offer in broadening the stories about what it means to be family in today's society.

Therapists who take stories outside of the therapy room (while protecting confidentiality and boundaries) can break silences, mystifications, and a sense of isolation for people. They can help people not blame themselves for larger societal dilemmas. For instance, all the personal stories that have been told of sexual abuse in the United States have resulted in a societal awareness that we are a culture with this problem. However, it is essential that this kind of sharing of personal stories be done in a respectful

---

*And doing this in a manner that respects the confidentiality and privacy of clients.

manner that does not oversimplify the issues. Unfortunately, with today's talk shows (there are now approximately 15 syndicated shows on the air), there is often a push for sensationalized telling of people's experiences that is not only exploitive but often detrimental to their well-being. This is *not* the kind of telling that I am encouraging.

The vigor of stories is that they can coherently intertwine many issues. And this intertwining is often captivating to us. In the autobiography *Black Ice* (quoted in Chapter 1), the author, Lorene Carey, tells her story of the transition from her teenage years to young adulthood. Within the story line the issues of gender, race, class, identity, and family relationships are braided together. In the telling of her story, she goes beyond reductionist explanations that only hold one variable at a time.

Therapists have the responsibility to hold the cultural and social contexts of stories up for ourselves and our clients so clients will understand their dilemmas in a wider field. Looking at the larger frame often offers people opportunities to move out of blaming cycles—cycles in which they blame either themselves or others. As they see the various constraints or beliefs that affected people's lives, they begin to empathize with family and individual dilemmas and become less judgmental. It can also help them to see other kinds of interventions that may be needed, such as political or community action.

In therapy, working at the intersection of cultural and personal stories provides many possibilities to hear and understand the multiple strands of our stories. A good way for clinicians to learn how to do this is to examine their own family stories and the frames within which they have been told. In the next chapter we'll look at a variety of techniques to hear, shape, and understand one's own trove of tales.

7

TRAINING THERAPISTS: LISTENING TO, SHAPING, AND ELABORATING STORIES*

I started to see the cut-off with my mom in more intergenerational terms. She kicked me out of the house when I was 17. She was 18 when she immigrated here from England and cut off from her alcoholic mom and sister. That was what she knew—abrupt leavings.

I have a way now too to think about what was happening between my mom, stepdad, and me—it was a powerful triangle. When my stepdad came into the picture, I liked the guy a lot, but I had had my mom to myself for a few years. A lot of times it felt like I was losing her to him. When my half brother was born, there were a lot of overlapping triangles. No wonder things felt so intense at home.

I've been having to rethink my whole family story. It makes me curious about reconnecting with my Dad. I haven't seen him since I was three and I have no idea where he is. But that was another dynamic I didn't have a name for—the triangle of my mom, Dad and me. She has been adamant about me not seeing him. I need to think about the impact on her too if I were to try to find my Dad.

—*Stephen, age 25, after his first semester*
of studying family therapy

Now, I am finding myself being an audience to others who have stories to tell. I recognize that in order to hold their stories, I must have room within me. The implication is that I must tell and retell my story to have holding space for the

*The foundation of many of the ideas in this chapter were laid for me by Evan Imber-Black years ago when I trained with her. Her creativity, sensitivity, and clear thinking are deeply acknowledged.

stories of others. This balance is crucial to my survivor as a helper. Writing down some of my own family tales caused me to bear witness to my own stories; a needed experience I often overlook.

> — *Greg Hocott, age 29, experienced clinician who has worked a number of years with Vietnam veterans and their families*

IN FAMILY THERAPY TRAINING, clinicians are asked to think deeply about generational and cultural history, intricate interactional patterns, dynamics between men, women, and children, as well as the societal and social contexts of families. For most people this study evokes reflection and thinking about their own experiences on a number of levels. For Stephen it meant that he now had a different vocabulary to name some of his life events — a vocabulary that seemed to help him understand his family story in some new ways as well as question the fact that one of the main players (his father) had been left out. Greg, the holder of so many others' stories, found he needed to make room for his own stories. For other trainees it might mean becoming aware of stories that have been painfully silenced for a long time, such as that of an alcoholic mother, sexual abuse by a brother, a violent father. Or it might mean cohering a story that was interrupted long ago and fragmented by migration, death, illness, and/or other losses.

Trainees may find themselves trying to create a new professional story for themselves, a story that bridges some of their personal and professional experiences. This can be complicated when part of the individual or work story is not told or acknowledged by the larger society, such as when a person is gay or lesbian or has experienced personal and/or professional blocks because of racism and sexism. For instance, Jocelyn, a lesbian in her early thirties, began to question if she could be a family therapist when, as a practicum student, she worked on a family therapy team with primarily heterosexual families and did not feel that she could share her lesbian identity with them.

Training programs help people understand and make meaning of how the study of systemic therapy touches their lives as well as how this understanding can add to and enhance their therapy skills. The frame of looking at and sharing life stories provides a flexible structure of support for this process for both trainers and trainees. For most trainees having protected time and space in which to examine their family story and then sharing it in a community of others going through a similar experience is an exhilarating and intense process. As they have said, "Be prepared to look at your own family of origin during these courses. It can be scary but it's also helpful to have new insights with which to look at your family" and "Knowing that other people in our group were also struggling with their own complicated dynamics was a comfort to me—I took solace in sharing our highs and our lows. And it took my interest keenly into the theories—I mean, trying to explain these true-to-life situations really made me look carefully at the concepts."

Working with trainees' stories in some depth facilitates family therapy training in a number of ways. First, it provides content that people are usually deeply involved in and know from the inside out—content that can be held up against family therapy theories to see where the models explain human behavior well and where they fall short. The contents of these family stories are also often much more diverse and complex than the family descriptions and case reports that are usually found in the family therapy literature. Second, for many trainees the systemic view is a shift from the more individualistic and blaming kinds of explanations for problematic interactions. This different way of thinking may jar some of the ways the trainees had previously framed familial dynamics. The frame of reworking family stories—either their own or others'—can offer a way to cohere and shape these new explanations. Third, many family therapy skills can be developed through the intense engagement with ideas that comes with linking theory, personal experience, and the experiences of others. And, most importantly, working with the story frame does not place students in the position of client (which is what happens when therapists are told they must be in therapy as some part of their training). Nor does it position the trainees so far from the position of client as to put them outside of the therapy process as an expert who is somehow removed from emotional dilemmas. (This sometimes happens with therapy models that use technical language and jargon to describe human interaction. This language seems to remove clinicians from a sense of shared humanity and common experiences with clients.) The story frame joins clients and therapists: We all have stories about difficulties, disruptions, healing, and change—they are not unique to therapy. And, finally, this framework also gives trainees the latitude to choose how much they want to examine and/or rework their experiences. Stories have multiple levels of meaning and trainees can decide whether they want to stay on the level of plot line and descriptive details, or go into the symbolic layers of meaning.

Using stories in training can involve exploring novels and plays, writing down one's own stories; using photos, floor plans, and genograms to expand and detail stories; and putting group stories together. Before going into these techniques, let's look at some exercises that can provide an essential foundation for all aspects of the story process.

The Sound of Silence: Exercises for Listening

As described in Chapter 1, the family therapy field has been very focused on the kinds of questions to ask in therapy and ideas about how to change interactions; little attention has been paid to listening. However, central to any inquiry-and-change process in therapy is the quality of the listening by both therapists and clients. Careful listening allows therapists to hear both the individual and familial stories of clients as well as to distinguish between family members' different values and beliefs, issues, concerns, and problem-solving strategies. Listening is also an essential part of the process for clients. Family members often need to listen to each other in some new ways, as well as to the therapist, if they are to take in some other perspectives from her. Therapists and clients also need to attend thoughtfully to themselves to "overhear" how they are communicating with others.

Simultaneous levels of listening occur in hearing family stories. There is a keeping track of the places, people, and facts; there is a taking in of the emotional inflections, nuances, and reactions; there is listening for the meaning of the content, and there is the interactive process of clients' feeling, or not feeling, heard.

To help people become more aware of the listening they do on multiple levels, I have developed several exercises. These are precursors to doing more elaborate work with family stories. Participating in them seems to enhance the training process as well as help trainees increase their skills. As they feel listened to in their training group, stronger links and greater safety are provided which give them increased support for looking at their own vulnerabilities and areas for development.

Exercise 1: Listening and Being Listened To

This exercise is a series of questions that focuses on how people have experienced listening and being listened to in their lives. As people articulate what they have gone through, they begin to be aware of how they have taken in that knowledge about listening and whether they have applied it to their work. The exercise ends by focusing on the kind of dual listening that happens in family therapy where the therapist not only needs to listen to each individual in the family, but also be aware of *how each person is being listened to by others in the family*. This is an important difference from individual therapeutic work where full attention can be devoted to one person; the therapist does not have to be concerned with balancing talk time among people or the reactions of others.

About an hour is needed to do the exercise. As a warm-up, people can be asked to think back to a time or times in their life when they felt most listened to or when they themselves listened well. Ask them to recall who was there, the things they were talking about, what people were wearing, and what the space was like that they were in. They can also be asked to remember how they felt physically in their bodies and/or how they felt in their mind when they experienced being heard or being able to deeply hear someone else. These few minutes of reflection can help people access their memories and recall them more vividly.

After doing this ask people, as they are ready, to find a partner. Give a copy of the following boxed questions to each dyad. For roughly the first 20 minutes, one member of the dyad asks his or her partner the questions, and then they reverse the process.

As the pairs finish with the questions, ask them to re-form the larger group to discuss some of the things they articulated about listening, as well as to comment on the activity itself. Then discuss ways the exercise applies to the therapy process as well as any ways it might be adapted and used with clients.*

---

*I do this with all the exercises I work with in training as a way to help people bridge the ideas we explore and treatment.

EXERCISE 1: LISTENING AND BEING LISTENED TO

1. What did you learn about listening while growing up at home, school, other places outside of the home?

   Was listening different for men? For women? For children? If so, in what ways?

   Who do you think was most listened to in your family? Least listened to? What is your explanation for this?

2. When have you felt really listened to? What elements contributed to that sense of being really heard?

   When did you *not* feel listened to? What contributed to that feeling?

3. Describe a time when you did some of your best listening. What helped and/or supported you in doing that?

   When have you done some of your worst listening? What would have helped you listen better in that situation?

4. Based on what you have learned and experienced with listening and being listened to, reflect on what particular strengths you might bring to a family therapy session and what areas you may need to be thoughtful about in regard to your listening skills.

5. In family therapy, with several people in the room who often have a complex history about listening, you need to listen to one person and at the same time listen to how others are or are not hearing them.

   What strategies do you think you use to do this kind of dual listening?

   What other kinds of strategies might you try? How might you experiment/practice with them?

The format of some of this exercise was suggested to me by a series of questions Evan Imber-Black developed on gift-giving; see Chapter 4 in *Rituals for Our Times*.

A Chinese school psychologist, Chieh Li, talked about growing up in China as a young child and how she was taught to listen to adults. She was repeatedly told, "Don't interrupt. Show your virtue." She told us, "I resented it. I thought I had sense too." She didn't feel listened to much at all until she was eight or nine years old. When the cultural revolution came, Chieh was twelve and both of her parents were taken away. She was left alone for a year to care for her two younger brothers, and for the two following years her parents were able to return only on some weekends. When her parents were able to rejoin them full time, she felt truly listened to: Her role had shifted into more of an adult one and now she could speak.

An Anglo-American woman, Marguerite, resonated to some of what Chieh shared. "I found myself thinking of the old adage, 'Children should be seen and not heard.' While I don't remember people saying that to me directly, it was certainly the pervasive sense I had in the house we grew up in. Now, in my practicum sessions, I sometimes find it hard to interrupt and redirect conversations, even when I think it would help us. I feel like the sessions get out of balance with one or more of the family members dominating the conversation. The parents I work with are mostly older than I am and I think I'm still influenced by that old saying. Besides, I'm still not confident enough of my skills to know that what I would say would be worth listening to."

Another graduate student, 32-year-old Mark, also linked some of his listening experiences to the therapy process. "I realized how different I felt when I was being carefully listened to—it was like the other person didn't have a different agenda for what they wanted me to talk about; they were open to whatever I was sharing. It made me wonder how clients feel with me. I know that when I am in the therapy room I always feel like I am so busy thinking about my next question or comment."

Other people have spoken about the dual listening inherent in family therapy. An experienced male therapist said, "Listening in family therapy is different than the individual work I've done because I'm not just hearing one person's story. I'm often told several stories about the same event. I can't just concentrate on one person and what he or she is thinking and feeling. On the other hand, I have access to the different versions and the listening dynamics of how other people hear the story." Chieh, the school psychologist, shared strategies about how she worked with these dual levels: If she feels family members are not listening, she asks them to help her out by listening and helping her to remember specific things; she may ask people to think of a question they would like to ask, based on what they have heard; she also reminds family members that they don't necessarily have to agree with the opinions of other family members, but that it is important to hear them and really understand what they are—that way they can know how their opinions are the same or different.

In regard to using this exercise with clients, some trainees have taken the first three questions and adapted them to the therapy relationship. Therapists and clients can reflect together:

1. When was a time in our therapy together when you felt really listened to? Not listened to?
2. What have you learned about listening during the time we have spent together?
3. In therapy, when do you think you do your best listening? What helps you to do that? Your worst listening? What would help you to listen better in those kinds of situations?

This exercise helps people think about the overall processes of listening they have learned about as well as begin to name aspects of their own style. It can also give them an opportunity to look at strategies for improving their listening.

Exercise 2: Stories, Styles, and Resonance

This exercise enacts the actual process of hearing stories by having people share some personal vignettes. To bring in some of the theoretical framework for stories, people are asked to think about the story styles discussed in Chapter 1 and apply them to the sagas they are recounting. A good way to familiarize everyone with the six story styles is to make a handout of Table 1, found on page 13, and to give brief examples of each style. Then, ask people to form dyads, with each person thinking of a family story that has been repeated over time either about him- or herself, the family as a group, or someone else in the family. Maybe it describes a dramatic event or a major transition that happened in someone's life. Perhaps it captures some vital aspects of a person's daily life. Or maybe it is a story that has been passed down from one generation to the next.

To get people involved in the exercise, you might ask them to imagine particular places where family stories were often told. For example:

1. Who might be there?
2. What was the atmosphere like?
3. What were the textures in the environment—the sense of the ambiance?
4. Who told the stories?
5. Were there special story-time rituals attached to the telling (such as during a holiday meal, or snuggling in bed)?

Direct the dyads to let one person tell their story while the other concentrates on hearing it and asks only clarifying questions. When the teller is done, the listener is encouraged to reflect on the story using guidelines similar to the ones used by reflecting teams (that is, utilize the language of the person speaking; comment on what seems important to the teller; use phrases like "it appeared that" and "I wonder if"). The listener is also asked to share anything about his or her life that resonates with the story that was told. The process is then reversed. The pair is then asked to converse about what story style or combination of styles might be applied to their two stories. The exercise ends with dyads reforming the larger group and sharing their thoughts on what they learned, the process, and how they might apply their ideas to their work with clients.

One trainee commented, "I appreciated just being listened to and not feeling like my partner was waiting to butt in to tell me about himself, as often happens with my friends. But most important was when my partner shared what echoed in his own life when he heard my story. In doing that, he shared some of his own vulnerabilities and I felt more comfortable with him."

Another trainee talked about trying to cohere a story. "My mother died five months ago and I tried to tell the story of her death but I found myself with only bits and pieces of it. I think I'm still very much in the middle of it and I don't really know what the story is. It made me think that families who have just had some kind of major change might not know exactly what the story line is or how to tell the story. But the reflections of my listener reassured me. She shared some of the different angles that she heard in what I said—about my sadness, my relief, the anger, the suffering my mother endured. It helped me to see that the story is all of these things; her acknowledgement helped me acknowledge it myself and will help me to keep trying to find ways to include all of them."

Amita, from Southern India, and Leon, a first generation American, shared some of their discussion about their two stories. Amita told the story of how her father had been crippled by polio in the 1950s when she was a young girl. He was very ill and she and her brothers were not allowed to see him except from a distance for several months for fear they might contract the disease. After he slowly recovered they never spoke about his shortened leg, yet they were reminded of it constantly, whenever he moved from place to place.

Leon, a man in his mid-twenties, told the story of his father who had escaped from Albania in the 1950s. "My father, Ahmed, died of a heart attack when I was thirteen, but the story of his escape was known and told by all in the household."

> My Dad always said the hardest part was the several years before he actually escaped and he was trying to decide whether to ask his cousin to escape with him or not. He was afraid to ask him because he knew what had happened when his aunt Leila had told her sister Jamila that she wanted to escape across the mountains to Greece. Out of fear of what would happen to Leila if she was caught as well as what would happen to herself, Jamila called the police and Leila was put in jail with a 20-year sentence for plotting to leave. Finally, my Dad got up the courage to ask his cousin and he said, "Yes." For a year the two of them planned their escape. From time to time, they stood on the hills looking over the frontier, studying the terrain. They told no one about what they wanted to do so that nothing would happen to them before they went and no one could get into trouble after they left.
>
> The night they headed for the border they put on dark clothing. They arranged their small packs with a few pieces of loose clothing on top to throw to the dogs. They tied their shoes in special knots that wouldn't get entangled in the brush. And then they ran.

Leon described his father's story as a rigid one—told the same way over and over. What he took from it as a child growing up was how brave his father was. Amita described her father's story as an untold one and commented that it didn't have the same level of details that were an important part of Leon's story.

When asked if they felt any particular resonation between the stories, Leon shared how hearing Amita's story made him think that in many ways the earlier life of his father was unspoken. "In fact, I know few details about his life in Albania before the escape. I wonder if it was too painful for him to talk about it and remember it. There wasn't anyone we could ask about it except his cousin, but he lived way out in California." Bravery was the theme that resonated for Amita. "Amhed's story focused so much on his courage and action. I was struck by how there must have been a strong bravery story in my father's battle against polio, but as we were so protected from his suffering as children, there didn't seem to be any way for the story of his courage to come through. I want to see if I can get any of this put back into the story." She then talked about how hearing this story, opened the possibility of a new take on her story and she wondered what this might mean in the therapy process as clients gathered new angles on their stories.

Leon also commented that hearing the story helped him envision Amita and her family in some new ways—that he felt taken inside of her experience. "I can see how hearing each other's stories in therapy could create some particular bonds." The resonation and listening that can be experienced in this exercise have a lot to teach about therapy connections and the power of stories to facilitate them.

Doing these kinds of exercises with the theoretical ideas described earlier in the book is a good way to help people understand and apply the concepts. The exercises may also help trainees have other frameworks to think about their experiences. Exercises 3 and 4 offer two other adaptations.

Exercise 3: Different Ways of Working with Stories in Therapy

To begin Exercise 3, hand out Table 2 "Different Ways of Working with Stories in Therapy" (p. 44). Then, after discussing the five categories (hearing family stories, theme stories, cohering a story, restorying, and inventing stories) and/or showing videos of clinical sessions that illustrate them, group the trainees in dyads or triads and ask them to share the ways they have been using them in therapy. (If you have an inexperienced group you can ask them to talk about either the ways stories have been shared in their family and work-related situations, or the ways they would like to work with stories in the future.) As part of this discussion, people can be asked to reflect on why they think they have been drawn to particular ways of working with stories.

My experience with this exercise is that people often start the dialogue thinking that they do not really use many of the five different ways; however, they soon realize that they work with stories more broadly than they initially thought. As one woman said, "When you handed us the chart, my response was, 'Oh well, all I'm doing is the first one, hearing family stories.' It was good to see that I was doing more than that and to have a way to name some of the distinctions."

Exercise 4: Examining Oral, Written, and Enacted Story Forms

Table 3 "Story Techniques" (p. 84), which distinguishes between spoken, written, and enacted stories, can be handed out to familiarize everyone with the three story mediums. Then, the following boxed series of questions can be used as a catalyst for small groups to think about and discuss them.

EXERCISE 4: EXAMINING ORAL, WRITTEN, AND ENACTED STORY FORMS

1. Are you most comfortable working with oral, written, or enacted stories in treatment?
   Which form of stories are you least comfortable working with?
   Why do you think that is?
2. In your own cultural background, which of the three categories do you think were most available to your ethnic group? Was there more of an oral or written tradition, or events that had elements of enactment?
   In your life experience, which of the three categories do you have the most exposure to?
3. Which of the three categories or particular techniques would you like to be more comfortable using in family therapy?
   What would help you feel more comfortable, or that you had more competence for using those particular techniques?
   How can you access this kind of help?

The most important thing is to keep adapting material to fit your own unique training and/or clinical situation.* Ideas to consider in adapting charts, ideas, and exercises include:

1. What kind of inquiry and learning are you hoping to facilitate?
   What kind of format is best for those goals:
   (a) Working in a large group? small group? some combination thereof?
   (b) With or without leaders for each group?
   (c) With written or spoken instructions?
2. What is unique about your training and clinical situation that you need to take into consideration? For example:
   (a) Do you have primarily experienced people, or a wide mix of people—some with work experience, others with very little?
   (b) Is it made up of predominantly one gender or one racial group?
   (c) How often does your group meet?
   (d) How much support do people feel from each other?
   (e) What confidentiality issues are there?
3. What are questions you ask of yourself that help you to grab hold of and communicate the theoretical ideas?
   What stories and vignettes can you tell to help illustrate the ideas?†
4. In what ways can you get feedback to modify and extend the exercises?

Feedback from trainees gives me the most useful information about how to modify and change the experiential activities. I do

---

*For creative adaptations, see "The Reauthoring of Therapist's Stories: Taking Doses of Our Own Medicine" by Clifton, Doan, & Mitchell.

†When I first started teaching 13 years ago, I remember writing out a list of the 15 families I had worked with in depth at that point, and another 20 or so that I had observed or had a few sessions with. For each family I identified several stories that could highlight different concepts. I took this list to each class. Gradually I was able to abandon the list as I learned to integrate it into my teaching. Students consistently note that this helps them understand the theoretical material. As one student wrote, "The powerful examples really help to make the material come alive." And another, "I always appreciate your anecdotes. The use of personal stories is a great teaching method."

this informally after each exercise by asking participants to comment on the exercise and suggest changes that would maximize a sense of safety for participants as well as optimize the learning possibilities and clinical skill development. For instance, in one course, as a way to get into narrative modes of therapy, I had asked students to write down a central family story and to analyze it by commenting on elements of voice, witnessing, position, and personal agency. Some of the feedback I received from them was that these four elements were too open-ended to help them articulate their stories. That helped me develop the categories of story styles as a more detailed way of looking at content, process, and time in the telling of central family stories.

I have also had trainees formally give me feedback by asking a small group of volunteers to keep a journal to respond to and critique each of the experiential activities we do. A few days before doing each exercise, I gave them a brief outline consisting of (a) what I hoped the exercise might begin to accomplish; (b) actual directions and questions I was going to ask, to help them give me feedback on them; and (c) questions and/or concerns I had about the exercise. After doing the exercise, each volunteer made notes on a feedback sheet regarding the clarity of the directions, the timing and rhythm of the exercise, and the ways in which it seemed to work, or not work, for individuals and the group. They also indicated any changes they would recommend. After several weeks, we met together and shared their notes on the exercises we had done. With people bouncing their ideas and reflections off each other, I found that not only did I get specific ideas for modifications, but I was also able to hear about problem areas across different exercises and the overall usefulness — or lack thereof — with a cluster of activities. The next listening exercise was designed after I received feedback that people wanted experiences that moved them more directly into the therapeutic process.

Exercise 5: Listening and the Therapy Process

This exercise is designed to help people become aware of the multiple levels that occur with listening in therapy, as well as teach them some skills to work with these different levels. A complex process is broken down into parts, to help people listen in specific ways. This exercise can be done while looking at videos, role playing, or observing clients and therapists behind the one-way mirror.

First, different categories to watch for are outlined for the observers to choose from. The box below is an example of what they might include. These categories will change depending on the setting, issues, therapist, and family. For instance, someone working in a hospital setting with families of a chronically ill patient might add other categories such as "beliefs about illness" and "beliefs about healing and caretaking." Or the hierarchy of doctor, nurse, and social worker might be highlighted as an important element to consider in the tallying and analysis of who talks to whom, when, and about what.

It is also helpful to discuss some strategies that will help with listening and gathering information about these categories. People might want to note key phrases and words, take dialogue verbatim in certain parts, draw pictures for metaphors, and make charts to tally interactions. (One easy way to tally interactions is to write down the names of all the participants in the session and to make a certain type of mark after their name each time they talk, a different mark when they make affirming statements, and a different mark when they cut someone off.) Phrases can be clustered under subheadings to juxtapose and link particular themes; people's nonverbal reactions can be noted too. Observers can also monitor their own internal reactions as they listen to different

---

EXERCISE 5: LISTENING AND THE THERAPY PROCESS

1. Listening for key phrases
2. Listening for metaphors and how they are used
3. Charting patterns of listening in the room (for example, who talks to whom, who interrupts, who cuts others off, and who affirms, restates, links ideas)
4. Listening for beliefs stated about a particular issue
5. Listening for key stories
6. Tracking actual talk time of each person in the session
7. Noting any comments about listening, being heard, and the overall quality of the conversation

---

styles of talking and sharing by writing down a few descriptive words about how they are feeling every five minutes or so.

TALK ONE, TALK ALL.   Bruce and Elana Grant had recently separated and their three children (two teenagers and an elementary-school-age son) were living primarily with the father in the family home. The therapist found the first session with them very chaotic and asked three team members behind the one-way mirror to observe them in relation to listening in three different ways. One person was asked to track who said what, when, to whom, and so on. A second team member jotted down key phrases people said. The third team member kept track of her own internal reactions as she listened, as if she were the therapist in the room tracking and guiding the conversation. During the intersession break, while sharing some of this information with the therapist, the team was able to note a number of patterns. First, the six-year-old son, Randy, was not stopped from interrupting any of the conversations. When the session became more intense, he ran around the room, cut into conversations more, and generally was more disruptive. Second, Bruce consistently answered first when the therapist asked any questions. Third, Elana usually needed to be asked something several times and encouraged to speak before she would say much. And fourth, the two teenagers frequently interrupted each other with put-downs, swears, and negative comments. When the therapist inquired about this the oldest daughter said, "Well, our Dad swears at us at home."

At the end of the session, the therapist described some of what had been noticed about listening in the family. Bruce responded by saying, "All of us are feeling bad about ourselves because of the put-downs and cursing. It's something I want to change." Elana shared that she had always found it hard to speak up—that she usually sat back to see what others were thinking and followed what they wanted to do. When the therapist commented on the interruptions by Randy, the two teenagers immediately jumped in with, "Yeah and he's just like that at home too." They finished the session by making a series of plans for home over the next week and for the following meeting. Each person agreed to spend a half-hour on different days of the week really sitting and listening to Randy. After that was in place, they were going to try some different strategies to ignore and redirect his interruptions. They also decided to begin with Elana at the next meeting to hear some of her ideas first. The therapist said she would bring in some quiet toys, masking tape, and a timer to make some activity circles for Randy where he could play and still participate in the session. The oldest daughter volunteered to make a chart to put up at home with each person's name on it and a place to check if that person made a put-down or a swear; this was intended as a way for all of them to listen and become more conscious about their language.

About half-way through the next session, a supervisor from another team, who had seen part of the first session with the family, passed through the observation room on her way to another session and remarked, "Gee, at first I thought you had a new family. They look so different and it's much calmer in there."

The exercises described so far in this chapter can help people become more aware of what they have learned about listening, practice some particular skills, as well as think specifically about levels of listening in the therapy room. The next exercises move more into the heart of the storying process and do not focus directly on listening. Rather, they emphasize needed skills to flesh out and develop story detail and meanings.

Shaping and Elaborating Stories: Exercises for Story Facilitation

Many of the techniques used in the practice of family therapy can be adapted to help both family members and trainees shape and thicken their own stories. Before having trainees do a more extensive analysis of familial dynamics with activities such as comparing their family story to the story of a family in a novel, there are a number of techniques that can be used to help them extend their understanding of their experiences as well as their descriptive capacities. Most of the traditional training techniques in family therapy can be adapted to have a narrative focus. I will share what I have added to the techniques of family photos, floor plans, and genograms to emphasize the story aspects of these activities.

Exercise 6: Using Family Photos in Therapy

Asking family members to bring photos into a session is a common method used to look at changes and life cycle transitions in a family, introduce members who are not able to come to sessions, and help the therapist learn more about the family history and environment (Anderson & Malloy, 1976; Sherman & Fredman, 1986). Having trainees bring in photos of their family of origin can be a good way to begin to teach them how to use photos in treatment; it will also provide them with input from other trainees about their family from what they observe in the photos (Akeret, 1974).

WORDS ILLUME THE PICTURE.   I usually ask trainees to bring in six or seven photos of their family at different stages of the life cycle. These are then examined with regard to spatial connection and distance between family members, kinds of activities they are doing, and overall affect. First, before people identify anyone in the photos, dates, or time in the life cycle, I ask them to tell the story of what they went through to get the pictures as well as how they decided to choose these particular photos. The point is to begin to explicate the meaning of pictures in family life in general as well as to understand the significance of these pictures for the person who brought them. For example, Peter Kearn brought in black and white photocopies of his family photos and told the following story:

> When I asked my mother if I could borrow the two albums that have most of our family pictures in it, she told me, "Curious that you want to see them now. What do you want them for? You never took that much interest in them." So I told her I needed them to bring to class. She asked me, "To share with people I don't know?"
> "Yes," I said.
> "Well, I don't want them removed from the house," she told me. Then she asked me what photos I wanted and she took them to the copy place and gave me these xeroxes.

In telling the story of getting the pictures, Peter began to introduce themes of control and care, and relationships to the outside world that were important in his family. The group that was to subsequently comment on what they saw in those pictures had an introduction into some of the familial dynamics. The story framed the rest of the activity.

WHAT STORY IS THERE TO TELL?   Another kind of story exercise that can be done after the pictures have been shared with two or three observers and they have described what they notice in them, is to pick one photo and make it come alive.* The person who brought the pictures should first title the photo, as a way to begin to encapsulate a story. Then, he or she tells a story about the picture as if the people in it could talk and move in and out of the picture. Yolanda, a 26-year-old woman from Cuba, chose a picture of her and her mother, father, three siblings, four aunts and uncles, and nine cousins at her father's 50th birthday party. She gave it the title, "My beloveds—I made it!" Her father's oldest brother had died in his late forties from a heart attack and her father hadn't been sure that he would make it to fifty. Then, in making the photo "come alive," she moved her father closer to his younger sister that he had been estranged from since their mother had died, and took herself and her siblings out from the middle between her parents and put her parents together. She had her father saying, "Another fifty, here I come." She and her siblings were saying to each other, "Go for it Mom and Dad."

Adding these kinds of story activities to the photo exercise gives different possibilities to think about the past, present, and future of one's life. Past family stories and events are presented through the photos, current family dynamics are often reflected in who is the keeper and holder of the pictures, and future wishes and desires can be presented in the framework of having a photo come alive. For example, Yolanda stated that in doing this, she realized how worried she had been as a teenager that her dad might die. After he reached fifty she felt safer to move out a little more. As she felt less fear that he was going to suddenly die, she had less need to hover around her parents. She also commented on the fact she grouped the siblings in a clump. "It made me realize that I am not as close to them now as I would like to be, especially to my

*This exercise is adapted from Robert Akeret, Ed.D.; see his book *Photoanalysis*.

brothers. I want to think if there are any particular things I want to do about that."

Exercise 7: Using Floor Plans in Therapy

Having family members or trainees draw floor plans of important places in which they have lived can provide a lot of information about daily interactions, the home environment, as well as the neighborhood context of the apartments or houses (Coppersmith, 1980b). After having trainees draw a floor plan, I ask them to note any rooms where they heard particular family stories and to write down any key phrases or dialogue from them that comes to mind. I encourage them to color, shape, and size the letters to reflect their feelings about the story. I also encourage them to think about what it meant to have the story told in that space and what they learned from that story in particular, either then or now.

For example, Burt drew on his floor plan the old nubby green sofa where he had sat as his father told him the story for the first time of the infant boy who had died two years before Burt was born. His name had been Burt too, but he had lived for only three hours. This second Burt, now 19, had never known there had been another son. Burt's Marine dress suit was hanging in the closet. He was ready to ship out the next morning to Vietnam. Looking back on that time, 20 years ago, Burt felt that upon hearing the story, he began to understand his father's cautious approach to him—his seeming wariness of getting too close. Perhaps his father was afraid of loss again. But he also recalled how hearing it had heightened his own fears about going to Nam. And when Burt returned to that same living room almost a year to the day later, the space was never the same to him. "Sometimes I would bury my face in that sofa and I could smell the sadness in it, a musky old smell edged with my raw fear about going into combat." He was glad when his parents bought a new sofa.

Another simple way to add story elements to a floor plan is to ask people to give a title to the place they have drawn, or write a caption under it. What would they name the apartment or house that they have drawn? What phrase or collection of phrases in a caption might capture a sense of their life in that space? For instance, after I drew the floor plan of the salmon pink house in which I grew up in Washington state, I wrote under it: "Lake Killarney House—Children's Paradise: Myth or Reality?" This caption held for me some of the mixed feelings I experienced living there.

Exercise 8: Using Genograms in Therapy

Genograms are an excellent tool to use to help track a story. People who are important characters can be easily identified right on the family tree. The fact that genograms span time, places, and different generations means that a story can be followed as it is passed from family to family and two and three stories can be located on different parts of the genogram and talked about at the same time.

Students in our program work in Bowen support groups of three or four people and coach each other on thinking about their family-of-origin dynamics. These groups provide a way to practice some of the techniques of the Bowen model, as well as a forum to explore the gifts they have received from their unique history, and areas to be aware of for further development. People usually introduce others in the group to their family by sharing what they know of their family tree. Another good way to help people get into the interactional patterns of each person's family of origin is to share some of the stories that go with the genogram. (The top of the box on the next page lists some questions I give out to the students to help them work with their family history.)

As a way to demonstrate to a training group how to create a genogram and use all the symbols, Rose Lowenstein (a Jewish-Italian trainee) and I were mapping out her family on a chalkboard. First we did three generations of her family (Russian Jewish on her father's side, Italian on her mother's). For about half an hour, we put in relevant dates, places, religious affiliations, work, illness, ethnic identification. Then, I asked Rose to share a story that would tell us something about the coming together of these two families with her parent's marriage. She thought for a moment and then said, "Yes, I have the story. As you can see, my father, Abe, is the first child in his family and the only son. His mother, my grandma Zelda, wore black to his wedding to my mother

EXERCISE 8: USING GENOGRAMS IN THERAPY

Working with Family History*

1. What is a key story that is passed down through the generations? Who tells it? When is it told? Who knows it? What are its variations? What is the affect with which the story is told?
2. What are themes embodied in this story?
3. How does this story speak to who you are as an adult? (e.g., What is expected of adults? Of men and women? How does it teach you to view the outside world?)
4. How are you connected to the story?
5. Are there key people that you want to ask about the details of this story and/or their versions of it?
6. Do you find yourself editing the story in different circumstances? Are parts of the story left out?
7. If you were going to reexamine, reframe, and/or remake the story, how might you do it? What different meanings might emerge?
8. With whom might you share this new version?
   Does it speak to you any differently about who you are or what others in the family are like?

Re-presenting Familial Dynamics

1. Who are the keepers of family stories?
   Who passes them on? At what kinds of events, in what settings are they passed on? Who is there when family stories are told?
2. What kinds of stories are told and with what affect?
   What themes link several family stories?
3. What do you think the effect of family stories is on different family members (eg., siblings, other generations)?
4. Are there untold stories? What might happen if they were told?
5. What family stories do you think should be available for the next generation?
6. What family stories do you tell (inside the family, outside the family, to closest friends, etc.)? Why do you tell these stories in particular?
   How are they the same or different than the kinds of stories other family members tell?
   What do you think would happen if you told different ones?

*The first eight questions are adapted from the work of Joan Laird; see her chapter "Women and Stories: Restorying Women's Self-constructions" in *Women in Families*.

Giovina. She said she was in mourning for her only son because he was marrying an Italian immigrant girl." People in the room leaned forward. "Aha," said someone from the group. Three hands immediately went up from trainees that wanted to ask questions. Their imaginations were now engaged with the people on this genogram in a different way; they were curious to see how this family drama played itself out.

A story coheres and holds information in a different way than the dates, names, places, ethnic background, jobs, and other information typically put on the genogram. Characters start to come alive. A sense of the quality of their life and the times they lived in begins to come through. They become human to us; we can identify with their foibles, contradictions, losses, and triumphs.

Questions about a series of stories in a family puts information together in yet another way. Familial patterns can be discerned and issues and concerns identified over time. If people find it useful to work with genograms and their stories, they may want to ask the kinds of questions listed in the box; the second part offers questions to think about how family stories can re-present* familial dynamics.

For instance, in my family, my mother is one of the main keepers of family stories. She usually tells them when several generations of the family are together and they focus primarily on the younger generation with any one of her four children as the main protagonist. Not many of the stories are about the siblings interacting together, nor are they about the family as a whole. They tend to center on idiosyncratic and creative things we did as children which fits with the family style of quite individualistic people who have each made distinctive life choices. Once in awhile my mother will tell stories about her childhood growing up, but these also tend to focus on a person of the younger generation, primarily her.

There are some secret stories that my brothers and sister and I have started to tell which include the story of my youngest brother's almost adoption, abusive parenting of my mother, and the suicide of our paternal great grandfather. (Our grandfather Hal

*The meanings of *re* and *present* are interesting here. *Re* signifies again, in return, in repetition, or reiteration. *Present* comes from *presente* (Spanish and Italian) and means offering or gift. See the Oxford Dictionary of English Etymology.

disclosed this to our father when Hal was in his nineties and near death.) Both of our parents had distance and cut-offs between people in their extended family. These secret stories seemed to have contributed to this pervasive pattern both because of what happened to people and because the stories were unspoken for years. We siblings have intentionally tried to find out about and elaborate these stories so that we can understand their impact on familial relationships as well as try to change the patterns of disconnection.

These patterns are reflective of a lot in our family. It was very child– and here-and-now–oriented. There was definitely an emphasis on "become your own unique self." There was little involved contact with the extended family and other generations. Looking at story patterns is a nonthreatening way to delve into complex family material. Most people enjoy telling and thinking about their family stories. Pulling stories together provides access into values and beliefs over broader time spans than is often available with just one story.

Many other techniques in family therapy can be adapted to focus on the narrative mode. For instance, with family sculpting, a story can be choreographed. With family art, a story can be drawn out, or part of it illustrated, or particular symbols that are key to the story can be sketched. Circular questioning can be taught by demonstrating different types of questions with the content focused on family stories (see Roberts, 1991, for a model of how to do this). As stories are filled out and probed for meaning, they lay the foundation for more extensive examination.

Tales of Others, Tales of One's Own: Working with Extended Story Frames

Beyond working with the skills of listening to and shaping and thickening stories, trainers and trainees may want to use more elaborated story frames to enhance their development. Novels and plays about families can be analyzed and compared and contrasted to one's own family. Family stories can be written down, shared, and used to explore different theories about narrative. Emerging trainee stories that speak to their professional development can be linked with the stories of other professionals already in the field.

Stories can be connected via videotape and enacting and telling group stories.

The power of using these story forms lies in the fact that they often hold the complexities and issues of today's families in a way that family therapy theories do not. Novelists, for example, are often ahead of therapists in describing configurations of families found today. Andrew Oxman, a student in his late twenties, found little in the family therapy literature that helped him understand his family situation. Growing up in the '60s and '70s with his mother, father, and sister, Andrew always thought of his father as heterosexual. However, in the late '80s his father told him that he was gay and while his parents continue to live together, his father now identifies himself as homosexual. Andrew, going outside of the family therapy field, found a novel, *Jack*, by A. M. Homes whose main character (Jack) is the son of a gay man. Jack also did not know his father was gay until he was older. This book allowed Andrew to look carefully at how Jack handled his father's shift in identity as well as how it affected his emerging identity and the interaction between Jack and his parents. Andrew was then able to compare Jack's experience to his situation.

The more elaborated story formats such as working with novels, plays, and written-down family stories, and interviewing other professionals about their stories are also relatively jargon-free. They don't use special vocabulary to describe complex human interaction, nor do they necessarily skew toward looking at only what is wrong in families—as many family therapy models do. They can be used with any of the theoretical models because they are not embedded in any particular theory.

One Story Provides the Backdrop for the Other:
Use of Novels and Plays

One of the most powerful ways to help trainees apply theoretical ideas and make sense of how their own story may be changing as they study family therapy is to have them do an analysis of a fictional family and then compare this family to their own.* Each family story provides a backdrop to the other story and as they are compared a rich tapestry is woven about the complex interac-

*See the Appendix for a list of suggested novels and plays.

tions of both. Let's go back to the work Andrew Oxman did in analyzing the book *Jack* and comparing it with his own family.

The novel is about Jack's emerging identity as the son of his parents, as a member of a divorced family, and as a unique person. Jack's parents separated when he was 11 as his father realized he was gay and began to develop a relationship with a man. Jack then lived primarily with his mother and was not told of his father's gay identity until he was older. Over time, Jack rebuilds a relationship with his father and his father's partner.

Andrew read this book and analyzed it by using life cycle theory (including stages, nodal and idiosyncratic events, and sexual development, identity, and autonomy issues); looking at family resources and strengths; creating an extensive four-generation genogram; and incorporating the Bowen model (including pattern repetition across generations, life events and family functioning, relational patterns and triangles, family structure, and sibling position). Doing this enabled Andrew to get inside Jack's story and write down his own story. He also began to highlight some areas he thought the field should be addressing in regard to families with gay members.

This writing (of the two stories) has given me ideas for future directions of gay issues in family therapy, particularly as related to the family life cycle. While there is a lot of information concerning homosexuality in the popular literature, this information has not disseminated to much of our society. Numerous questions were raised for me, such as: What does it mean to be gay? What does it mean to have a family member who is gay? How does this affect our sense of "family"? How does this impact the members of the family with respect to their gender, sibling position, stage of the life cycle, age, cultural and ethnic heritage, social experience, and relational patterns? What are possible steps to take in redefining and making sense of our relationship with a gay family member? Could these be integrated into the life cycle perspective? What are the stages of impact on the person who has a family member come out to them?

I believe there may be stages for this process. This is evident in both Jack's and my experience: at first we were angry and confused about our father's being gay; then, as we began reading about homosexuality and spending more time with our fathers, we were able to accept them more, and eventually realize that their homosexuality does not have to threaten our sense of self. It does mean we have to redefine our sense of what 'family' means, and what our relationship with our fathers will be.

These are vital issues which the family therapy field has yet to consider in depth. I believe the impact of a person's coming out will be felt by the entire family, at all generational levels. The above questions offer a starting point from which to consider these issues.

Andrew used the story of Jack to expand his understanding of himself and his family dynamics, and as a stimulus to critique the field of family therapy. The scope of the novels and plays available to do this is broad. Almost any situation can be found in literature.

Whatever modes of assessment are being studied (family rules, roles, myths, structural mapping, rituals) can be used for the analysis. I usually encourage students to pick modes of assessment they are the most unsure of, the most intrigued by, or ones they want to learn more about. They have a couple of months to work on these papers; I also encourage them to pick up on subtexts of gender, race, class, and sexual orientation in both their families and the novels.

Jennifer Iré, a West Indian woman in her late forties, compared her family to the family in the novel *Ordinary People* by Judith Guest. She chose to highlight class, among other things, in her analysis.

> Beth (the mother in *Ordinary People*)—given the life style we heard about prior to marriage—came from the upper socio-economic class and married Calvin (the father) whose class identification was definitely not on a level with Beth. Having come from an orphanage, it would imply working class or middle class. His professional potential when she met him and the entree provided by Arnold Bacon forecast that he could rise. However, I think that Beth married below her class but was able to recover this status as Calvin became successful.
>
> There is a hint of that when she is trying to coerce him to have the family spend Christmas away from home and he balks. She leans towards him, "All the wonderful places we've been . . . I know it's a lot to ask, Cal, I know we have expenses." He responds, "It's not the money" (p. 29). Earlier Calvin admits to himself that

he had been proud to have been able to afford expenses like the orthodontist. "He was supporting his family, his boys in style: whatever they needed, whatever they wanted, they got. He had arrived. Not bad for the kid from the Evangelical Home" (p. 10).

In my family, the class distinction was there. In Trinidad it is a little different, as class then, I think, was distinguished by ownership of property, education and occupation, as well as money. My father's extended family were property owners. He says, "After my father died, my mother took us back to her mother's property where they lived." His uncles had been, and still were, businessmen. My mother's mother, on the other hand, did not have either property or money in her background and, furthermore, she had been orphaned. She had no connection with her extended family in Grenada so there was a definite moving-up for my mother (though I would say it was nebulous since over time my father's family, I believe, lost or sold off the property). I suppose that envy was generated between mother and daughter because of this. Envy of the daughter getting what she could not get herself?

Adding class, gender, race, culture, and sexual orientation to the analysis can bring other layers of investigation to stories that are often poorly addressed in family therapy theories. It also provides a wider scope for students to discover the most salient aspects of their family's experience to comment upon. It is fascinating to see how the same text can be used in very different ways to examine story significance, depending on the ways the fictional stories resonate with the trainees. Students sometimes ask whether they should deliberately choose a book that is similar to their family on key dimensions, or one that is very different. I tell them that it usually does not matter because each text has many different levels. What seems to be most important is finding a novel or play that they feel passionate about. For instance, Stephen, the young man quoted at the very beginning of this chapter, also worked with the novel *Ordinary People*. In the summary to his paper, you can sense the meaning he made of the story in the novel and his family story:

> I feel that both Conrad (the younger son in the family that tried to commit suicide after his brother drowned in a sailing accident) and myself have a strong sense of self having come through the

experiences that were central to our life. Trauma simply under-scores the process of facing oneself in order to heal. For an adoles-cent, this process of self-reflection can speed up the process of completing tasks associated with this stage, and lead to healing in both intrapersonal and developmental realms.

Within the two family systems, I see two trends. Conrad's family split up at the end of the story. My family appears to have the opportunity to move closer together. I am taking advantage of this opportunity, and hoping that the issues associated with my own family can be processed enough for me to have sufficient meaning to move on and start my own family. Of course, that will be a learning experience in and of itself!

The response of people reading these papers is an essential part of the process. Sometimes people come up against painful issues, unresolved conflicts, and family secrets. It is important that they feel the reader is supportive of them and their development, thoughts, and feelings. People may need assistance along the way in the analysis and writing as well. Support groups can be formed at the beginning of the training group with the express purpose of helping each other learn material, as well as offering emotional support.

It seems to be an easy step for trainees to go from comparing a fictional family with their own family, to respectfully thinking about the stories of families going to a mental health clinic. Train-ees bring their experience of seeing the power of stories—how they can explain complex dynamics in a nonpathologizing way, how one story can illuminate the other, and how resonation between stories can bond and link people together.

Writing Out Specific Family Stories

Another variation of working with stories is to focus on a few central stories, write them out, and use them to look at ideas about narrative. It is not the broad-brushed look at the family saga over time that happens in working with novels and plays; rather, it is a detailed look at the process of storying. I usually have trainees do this after we have worked with structural and Bowen models, some of the strategic work of Jay Haley and Cloe

Madanes, as well as some exposure to Satir's ideas (as a way to get into Milan, narrative, and reflecting team models of treatment).

People are asked to write down a central family story and examine it for the following elements: voice, witnessing and listening, position and personal agency, and themes. They are also asked to use the six-family-style typology to see if those categories work for them.

Claire wrote the story of her two-year-old brother becoming wedged in an abandoned barbecue chimney. She was ten, another brother, Sean, was seven. They tried to pull him out but couldn't, so they devised a plan to rescue him. Claire sat next to him and tried to distract him by telling him stories and singing songs. Sean went to sit at the beginning of their driveway to wait for their dad to come home to pull him out. Claire wrote:

> This story used to end right there, or with Dad plucking my little brother out of the chimney. A recent addition was the revelation by my mother about a year ago that she really didn't appreciate that story, or the way we told it, because she can't figure out why we didn't ask her for help. My mother did not work outside the home when we were growing up, so it is likely that she was at home. But for some reason my brother and I don't remember that asking Mom for help was an option. It is sort of painful for me to realize now that my brother and I told that story for years, to poke fun at my little brother and also to show how responsible *we* were, while my mother remained silent about her feelings that her years of parenting were being denied somehow. And Dad gets all the credit for swooping in for the rescue.
>
> I wonder, in terms of developing voice and personal agency, how often it happens that parents allow their children to tell a restricted or slanted version of the story that fulfills some need on the part of the child, but does not reflect the parents' perspective, or even denies their existence.

This trainee raises questions beautifully about a unique generational process. By intricately capturing nuances in this changing story, she was developing skills that will hold her in good stead in many therapy sessions. She went on to write more about stories that are untold:

The Stories that are Not Told, and Some Reasons Why

I have referred to one piece of this already in discussing my mother's reaction to the chimney rescue story. There are stories of heroism and wisdom about my mother, but they are not told as often as stories about when she got mad or embarrassed us as teenagers. One reason for this is that she is not one of the skilled story tellers in the family. She gets a good one in every now and then, but not often. So her story is told (or not told) by others. I must admit that I am one of the story tellers in the family, and therefore feel partly responsible for the skewed image of my mother that has grown over the years. As one of the "in" crowd in some ways, it is hard for me to identify precisely why it happens this way. The stories that are told often poke fun at the subjects, and this may be one reason why my mother is described in uncomplimentary ways. But that does not address the issue of why she gets left out completely. Internalized sexism is one explanation—that the stories we tell embody societal attitudes of devaluing housework and taking women for granted.

In this analysis, Claire provides a strong example of how looking at the story process allowed her to reconfigure how she understood the relationships of people in her family. The ways stories were shared and told in her family directly influenced how people were seen. As she understood this, she began to see her mother differently.

I have consistently been impressed with the ways in which this kind of writing down and analysis of stories gives trainees rich possibilities to both explicate familial dynamics as well as look more closely at story processes. Another person looked at how stories shifted in her family over time when there was a major change—the divorce of her parents.

One overt change involves the story of my parents' courtship and marriage. Pre-divorce, this was the story:

My father and a friend of his wanted to improve their social life so they founded a singles club in the Cincinnati area where they were living. (Incidentally, my father's parents met through a church group—a singles social group.) Dad met Mom through the group, they liked each other (words like "fell in love" were never used), and eventually got married.

After my parents separated (they were separated for almost three years before they divorced), Mom decided to fill in some other details:

Well, actually, Dad was more interested in Mom than she was in him. She was a teacher working in the Cincinnati area, but she spent summers at home on the farm in eastern Iowa. The first summer after she and Dad met, he wanted to visit her in Iowa, but she wouldn't let him. Also, his mother didn't like her very much. (My father lived in the same house as his parents until he married at the age of 35.) According to Dad, though, his mother treated her just like she treated any of his other female friends. Well, finally Dad won her over and they were married.

The details that were remembered *and shared* by my mother certainly shifted when it became clear that the marriage was ending. Perhaps the function of the story also changed, from providing a pretty straightforward account of an important event in family history to justifying a more recent development in the marriage. If she never liked him that much in the first place, the divorce couldn't be as devastating. My father was also given more of an active role in the newly fleshed-out version, although there was no sense that Mom had felt pleased to be pursued so actively. This parallels the fact that Dad initiated the divorce, too, leaving Mom feeling pretty powerless.

As these kinds of analyses are shared among students, they are invited to think about how stories function in families in a variety of ways. They open up many possibilities for teachers and students to keep exploring what can be done with stories.

Hearing Other's Stories to Help Make Sense of One's Own

There may be times when it is helpful for trainees to move beyond their personal stories to their emerging professional stories. The stories of others already in the field may be an important resource. Hearing stories of how they have developed their work identities can help beginning family therapists understand that others have gone through similar periods of questioning, concern, and/or qualms. Ideas about how to handle various work transitions and issues are often embedded in the stories as well. It may be especially important for some of this to happen when part of the trainee's story has been silenced and yet has direct bearing on their professional identity. Let's go back to the situation described at the beginning of the chapter (p. 148) in which Jocelyn found herself.

As Jocelyn Robinson worked with her first families, she began to have concerns about what stories to share about her own personal life with both families and other beginning professionals with whom she was working. A lesbian in her early thirties, she wore a ring as a symbol of her commitment to her partner, Michelle. She and Michelle had no children. Working on a team with primarily heterosexual families, her questions about being a lesbian and a therapist—especially a family therapist—intensified.

> I have noticed the value for some families of a therapist sharing his or her life experience as a parent and a spouse. I have felt the shift in the relationship between the therapist and the family when the therapist shares this information in a way that lets the family know that she, too, has struggled with the mix of love, exasperation, fulfillment, and desperation involved in relationships between family members. That shift has felt to me like a move toward a more open, meaningful level of communication, yet I have found myself stiffening and holding back at moments when I might have done the same thing. I have not found a way to say, "My partner and I . . . " that fits in the way some of my colleagues say, "My husband and I . . . "
>
> I do not believe that I have to be a mother and/or wife, or otherwise have lived the experience of clients, in order to be a good or effective family therapist. But I know that for me at this point, my identity as a lesbian is a like a secret that spreads to encompass other topics of conversation and the ways in which I relate to clients. Instead of feeling free to share something of myself and my experience, I feel fear. Fear that I'll forget to be careful about the pronouns and "come out" unwittingly, or fear that an intentional revelation on my part will cause them to dislike/revile, distrust, or dismiss me. Some of this is my own internalized homophobia, some is my knowledge of other people's homophobia, and some is concern that this information may not be relevant to the issues the family needs to address.
>
> A rapid-fire series of questions swirls in my head during sessions: "What if they ask me if I'm married? What if she asks me if I'm a lesbian? What if he assumes from my ring that I'm married and asks me what my husband would say about this? What will I do if

they ask me? What would they do if I told them?" This internal dialogue/battle wages on, distracting me and causing me to feel stiff and uncomfortable. If they don't ask me and I assume that they assume that I'm straight, I feel like an imposter. Yet I live in fear of being asked directly. And I'm not sure that I want to tell them or that they want to hear it. This is not just a double bind, this is a triple backflip bind!

Jocelyn said that once she articulated and shared with her team what she was experiencing, it began to be easier for her to be in the therapy room. As she named and voiced her concerns, she had a way to hold and examine her reactions. However, she decided she wanted to go another step in her training and interview experienced family therapists who were lesbian and to find out "how they had navigated rough stretches of doubt" like the one Jocelyn found herself in. She also felt that others in the field could benefit from her retelling of the women's stories as it would offer information about how people whose stories were silenced in the larger culture dealt with this in the professional arena. So Jocelyn interviewed three women, both in person and on the phone. Her conversations with them focused on how they saw the relationship between the personal and the professional, including how "out" they were when they were in training for family therapy and how much they shared about their own familial life. She also asked them about ways they saw their identity as a lesbian as an asset in their therapeutic work, and/or as a barrier to sharing and creating relationships, as well as how they wished things would be for lesbian family therapists in the future. Over the next couple of months, Jocelyn wrote up these stories to share with others in her training program and reflected on the process for herself.

Looking back on what I wrote before the interviews, I am amazed at the negative and panic-stricken quality of what I was feeling. I was not even considering the possibility that clients might *like* me because of or in spite of my being lesbian. My attempts to think in terms of resources had produced meager results. And I was focused so completely on that one aspect of my identity that I had lost track of the fact that I am more than "just" a lesbian.

Something has shifted for me in the weeks that have passed since I wrote that section. Talking with lesbians who have fielded the big coming-out question from clients and lived to tell the tale, who have carved out careers that encompass the broad range of their abilities and interests, and who have a long-term, more balanced perspective which encompasses the extremes of pain and joy, has given me hope and expanded my focus.

I feel like a client who has just been visited by a reflecting team. Some of the things the women had to say were familiar to me and fit with my experience. Others were just different enough to start me thinking in new ways.

In the listening, putting together, and retelling of the stories of those who had walked before her and dealt with some of the same issues, Jocelyn found ways to locate herself differently in relation to her own story. The stories of others' experiences helped her to find her own blueprint.

Similarly, stories of clients can be put together as a resource for other clients in making sense of their dilemmas. Greg, the experienced clinician quoted at the beginning of this chapter, decided for one of his final course projects to do a video of the Vietnam veterans and their spouses that he worked with. He asked them to share their particular stories about how Vietnam affected their life. As he wrote: "I see two benefits to this project. First, for the family telling their story, the act of sharing is beneficial. Second, the recipients of the story receive alternative realities in addition to identification with the families. This process of generating alternative realities and identification is enhanced if those bearing witness are also veteran families."

The Sagas Continue

Back to the opening vignette of this chapter: At the end of a year working in family therapy, Stephen brought to the last class pictures of himself with his biological father. Stephen had discovered that he lived in the next state, only an hour and a half away. Two days before, they had met for the first time for lunch. Here is the next chapter in Stephen's story:

This Bowen group was a phenomenal experience for me to participate in. Through the process of meeting with the members of my group I was able to receive the support and encouragement that prompted me to make contact with my biological father in an effort to explore and heal a long-standing cut-off in my genogram. I was successful in this endeavor, and now having met with my biological father, I am in a new position in terms of my family of origin as well as with my understanding of the larger system that I am now aware of being a part of.

A new "I" position that I can take in my family of origin is that I am committed to preventing further cut-offs in my life whenever and wherever this is possible. There are a number of reasons for this position. First of all, I feel that it is important for me to stay in touch with people that mean a lot to me. As a child, I did not choose to be separated from my biological father. I was powerless and as a result became a participant in the cut-off that took place between my mother and my biological father. This has affected me profoundly throughout my life and played a particular role in my family while I was growing up. In a nutshell, I always felt like I was the "outsider" in my family. There was always this question mark of not knowing who I was or where I came from, just the knowledge that I didn't fully fit in.

Now as an adult, I have chosen to fill this question mark as best as I can with the knowledge of who I was then, and, more importantly, who my biological father was then as well as who he is now. I am committed to maintaining contact with him, although I do not know what form this contact will take or how often we will see each other. All of this remains to be seen.

If we can honor our own stories and those of others close to us, we can learn a lot about how to hear and honor the stories of intimate strangers—our clients. Working with stories with trainees on multiple levels will give them enough experience so they can discern the scope of what stories can bring to therapy. As people move in and out of myriad story frames and activities, they have possibilities to deeply take in the systemic perspective and all it entails with looking from different vantage points, including contexts and highlighting people's resources and strengths. Hopefully, working with stories will help them bring to their work the warmth, affection, and clear eye that good novelists give to their plots and characters. And most of all, trainees and trainers have an incredible gift together—to be able to share in, celebrate, and treasure our trove of stories.

8

TELLING TALES OUTSIDE
OF THE THERAPY ROOM

CHILDREN AND STAFF at a residential treatment center, with the help of an improvisational theatre group, tell their stories of what it means to live or work there. They break out of their usual roles and interactions and appreciate their unique experiences as well as find new commonalities. When there was discontent with the leadership of a public agency and numerous disparate stories began to emerge about what the director was doing, he called the staff together and told his story of the pressures he was under—then asked for comments from all of them. With a way to openly speak about their difficulties, the organization began to pull together. In supervision, a trainee told the story of her client Lorna and the wild turkey—a metaphor for building trust and connection. This affirmed the humanness of Lorna and the trainee's own connection to her in a way that a litany of Lorna's problems could not. Besides working with stories in training, there are many other ways to tell tales outside of therapy that can enhance and inform narrative work. In supervision, the story frame can help supervisors recollect, share, and analyze their development as supportive advisors to others. Stories can also provide a resource frame for complex cases where trainees in supervision are encouraged to become engaged with the ongoing life of the family, rather than overwhelmed with the difficult details of the case. As Lynn Hoffman stated, "My motto, in this regard, is 'every family is its own

Shakespeare play.' Shakespeare too took hackneyed plots, covering the whole grim list of human failings, made them into astonishing fables and peopled them with characters that were larger than life" (1989, unpaginated).

The stories that are told about clinics and professional associations tell much about the culture of these groups, including the relationships among people working in them as well as their community connections. Telling and examining these stories can help professionals look at larger system dynamics and understand the place of their own work within the organization: They can also offer possibilities for collegial links. For example, in one mental health center after there was a fiscal scandal in which several people were fired for handling money inappropriately, the staff was very fragmented and wary. People did not know whom they could talk to safely about rumors they had heard or what they themselves had experienced. The clinical director proposed a series of in-house workshops with protective ground rules for people to begin telling the stories of what they had seen happening within the agency and what they hoped it could now move toward. This began a process of reexamination and healing for the agency.

Exciting work is being done in communities with oral history, theater stories, and literacy training that brings people together from different backgrounds, honors the multitude of traditions we have in this country and lets people who are often ignored be heard. This work offers ways for therapists to expand their skills of working with stories, especially in understanding the larger social and cultural context. It can also be a resource for clients and therapists for new connections outside of the therapy room. Families need places other than family sessions to tell their stories.

As therapists work with stories in domains outside of the treatment room, and experience their potential for communicating key values and beliefs to themselves and others, they will be more likely to feel comfortable working with the story modality in therapy. This chapter will explore three different arenas in which tales can be told outside of therapy to help clinicians partake directly in story processes in their professional work.

Stories and Super Vision

According to the Oxford Dictionary of English Etymology, the word supervision can be separated into two main parts: *super* carries the meanings of "beyond, besides, and above"; *vision* comes from "videre" to see, and has its roots in signifying "something that appears to be seen otherwise than by ordinary sight and seeing something not present to the eye" (Onions, 1983, p. 983). If you think about visionaries, they are people that look beyond the day-to-day routine.

There has sometimes been too much focus on the "above" meaning of *super* in supervision. The supervisor is viewed as someone who is higher than the supervisee in the hierarchy and therefore knows better. In supervising, she or he then hands down to the supervisee this "better" knowledge. This does not hold a sense of learning that helps people put together information in new ways and discover things themselves. I prefer to emphasize the "beyond" and "besides" meanings of *super*, and think about supervision as "extraordinary vision." The supervisor's role is to facilitate an exploratory and expansive view. Work with stories has the capacity to help people recollect, examine, and cohere diverse elements—which can help capture this meaning of supervision.

Exercise 9: Developing as a Supervisor

To introduce stories into the process, supervisors can be asked (for instance, in a group of supervisors) to share their stories about how they first imagined themselves as supervisors, what stories they tell now about themselves as supervisors, and what stories they imagine might be told about them upon retirement. The open-ended sentences in the top of the box on the next page can be used as a warm-up to help them get into their stories; this takes about 15 to 20 minutes.* After asking people to form dyads, I read the first phrase aloud, then each person in the pair responds

---

*These sentences can also be a good way for a supervision group or dyad to open discussion about how people want to work together. Supervisees and supervisors can complete them and then share what kinds of good supervision they have experienced and ways they might build this into their current situation.

with the first thing that comes into mind. I encourage them not to think about it too much before responding. Then, a minute or two later, after the people in the dyads have explained and elaborated their responses to each other, I read the next beginning phrase for them to complete. I tell people not to worry about writing the phrases down because at the end I'll give them a copy of all of them written out.

EXERCISE 9: DEVELOPING AS A SUPERVISOR

Open-ended Sentences for Making Meaning of Supervision

1. Supervision is . . .
2. When I was a child, supervision was . . .
3. To my parents (guardians), supervision . . .
4. In my first job, supervision . . .
5. In school, supervision . . .
6. Supervision in mental health . . .
7. When supervision is problematic, . . .
8. When I am being supervised, I . . .
9. When I am a supervisor, I . . .
10. When supervision works well . . .

Looking at Yourself as a Supervisor

1. Before you had ever supervised:
   What story would you have told about yourself 5 years ago as a future possible supervisor? 10 years ago? 15 years ago?
   Did you imagine yourself doing it or not?
   What picture did you have of yourself (if any) in the future as a supervisor?
2. What story do you tell people today when they ask you about your supervisory work?
3. What story would you like to tell 10 years from now about yourself as a supervisor?
4. Imagine your retirement party. Numerous people are there that you have worked with over the years. They are feting and honoring you. What are 2 or 3 vignettes that you would like people to be telling about you?

Common issues that often emerge after these sentences are completed include the fact that few people are trained in supervision — they just jump in and do it. People also comment on the tension found in many supervision set-ups where the supervisor has to both evaluate people *and* support them to do their best work. Another issue is that the word itself seems to have a number of negative connotations for people (especially when they were younger).

After this warm-up, I have the same dyads begin telling their supervision stories. I encourage them to have one person answer all of the questions in the lower part of the box, and then the second person do the same.*

Listeners are also given some brief instructions; they are asked to listen for and think about:

1. Common themes that they hear that link the stories
2. Key phrases (they may want to jot down a few)
3. Possible titles or subtitles to stories that are being told to them by their partner.

Having people write these titles on large newsprint and putting them up on the wall is a quick way to share some of the ideas that emerge. Give people large paper, markers, and crayons and encourage them to draw the titles in lettering, shapes, and colors that illustrate their meaning. Here are some of the titles that have been put forth by different supervisors:

MY STUDENT IS MY TEACHER IS MYSELF

Finding, Becoming, and Giving [scripted in black calligraphy]

The Pleasure of Not Knowing

What's love got to do with it? [in vibrant red]

*This exercise can be easily adapted for clinicians by substituting the word "therapist" for the word supervisor and inserting "therapy" in place of the word supervision. It could be used in a supervision group or dyad with the supervisee(s) putting in the words "therapist" and "therapy" and the supervisor(s) answering the questions as written.

Coming ALONG Way

In time, everything will fall into place!

Gentle Power

THE BIRD WHO TAUGHT THE TURTLE TO SING AND
FLY [in large purple letters with birds flying above the Is]

The Princess who picked up the fish with tenderness, let her go
and continued, with a tad of ambivalence, on her adventure

People can be asked to share some of the content of the stories
that went with their titles. David Holdzkom, who had written
"MY STUDENT IS MY TEACHER IS MYSELF," described supervising as like a Mobius strip where roles are fluid and vantage
points are everchanging. "I keep learning and discovering myself
because I see supervision as a time to look at that which we least
know, can name, or understand. It's not just questions supervisees
have, it's questions we all have."

Jonah Gow, whose title was "The Pleasure of Not Knowing,"
talked about how anxious he used to become when he first supervised because he knew he "didn't know all the answers." He was
afraid that something would come up in therapy that he wouldn't
know how to "solve." In thinking about this, he realized that there
were probably some parallels between his anxieties and fears and
the feelings of his supervisees that they didn't know about numerous things either. So he started moving his supervision toward a
frame of the pleasures of discovering new things and *not* knowing
all the answers. This opened up an atmosphere for both him and
his supervisees of exploration rather than *the best* or *the right*
response.

As a way to help people remake connections with their work
settings, ask them to consider the following three questions:

1. How might you adapt and use this exercise in your own
   supervisory setting?
2. What is important to share about your supervisory story?
3. How might you do it in tandem with people telling their
   therapist story?

David thought it would be useful for all five people in his supervision group to imagine themselves as supervisors to get a common picture of what they thought was supportive supervision. He also thought he would share what he called his "anti-image" of himself as supervisor. As he said, "Having gone to boarding school and been supervised around the clock there, I never thought of myself as someone who wanted to be looking out for someone else. I felt too looked after myself! I'm sure that has influenced how I supervise. The last thing I want is for it to be a process of checking up on someone."

People may want to do a more formal analysis of their supervision. One supervisor decided to have a colleague come up and observe her supervision and then they wrote together about the session, the team interactions, and her supervision. They thoughtfully described the session, including pre-, post-, and intersession discussions, and commented on shifting team dynamics, experimentation with reflecting and Milan style teams for feedback, as well as supervisor-therapist and supervisor-team interactions. At the end of this analysis, the supervisor wrote:

> My areas for development are to continue the process of developing my own voice as a therapist and my confidence as a supervisor. This process of growth, of course, involves risk and struggle that I am willing to undertake. Too frequently I have discarded my own ideas and listened to someone more senior. However, now I am beginning to hold on to my own ideas and risk my own thinking. Perhaps as a woman, this process is more painstaking. In tandem with this personal process, I am becoming more deeply interested in gender, power, and the subject of voice in families. I wish to develop my skill and my own questions to elicit these issues. An example is the new question added to our format on the reflecting team: "Who has the power to story other's lives?"
>
> This paper has been a chance to express important recent experiences of discovery, transformation, and voice. It is the telling of my story. I have noticed that since writing it, I have felt a great liberation from anxieties that were plaguing me as a supervisor. This storytelling process has impressed on me the restorative power of claiming a voice. (Olson, 1990, p. 16)

This supervisor reclaimed her work through observation, reflection with others, and in her own writing.

Michael White (1994) suggests another way to have people tell their training and supervision stories. Groups of three to five people, using a reflecting team format, interview each other about their counseling career. He encourages them to ask about "sparkling moments" (unique turning points in their counseling history) and then to examine how these moments inform them about distinctive resources and strengths that they bring to their therapeutic work. This exercise could easily be adapted to supervision by asking people to share unique times in their supervision history and how these "sparkling moments" inform their current supervision.

Other Uses For Stories in Supervision

Stories can also be a tool to facilitate talking about and seeing families in a different way in supervision. When Lynn Hoffman was supervising some of the practicum students at the University of Massachusetts, she described how using a story frame changed the dynamics around a hard case.

> It is often useful to find an image or analogy that by itself provides a benevolent framework for a story that is otherwise one more version of the clinical trinity of alcoholism, incest, and violence. How many of us have reacted to the usual intake sheet with its dreary and reductive description of clinical problems with the wish not to see the families it describes. Only after due acquaintance do the families become fleshed out as real people, with hearts and minds, remarkable histories, and hopes of change. (1989, unpaginated)

She then went on to describe the family that Jean Flegenheimer, a trainee, was seeing. Lorna, the mother of two young children, called a mental health agency because of her fears that she would "fall off a line" or "go crazy" in her grief for her mother. Lorna would not leave the house and had no friends and did few activities. Her mother, who was said to be agoraphobic, had recently died of complications from anorexia. Lorna's father was a World War II veteran who suffered from flashbacks; he also physically abused Lorna's mother. When Lorna was younger he would hold her and her siblings and mother at knife point and threaten to kill them. Lorna and her younger sister had both been sexually abused by their father. Lorna felt guilty because she had not prevented her mother's death.

Jean found it hard to help Lorna. Lorna would not come to the clinic, so Jean took to going over to her house and sitting in the kitchen with her over coffee. Enter a story. And a story about the story.

The Wild Turkey

One day Lorna told Jean about a wild turkey she had seen in the field in back of her house. She had put out some seeds and crumbs. The turkey came back and fed on the food she left for it. Soon the turkey was coming regularly and began to be tame enough to come close to the house. Jean felt that she also was trying to connect with a wild creature. The story of the woman and the turkey symbolized many things: the preoccupation with food that was such a problem in this family; the fear of becoming too close to other humans; the need to reach out and nourish and to know that one's efforts are accepted, the problem of "wildness." All these issues were contained in the conversation about the turkey and in Lorna's story about her efforts to care for it.

Gradually Lorna began to show hopeful signs of moving out of her inertia. She enrolled her three-year-old in a participant play-group; she got the children's father to take more responsibility for them; she began to re-connect with her sisters, and even mulled over the idea of going to church.

This "embracing metaphor" of the wild turkey became a way Jean also communicated to the [supervision] group about the case. Instead of another hopeless-sounding situation, bringing thoughts of burnout to all who heard it, the group felt inspired by Jean's story. It seemed as if the image was a healing analogy, stumbled upon accidentally, but used by Lorna and Jean to communicate about the way Lorna was handling the dilemmas of her life. (Hoffman, 1989, unpaginated)

In this case, a story emerged on its own. This often happens, but if it doesn't and people want a different way to conceptualize a case, a story might be stimulated by having the therapist bring in an object that symbolizes the case (Imber-Black, Roberts, & Whiting, 1988) or describe an image that comes to mind when the therapist thinks about going into a session with that particular family. People can also share stories from their own experience or of other families that come to mind when they think of a specific family.

Celeste Wilkerson was working with a family with which she felt very bogged down. The Sterns were a remarried couple with two teenage boys, aged 14 and 16. The stepfather was an alcoholic and wasn't involved much with the family and so far had not come to any of the sessions. Both boys had been in foster care for a few months two years earlier when their mother's drinking had gotten out of control. The supervisee, Celeste, suspected that the older son had problems with drugs and alcohol. The sons reluctantly came to sessions after having been forced to see a psychologist while in foster care that they did not like.

In her supervision group, Celeste described feeling that after two months she and the family were not getting anywhere. Often only one or two family members would show up if at all. It was hard to get anyone to talk about the topic of substance abuse. If the boys did come, they made it clear they didn' t want to be there. The more Celeste directly confronted them, the more they backed away from her. Celeste found herself dreading the next scheduled time with them and hoping that they wouldn't come. Asked to bring in a symbol of the family to the next group meeting, Celeste brought in a brown mug. "Not just an ordinary mug," she said, "it's hefty—solid, yet it fits comfortably into one hand. When it has hot liquids in it, because it is so thick, the cup is not too hot. You can snug your fingers around it and it will warm your hand. I've had it for over 20 years—it was one of a pair from a very good friend of mine." She then linked this symbol to a story she wanted to build for this family which she entitled, "The Hot Cup." The family members all seemed to be looking for sustenance, and she wanted to be able to hand them a hot cup (with some of the hot issues) but to do it in such a way that it would warm them and offer them some of the things that they seemed to be searching for. Celeste continued to bring this cup to supervision and used it and the story it represented to help ground her in a different attitude toward the case. As she said, "It seemed to help me relax more about the case—to feel less responsible to 'make' them do some- thing. And as I was calmer, the more comfortable they seemed to become in sessions. Rather than me 'chasing them,' they began to get more involved."

Haley (1987) talks about the importance of the supervision model fitting and supporting the frame in which therapy is done. As trainees and supervisors experience how stories can help them develop themselves, their understanding of the ways stories can be used in therapy is heightened.

Similarly, looking at organizational stories and seeing how they inform us about the dynamics within groups can help clinicians understand more about the power of stories. This kind of exploration can also help them know more about the context in which they are doing their therapeutic work.

Stories and Organizations: Telling It Like It Is

Most therapists have an affiliation at some point in their career, if not during most of their career, with various mental health agencies and/or professional organizations. The stories that are told within institutions about their history, foibles, and working conditions can inform others about the culture of that group as well as give a good idea of what kinds of working relationships people might have there. Similarly, stories that are told outside of the institution present an image of that agency and what it is like to go there for therapy and other kinds of help. Looking at the stories told about organizations can help people understand the values and beliefs that are represented by them, as well as how stories take on meaning beyond just an individual, family, or small group. As in families, a particular legacy may be passed down and some stories may be silenced or hidden while others evolve and change over time, capturing unique nuances of the organization.

An organization espousing an Eastern religion began public service work with the story that their key mission was to provide permanent housing for the homeless. The group ran a bakery to generate the income to provide the housing. This soon became an "official" story, cannonized in the media through newspaper articles and a short TV clip. Meanwhile, outside of the agency, a different set of stories began to be told. As people who were supposedly next in line to get permanent housing were repeatedly shunted aside, community members started to talk about how the bakery was really a front to obtain public monies for the homeless, but that this money was not getting to them. No autonomous governing board existed to oversee the distribution of funds and it appeared that funds given to the group were being moved from one part of the organization to another to support other programs—*not* housing for the homeless. As this "unofficial" story began to circulate more in the community it began to generate mistrust of the agency. Workers within the agency started to hear this story, and ongoing events within the organization began to corroborate the second story. Some of the workers quit; the discrepancies between the official story and the unofficial story made it impossible for them to stay there.

Looking at stories told both within and without agencies can help clinicians identify congruency or lack of it between actions of the institution, stated goals, and how the institution is perceived by others. Widely disparate stories, or unspoken and/or hidden stories are often a sign of difficulties in agencies. Healthy institutions generally have low levels of gossip and innuendo, and high overlap between the kinds of stories that are told by different people from various vantage points—which is not to say that gaps cannot occur between the kinds of stories told within groups. However, how this kind of rent is addressed is crucial.

In one nonprofit human service institution, the director began to hear bits and pieces of stories that criticized how he was handling the agency at a time that they were buffeted by both the recession and more public recognition. These two factors meant a considerable increased workload for all the staff as they expanded services to broaden their economic base; they also needed to commit scarce resources in order to respond to their higher visibility. As a result of these changing needs, the responsibilities of the director also greatly increased. He began to have difficulty following through with details, letting others know about important decisions, and he made several public gaffes. Staff began to express discontent with his leadership, but he did not say anything openly about what was happening with him. In this vacuum, a number of stories began to be told about him behind his back. In the absence of any public story about what was happening with him and the institution, rumors emerged. As the director began to hear more of this, he called a staff meeting and announced ahead of time that he was going to share the story of what he felt had happened to him and the agency. At the beginning of the meeting, he asked for two ground rules: one, that he be permitted to share his remarks in their entirety without interruption, and two, that when he was done, each staff member have a few minutes to speak to respond to what he said. He then went on to share the increased commitments he had had to take on including important job searches for the parent organization, licensing and accrediting issues, as well as the opening of a new program some distance away which had run into major problems. He took responsibility for mistakes he felt he had made and then proceeded to outline steps he was beginning to take to turn the situation around. A staff member described what happened:

> The power of this presentation was palpable. Every respondent, of which there were over 20, noted an appreciation for his candor and courage. In responding, all affirmed the need for change, some noting the negative effects his neglect had had on them personally or on others, others urging immediate action, others less directly affected nonetheless hoping for a redress of the situation.
>
> Perhaps most clear to me was the power of the narrative as a means of response to the diverse concerns of the staff. The director himself acknowledged the extent to which "people talking behind his back" had bothered him. It is clear this was, for him, a way of taking back a sense of "personal agency" in the situation, of weaving together the fragments of the different stories people had been recounting. For some faculty, his story had been a "secret" one, for others his story was intertwined with the many other frustrations of their professional lives. His narrative in many ways served to sort out what he viewed to be his responsibility and to make room for the evolution of a new dynamic in the program. (Lise Sparrow, personal communication, October, 1993)

Once the director directly shared his story, people could respond genuinely to him—there was room to share the stresses they had all been under. The staff went on to try to create new stories about the institution that included themes of collaboration, accountability, and struggling together to take on new tasks.

Looking at stories within an organization as a tool to understand them, and to examine problem-solving styles and managerial modes has already been done in the business world.* These ideas can be applied within family therapy institutions as well. For instance, one can look to see if there are similar common theme stories, such as the ones found in businesses: relations between people in the hierarchy; how the organization handles obstacles; what happens if there are job changes and/or forced moves. Here are some ideas about how to access stories that are told about your organization or agency.

Exercise 10: Finding the Stories

Ask long-time staff members what stories they tell about the agency. Ask clients and community people to share with you stories they have heard. Tell them the stories will help the agency to understand how they are viewed in the community and how people see the work of the institution. To let them know that you are open to hearing a range of stories, you might share a story you yourself know about the agency that exposes some of its vulnerabilities. In the next box are some examples of the kinds of questions that can be asked to elicit institutional stories.

"WATCHING OVER."   The director of our counseling program at the University of Massachusetts dedicated himself to doing many administrative tasks that others did not want to add to their teaching and advising responsibilities. At a faculty retreat, each faculty member had been asked to share any particular stories they told about the program. The director told this story: "Some 22 years ago I was hired to work in the counseling program. The program had recently begun and we had just a few faculty members. I'd only been working in it about a year when the dean that hired me took a job elsewhere. Just before he left, he put his hand on my shoulder and said, 'Watch over this fledgling program. I'm counting on you to keep it going.' I took his words very seriously and I've been watching over it every since."

Although I had worked with the director for more than six years, this was the first time I had heard this story. It helped me to

*See Joanne Martin, Martha S. Feldman, Mary Jo Hatch, and Sim B. Sitkin's "The uniqueness paradox in organizational stories" in *Administrative Science Quarterly* and Ian Mittrof and R. H. Kilmer's "Stories managers tell: A new tool for organizational problem solving" in *Management Review*.

EXERCISE 10: FINDING THE STORIES

1. Gathering background: What stories are told about the meaning of the agency name? Its location? The logo (if it has one)?
   Are there nicknames for the organization? If so, what are their origins?
   What descriptive words could be used to describe the agency (enticing, comforting, cold, busy, preoccupied, quiet, active, safe, noisy, dingy, unorganized, inviting, etc.)?
2. What kinds of stories are told within the agency? Outside of it by community members?
   Where do these stories intersect? Where are they different?
   What common and/or disparate themes emerge from them?
3. If you were to give a title to your typical week at your organization or to a typical encounter there, what would it be?
   Put together such titles for several people—what kind of story line starts to emerge?
   If you were to bring in symbols to go along with agency stories, what might they be?
4. What future stories would you like to tell within the agency? Outside of it?
   How are they the same? Different?
   What do you hope that these stories will communicate about the institution?

---

better understand his willingness to do this work for the program, his solicitousness, as well as the amount of control he liked to have over the office, curriculum, and other decisions.

Using some of the constructs presented in this book to analyze family stories, the life of organizations can be investigated as well. Are there particular story styles that predominate? What are the themes of the stories that are told? Are there hidden stories? When, where, and how are the stories told? Who tells them? Within professional organizations, the telling of personal stories that relate to clinical and theoretical ideas that are being worked with presents other possibilities, and raises questions about where and how to make links or keep boundaries between one's personal and professional life.

Telling One's Story Within a Professional Organization

Over the 17 years that I have been going to professional conferences, I have noticed a change in workshops and plenaries: Presenters are more likely to share quite personal stories about their experience as a way to illustrate their conceptual ideas. This kind of sharing can enhance a professional presentation because therapists often have particular skills to be reflective, and to name and describe their experience. Also, a lot of the clinical literature still fails to capture the changing faces of today's families; clinicians represent the many configurations of families we find and as they share their lives, they can inform all of us. For instance, Dr. Gary Sanders at a plenary at AFTA (June, 1992) on gay and lesbian families, showed a videotape of himself, his partner, his mother, and some members of their family of choice (friends who were close to them and acted as extended family). In the video, they talked about how many gay and lesbian couples often have these kinds of extended families and the ways in which they provide support to the couple and family. Dr. Sanders went on to use his personal story as a jumping off point to discuss how this kind of family of choice may be a key resource for clients and how therapists can ask about and access their support for gay and lesbian couples. As he took us inside of his experience, he vividly let us all learn more about this kind of family structure.

At the same AFTA conference in a different plenary, three people talked about death and loss. Out of those three presentations, I will always remember Peter Lynch's (1992) story of his grandfather's death in Ireland. He described the wake, with the body center stage in the parlor. He told of softly touching his grandfather's dry wrinkled face. What it felt like to sleep with the body in the house — both comforting to know his grandfather was still with them, but sad because it was in such a different way. He described carrying the heavy coffin with its front corner digging down into his shoulder and the heaving in of the first shovel of dirt on top of the coffin — that sharp splatting sound. For Peter, the contact with death in so many different ways helped him make sense of what it was. I myself imagined taking a shovelful of dirt and splaying it on the coffin.

Peter contrasted this with with a funeral he had recently gone to here where the body was not even present at the service in the church. It had been "preburied"; after the funeral people went out and stood around the gravesite with the outlines of the grave hidden under green astroturf. The mourners did not have opportunities available to them to "touch" death directly.

I tell Peter's story now with my own imagination and interpretations. It viscerally taught me two quite contrasting ways to think about death and rituals of loss.

However, sharing personal stories within a professional organization is quite different from sharing client stories. First of all, the tellers are known and known in a particular way, i.e., for their professional work; and second, people within the organization have an ongoing relationship with each other. When client stories are shared, the characters are anonymous and no one but the person sharing the story knows them or has an ongoing relationship with them—boundaries are more distinct. The telling of personal stories by professionals does not have the protection of the clearer boundaries that are in place when client stories are told.

While sharing personal stories can enhance the development of ideas, it can also be handled in ways that are not appropriate. People may inadvertently disclose more than they care to, or they may feel misheard, depending on how people respond to them. If intense material is to be shared, there must be ways to process emotional reactions. Therefore, how to present stories in a professional arena needs to be thought through carefully. Traditionally in academia, these stories have been disguised. For example, in family therapy we have the Anonymous story (by Murray Bowen) of his family-of-origin work with his own family. Entitled "Toward the Differentiation of a Self in One's Own Family," it was published as "By Anonymous" (Anonymous, 1972), and is still referred to as the "Anonymous article" even though most everyone in the field knows it was written by Bowen.

Telling personal stories in a large group is different than telling them within the confines of a small therapy room with people with whom you have an ongoing relationship. The ground rules for presenting in academia (talk in the third person, be objective, present the facts in a scientific manner) do not necessarily support what happens when people share their stories. People should develop ground rules carefully to create an environment that draws upon the power of people's stories, supports them in the telling, and provides safety and respect for both the tellers and listeners. Some suggested guidelines include:

- Prior to the presentation, talk with presenters about the size of the audience, its composition and what level of disclosure they wish to choose.
- Structure the presentation so that presenters know how they have been heard; affirm their experience before asking the listeners for their critiques and questions.
- Encourage audience responders to speak about their own experience rather than telling how someone else should think or feel about something.
- Speak to tensions that may arise if the material is about areas that are sometimes hard to discuss, like racism or gender oppression. Or, better, strategize on ways to handle such tensions together *before* they arise.
- Organize formats such that individuals have a chance to tell their various stories, not just listen to one person share their experience.

Listening to and examining the stories told about agencies and organizations can tell a lot about their ambiance and working relationships. Employees of the institutions can gather a lot of feedback about how various people who are served by the agency view it. The sharing of personal stories within organizations can be a powerful resource, especially for looking at complex family dynamics that have not been well-described in the family therapy literature. However, care needs to be taken that it is done in a way that both enhances the sharing of knowledge and ideas and respects personal boundaries.

Communities and Stories: Braiding Individual, Family, and Community Tales

Work done with stories in oral history projects and theater groups offers another arena to inspire and nurture story work in therapy. Oral history centers, theater groups, volunteer literacy, and school-family groups are all using stories to access people's experience, share them with others, and build skills. These kinds of projects can be adjunctive to therapy in that they provide resources for people outside of the therapist's office. They also have many things to teach us about how stories can knit together communities of very different backgrounds, and link generations while teaching skills. These grassroots projects can be found all over the United States and in other countries. I will describe a few of them here to share some of the ways in which I think their work overlaps with that which we do in therapy. I encourage readers to look for and find these groups in their home communities as a resource for both their clients and mental health professionals.

Oral History: Essence and Essentials

> We celebrate the diverse accomplishments of the many people who have joined us over the past decade in using the power of everyday life stories to reach beyond prejudice and toward a world where everyone has a voice.
>
> *—Oral History Center, Cambridge, MA, May 16, 1992*

Oral history projects have been the gatherers of our day-to-day history—essential stories that tell who we are, where we came from, and where we might be headed. These stories do not usually find their way into the history books, and yet they weave the very fabric of who we are.

For the past eleven years the Oral History Center in Cambridge, Massachusetts, has built bridges between people and communities by facilitating the sharing of life stories between Palestinian and Jewish women; Latino, Anglo, Asian, Portuguese, and English-speaking students; African-American youths and elders; parochial and public school teens; Chinese and Syrian adults; and Mayan, Creole, and Garifura women from Belize. A Palestinian woman, Feryal Abassi Ghnaim, and a Jewish woman, Cindy Cohen, co-directed the project on the stories and folk arts of Palestinian and Jewish women. They emphasized finding ways to honor multiple strands of stories that can inform people about the same events and situations. As Gail Reimer, the Associate Director of the Massachusetts Foundation for the Humanities, stated, "Think for instance about the Columbus quincentennial. For one group of people it's a date to celebrate; for others, a day of mourning. The challenge for our multicultural society is that we need to learn to allow these two stories—stories that seemingly undermine each other—to coexist, to be heard simultaneously in the same time and place." (Voices, 1992, p. 2) This description sounds like some of what needs to happen in family therapy sessions, along with a deep recognition that not all stories are equal. Where people have been abused, traumatized, and in other ways hurt and exploited, their stories and the stories of their attackers are on different distinct levels. In order for the stories of the less powerful to come forth, the therapist needs to acknowledge and hold the power differential between the stories as well as hold people accountable for their actions. As Evan Imber-Black has noted, "The story of the Nazis is not of 'equal' moral validity to that of the Holocaust survivors. The oppressor's story does not have the moral equivalency of the oppressed story" (personal communication, October, 1993). Therapists have the responsibility for always asking themselves who has had the power to have their stories heard, along with making ethical and moral decisions about societal injustices as reflected in stories.

Many oral history projects focus on supporting silenced voices coming forth. "Let Life be Yours: Voices of Cambridge Working Women," a video of an intergenerational project by the Oral History Center, powerfully demonstrates this. It grew out of high school girls' interviewing older women about transitions in their lives and particularly how they were affected by economic situations, cultural background, immigration, and the Civil Rights movement. In the video, the women eloquently share their own labor histories, experiences of aging, as well as their views on gender, race, and class. This video has been used as a teaching/networking tool in "over 600 community education programs on women's history, multicultural issues, older people's lives, and oral history. The entire show has been translated into Portuguese, Haitian, Creole, and Spanish, and used as the basis for discussion of women's roles in those communities" (Cohen, 1986, p. 8).

In the Griots of Roxbury project, young African-Americans, aged 17 to 20, raised questions about "why they were born into this time of violence." They are interviewing five generations of Roxbury residents about their lives as teenagers to see if they can get some answers to their questions. "And they are cautiously hopeful of intervening in the violence that has taken the lives of family members and friends." As one participant said, "It's out there every day. It's life and you deal with it. If we make this video and people really start listening to us—well . . . "(Voices, 1992, p. 4).

The focus of many oral history projects is on gathering the least recorded aspects of people's lives and using them to strengthen communities. To that end, they work particularly on intergenerational communication as well as intercultural communication. A shared sense of history and understanding of dynamics in their current lives can help community members be active in shaping their future.

Oral history projects also try to draw upon arts indigenous to communities to facilitate the storytelling, arts such as songs, quilt-making, batik, embroidery, making lace, arpilleras, and photos. As well, they structure their projects to respect cultural rules. For instance, in working with young Portuguese women in Cambridge, the Oral History Center staff arranged to interview the teenagers at the Portuguese community center rather than in their homes. Community members wanted them to be talked to in a public and known place; it was felt that their houses were too intimate of a setting to have this kind of interview with people from outside of the family.

Therapy and Oral History

Oral history techniques, with their emphasis on creating intergenerational affiliation and interchange across different cultural experiences, can be supportive of family therapy work. There is a lot of overlap between teaching people to facilitate oral history and doing therapy. Oral history gatherers are trained to dialogue with their interviewees about what they want to get out of sharing the stories, how they will be accountable to each other, how to ask questions, audio- and videotape, and put the information together in a way that it can be shared. These skills can be particularly useful for therapy interventions that are designed to pull together some of the unique experiences of an individual or a family and link them to the lives of others.

Workshops are often offered on topics such as designing a family oral history project, using oral history in organizations, oral history for advocates, and oral history techniques for artists. Oral history techniques can be used to help gather the stories of organizations, thus helping mental health professionals understand the philosophy and work history of a clinic. They can also be used by clinicians as well as by clients to gather information on their own extended families.

"MEMOIRS AT AGE TEN."   In the Saari-Moriarty family, Laurie, the stepmother, wanted help connecting more with her ten-year-old stepdaughter, Emily. Emily was ambivalent about her stepmother because her biological parents had gone through a bitterly contested divorce with custody of the children being the primary issue they fought out in the courts for three years. Emily said, "I'm just getting clear how I can be with my mom without hurting my dad and how I can be with my dad without hurting my mom and then this new person comes along." As the therapist talked with them, they tried to come up with something that could help them get to know each other better, but without Emily feeling torn between people. The therapist, trained in oral history techniques, made some suggestions about various small history-gathering projects that they might do to create a greater sense of a shared life story. She talked about the importance of doing it in ways that acknowledged all of Emily's complex connections, yet let Emily and Laurie do something unique together.

They hit upon the idea of Laurie and Emily doing a memory book together in which they would record their memories from ages one to ten, and which they could then give to her dad as a birthday present. Emily dictated to Laurie some of the special memories she had of each year of her life and Emily then illustrated them. Likewise, Laurie dictated her memories to Emily, and then Laurie illustrated. Emily told about first learning how to ride a bike when she was six, with her older sister holding onto the seat, running down the dirt road with her, and then pushing her off to zig-zag over the packed earth. That made Laurie think of something that had happened to her when she was six. "I was on the back of Dwight Madsen's bike, sitting on his fender and when we went riding out from the front of my house, his tire got caught on the edge of the walk, my foot slipped into the wheel, and the toe-nail of my big toe was torn off. That was the first time I was really hurt. And my toenail has never been the same since." Laurie then reported how she took her shoe off and showed Emily her scars, and then they compared scars on their knees.

Emily could not remember much from the first three years of her life so she asked her parents to tell her stories about things she had done at those ages. Structurally, the project gave Emily a way to touch base with and include all the adults in her life, while also giving her and her stepmother a unique way to be together.

Later, for Christmas, Laurie and Emily made a "grandparents book" for all the different sets of grandparents Emily now had. (This is often an unaddressed issue in remarried families—how to build connections between the grandparents and their new step-grandchildren.) Together they made up questions to ask the grandparents: "What did you do in World War II? What was your most embarrassing moment as a child? Who was your best friend?" These and other questions were written at the top of a blank sheet of paper, border designs put in, and then color-xeroxed and sent to all of the grandparents to fill out. Both the making of the book together and then the sharing of the responses continued the connections on multiple levels. Laurie and Emily worked together on the project, but at the same time, the way it was structured made new ties between the grandparents and the family.

Oral history techniques can be called upon in therapy to help elicit stories. Clients can also be helped to build support networks in communities through participation in oral history project; as one participant said,

> Some of them stories is equal to mine,
> and some of 'em is different—
> And it do me good just to hear.
> (Cohen & Engel, 1988, p. 3)

Playback Theatre: Criss-Crossing Personal Stories and Community Stories

> In this reductive age of therapeutic scripts and programmatic recovery, the building of community through sharing and wit-

nessing deep stories comes like fresh water after a long hike, reconnecting us with the extraordinary array of human experience and the irreducible poetry of the self.

— Mimi Katzenback, Playback Theatre Director
(Interplay, 1991a, p. 1)

The drama of stories can be shared even more vividly with theater techniques. Playback Theatre was developed in the 1970s by Jonathon Fox. Fox had a background in literature where he was particularly interested in epics and oral traditions; he also had training in theater and psychodrama. Playback was conceived as a way to tell stories in a group in a manner that honored both individuals and their collective experience. Based on a model of constructive social dialogue, its focus is on collaboratively telling many stories.*

Using improvisational and psychodrama techniques, small troupes of actors go into residential treatment centers, prisons, hospitals, recovery clinics, shelters for battered women, schools, community centers, and conferences to help people tell their stories. The basic format consists of an opening (often with music, a procession of the actors coming in and then welcoming the gathering) and perhaps a fluid sculpture (a movement piece where the actors express a particular feeling). Then, a scene is created by asking a "teller" to come up from the audience and sit in the teller's chair and share a story. "Interviewed by a 'conductor,' he or she narrates a moment of life, which is then enacted, or 'played back,' by performers using mime, music, and spontaneous spoken scenes. In the course of a playback event, many tellers tell and many stories are made into theater, revealing collective themes. Like other kinds of improvisation, the process has an informal aspect, since the actors are present on stage as themselves. Nevertheless, the enactments frequently evoke archetypal images and strong emotions" (Fox, no date, p. 1).

The scenarios that are acted out are sometimes interspersed

*A few pages in this book will not do full justice to the depth of this work. For more complete descriptions, the reader is referred to *Dramatized Personal Story in Playback Theatre*, an unpublished manuscript by Jonathon Fox, "Culture and Community: Playback Theatre" by Jo Salas, and "Playback Theatre: The Community Sees Itself" by Jonathon Fox. More information can also be obtained from the International Playback Theatre Network (an association of Playback performers and teachers) at PO Box 1173, New Paltz, NY 12561.

with pairs (in twos, the actors successively act out two feelings that are central to a situation), musical interludes, or perhaps an invitation for audience members to come up and be part of the troupe for a scene. Lighting, music, cloths, props, and a few crates are all used to help create a sense of "theatricality."

Jo Salas, musician, writer, and founder of playback groups in New York, organized a playback group, at a residential center for children. The staff from the center makes up the group, which includes one high-level administrator. They have done shows for the people who work there as well as for the children. As Jo described it, "Children and staff alike seem to recognize the opportunity to find affirmation and new ways to connect with each other. The children's stories have tended to be on the theme of nurturing parents. They tell about one cherished moment—when a father showed up on a birthday, or about finally finding loving adoptive parents after a wretched early childhood with a harsh mother and a series of inadequate foster placements. The adults have told about the special challenges—and sometimes the satisfactions—of working with these children, with their difficult behavior and often tragic backgrounds" (Interplay, 1991a, p. 3). Playback offers ways for this group to bond around its unique circumstances and work. It also provides an ongoing forum that names and honors work that is often unseen in society. The members of the troupe, despite very demanding job and family commitments, keep squeezing in rehearsal time because they find it is both invigorating and healing for them.

Playback theatre can also be done in communities that are not a formally organized group or agency. For instance, the San Francisco group has worked with Germans and Jews, bringing them together to commemorate the Holocaust. And the Schaffhausen (Switzerland) Playback Group, right after the war in the Persian Gulf started in early 1991, offered playback sessions in various neighborhoods at community centers and school auditoriums. Everyone in the community was welcome to come forth and tell their stories about what it meant to them to have war break out in the Middle East. As the director, Annette Henne, said, "It was very important for people to tell and look and share. It was something special I really can't find words for. In these days of war, I had the feeling that Playback Theatre was very important. It is not enough to talk about war and share opinions. People need to have a place where feelings can be aired." (Interplay, 1991a, p. 8) People can get a sense of community support and not feel like they are so alone with these kinds of large-scale events. It is quite different to sit with a large group of concerned people and share your responses to a world-wide crisis than it is to sit around the dining room table with a few friends and/or family members and discuss it.

Playback may also be done with groups that come together for brief periods of time at conferences, teacher seminars, or village fairs. For example, a television crew came to the United States from the former Soviet Union just four days after the failure of the coup attempt in 1991. This crew had made a film of the playback troupe in Moscow, and they came here to get footage of playback groups to add to their documentary. The last night they were in the United States, a playback group from New York asked all the members from the television crew to become tellers to share with the playback community what was happening in their country. Scriptwriter Lyudmila Shevstova, when asked why they came to the United States from Moscow at such a historic time, said, "There is no more important time than now, when there is new freedom from fear, for playback to play a role in offering a forum for Soviet citizens to tell their stories, whatever they may be—in public" (Interplay, 1991b, p. 7). For groups that come together for short and often intense periods of time, doing playback offers a chance to communicate the meanings that are being given to the event in a public arena.

Theater and Therapy

Playback theater and other improvisational groups like them* have a number of things to offer both therapists and clients. The training to become a member of these groups can enhance therapy skills. As one social work student wrote, "I've been keenly aware in my fieldwork [in a psychiatric unit of a hospital] of how Playback and psychodrama training have helped me with two essential therapeutic skills: 1) empathic skills, 'being with' the patient/cli-

---

*A wonderful group is Rehearsals for Growth. Contact Gloria Maddox and Dr. Daniel Wiener at 251 Fifth Avenue (Floor 3), NY, NY 10016 (212) 684–6776 for information about their newsletter and workshops. They use improvisational theater to both train family therapists and work with clients. See also Daniel Wiener's forthcoming book, *Rehearsals for Growth: Theater Improvisation for Psychotherapists.*

ent and not being afraid of their powerful feelings; and 2) listening skills, getting a sense of the latent content behind the manifest expression [this is obviously the same thing as the Playback skill of grasping the *essence* of a story]" (Interplay, 1992, p. 6).

Beyond these skills, playback can help people feel more comfortable doing the more active kinds of story techniques described in Chapter 5 (such as sculpting, puppets, and role-playing). A range of workshops are offered by playback groups, including looking at personal stories in action, spontaneity, acting, playback with youth, conducting, and playback for community change.

There are also many things to learn from playback theater about how to knit individual stories together as one after the other are told. This can be a central part of working with stories in family therapy, especially with family members who are very disconnected from one another. People in playback have commented on the evolution of this focus on building one story upon another. "More important, however, has been the growing appreciation of the connection between the stories. The next Teller, we have found, will tell a story which, while just as personal as the one before, nevertheless provides a comment on the previous story. In this way, the Playback audience engages in a discourse through the medium of the stories" (Fox, no date, p. 4).

As with oral history work, playback offers clients and therapists a public forum for telling stories. Many playback companies have been asked to present at psychological conferences. A troupe performed at a family therapy conference at the University of Massachusetts a few years ago. They set a wonderful exploratory and respectful tone for the conference by providing a place for people to share why they had come, what they expected, as well as the story of the conference from conception to actual implementation. Playback work offers a way to look at what happens when individual stories enter the public domain and as stories are linked together. It also provides ways for clinicians to learn more active ways of working with stories.

Interweaving Stories

Work with stories outside of the therapy room can support narrative work in treatment. If stories are used in supervision to help articulate ways people support each other in doing good therapy, and supervisees and supervisors directly experience their potential to help with their own development, they are more likely to use stories in therapy. As they explore the possibilities of stories in their own life they will be more comfortable using them in treatment, and will probably use them more imaginatively as well.

Organizational stories can be an evocative tool for studying larger systems. As people understand and make meaning of their work contexts, they are often able to do better work within that setting. Gaining an understanding of their work sites by examining the stories told about them can also help clinicians structure, ask for, and have clearer expectations about what they need in that situation to do good therapeutic work. In reflecting on their own larger system relationships, they can also become more skillful in helping families look at their larger system affiliations.

Knowing about and joining with community groups that use the story frame supports families in having places other than in the therapy room to tell their stories and be heard. Working with stories in a larger context can expand the skills and repertoire of therapists.

Therapists are in a unique position to facilitate the sharing of stories in many arenas. Families often recognize this. For example: Two therapists went into the Schutte home to work with the stepfather, Dennis, his wife, Janis, and her two teenage children. Dennis was paralyzed from the waist down because of an accident, and therapy took place around the specialized bed that had been made for him. He and Janis had married after his accident, and he had become actively involved in the family, including the parenting of the two children. At the end of therapy, he was asked what he wanted other professionals to know about the work they had done together. Dennis said, "I've only asked these two therapists to come—the reason I appreciate them being here is because they see other families and they can give us ideas on how to help our situation from what they know about the stories from other families. And that's what therapists will be able to bring to another family. We have so much diversity in our family, and more family unity came out of this. If other families hear about what we did, maybe they can learn from us. You could tell us what others had to say. Now you can pass it on from us."

Therapists have an incomparable vantage point from which to help rework, pass on, and link our tales. It is a large responsibility because with these stories, therapists have tools to support society with the complex evolution of that always-changing, yet always-enduring institution we call the family.

APPENDIX:
SELECTED LIST OF
FAMILY LITERATURE

Novels

Achebe, Chinua	*Things Fall Apart*
Allende, Isabel	*The House of the Spirits*
Alvarez, Julia	*How the Garcia Girls Lost Their Accents*
Austin, Doris	*After the Garden*
Bainbridge, Beryl	*A Quiet Life*
Baldwin, James	*Go Tell It on the Mountain*
Brown, Rosellen	*Civil Wars*
	Tender Mercies
Chase, Joan	*During the Reign of the Queen of Persia*
Chin, Pa	*Family*
Chute, Carolyn	*The Beans of Egypt, Maine*
Colwin, Laurie	*Family Happiness*
Curran, Mary Doyle	*The Parish and the Hill*
Dann, Patty	*Mermaids*
Dew, Robb Forman	*The Time of Her Life*
	Fortunate Lives
Dillard, Annie	*The Living*
Dorris, Michael	*A Yellow Raft in Blue Water*
Drabble, Margaret	*The Middle Ground*
Dostoyevsky, Fyodor	*The Brothers Karamazov*

Erdrich, Louise	*Love Medicine*
Findley, Timothy	*The Last of the Crazy People*
Flynt, Candace	*Mother Love*
Ford, Elaine	*Missed Connections*
Garcia, Cristina	*Dreaming in Cuban*
Godwin, Gail	*A Mother and Two Daughters*
Gordon, Mary	*The Other Side*
Guest, Judith	*Ordinary People*
Hearon, Shelby	*A Small Town*
Hijuelos, Oscar	*Our House in the Last World*
	The Fourteen Sisters of Emilio Montez O'Brien
Irving, John	*The Hotel New Hampshire*
Jen, Gish	*Typical American*
Kadohata, Cynthia	*The Floating World*
Kennedy, William	*Very Old Bones*
Leavitt, David	*The Lost Language of Cranes*
Lee, Harper	*To Kill a Mockingbird*
Mahfouz, Naguib	*The Beginning and the End*
Markus, Julia	*Uncle*
	American Rose
Marshall, Paule	*Brown Girl, Brownstones*
McDermott, Alice	*At Weddings and Wakes*
Miller, Sue	*Family Pictures*
Moore, Susanna	*My Old Sweetheart*
Morrison, Toni	*Beloved*
Ng, Fae Myenne	*Bone*
Paton, Alan	*Cry, the Beloved Country*
Porter, Connie	*All-Bright Court*
Potok, Chaim	*In the Beginning*
	My Name is Asher Lev
Quindlen, Anna	*Object Lessons*
Rivera, Edward	*Family Installments*
Robinson, Marilynne	*Housekeeping*
Sayles, John	*Los Gusanos*
Sexton, Linda Gray	*Rituals*
Smiley, Jane	*A Thousand Acres*
Smith, Lee	*Black Mountain Breakdown*
	Family Linen

Stark, Sharon Sheehe   *A Wrestling Season*
Steinbeck, John   *The Grapes of Wrath*
Tan, Amy   *The Joy Luck Club*
Taylor, Peter   *A Summons to Memphis*
Theroux, Paul   *The Mosquito Coast*
Toson, Shimazaki   *The Family*
Tyler, Anne   *Dinner at the Homesick*
                           Restaurant
                           Searching for Caleb

Nonfiction

Brady, Katherine   *Father's Day: A True Story of*
                           Incest
Chernin, Kim   *In My Mother's House: A*
                           Daughter's Story
Gage, Nicholas   *A Place for Us*
Hoffman, Eva   *Lost in Translation*
Ione, Carole   *Pride of Family: Four*
                           Generations of American
                           Women of Color
Kingston, Maxine Hong   *The Woman Warrior:*
                           Memoirs of a Girlhood
                           Among Ghosts

Plays

Albee, Edward   *A Delicate Balance*
                           Who's Afraid of Virginia
                           Woolf?
Bergman, Ingmar   *The Marriage Scenarios*
Chekov, Anton   *The Cherry Orchard*
Hansberry, Lorraine   *A Raisin in the Sun*
Ibsen, Henrik   *A Doll's House*
                           Hedda Gabler
Marquez, R.   *The Oxcart*
Miller, Arthur   *All My Sons*
                           A View from the Bridge
                           Death of a Salesman

Pinter, Harold	*The Homecoming*
Sanchez-Scott, Milcha	*Roosters*
Shepard, Sam	*Buried Child*
Sutherland, Efua	*Edufa*
Wilder, Thornton	*Our Town*
Williams, Tennessee	*Cat on a Hot Tin Roof*
	The Glass Menagerie

REFERENCES

Akeret, R. U. (1974). *Photoanalysis*. New York: Wyden.

Allen, J., & Laird, J. (1990). Men and story: Constructing new narratives in therapy. In M. Bograd (Ed.), *Journal of Feminist Family Therapy*, 2, 3–4, 75–100.

Anderson, C., & Malloy, E. (1976). Family photographs: In treatment and training. *Family Process*, 15(2), 259–264.

Anderson, H., & Goolishian, H. (1988). Human systems as linguistic systems: Preliminary and evolving ideas about the implications for clinical theory. *Family Process*, 27(4), 371–393.

Anderson, H., Goolishian, H., & Winderman, L. (1986). Problem determined systems: Toward transformation in family therapy. *Journal of Strategic and Systemic Therapies*, 5(4), 1–11.

Anonymous (1972). Toward the differentiation of a self in one's own family. In J. Framo (Ed.), *Family interaction* (pp. 111–166). New York: Springer.

Bass, E., & Davis, L. (1988). *The courage to heal*. New York: Harper & Row.

Becker, A. L. (1991). A short essay on languaging. In F. Steier (Ed.), *Research and reflexivity* (pp. 226–234). London: Sage.

Belenky, M. F., Clinchy, B. M., Goldberger, N. R., & Tarule, J. M. (1986). *Women's ways of knowing: The development of self, voice and mind*. New York: Basic.

Benjamin, W. (1969). *Illuminations* (H. Zohn, Trans.). New York: Schocken.

Berger, J. (1992, January 5). Review of Keeping a Rendezvous. *New York Times Book Review*, p. 11.

Billingsley, A. (1992). *Climbing Jacob's ladder*. New York: Simon & Schuster.

Blythe, R. (1983). *Characters and their landscapes*. San Diego: Harcourt Brace Jovanovich.

Boscolo, L., & Bertrando, P. (1993). *The times of time: A new perspective in systemic therapy and consultation*. New York: Norton.

Brady, K. (1979). *Father's day: A true story of incest*. New York: Seaview.

Carey, L. (1991). *Black ice*. New York: Vintage.

Carter, E. A., & McGoldrick Orfanidis, M. (1976). Family therapy with one person and the family therapist's own family. In P. Guerin (Ed.), *Family therapy: Theory and practice* (pp. 193–219). New York: Gardner.

Chasin, R., Roth, S., & Bograd, M. (1989). Action methods in systemic therapy: Dramatizing ideal futures and reformed pasts with couples. *Family Process*, 28(2), 121–136.

Clifton, D., Doan, R., & Mitchell, D. (1990). The reauthoring of therapist's stories: Taking doses of our own medicine. *Journal of Strategic and Systemic Therapies*, 9(4), 61–66.

Cohen, C. (1986). *Using the arts in political education.* Unpublished manuscript.

Cohen, C., & Engel, B. (1988). *Lifelines oral history project: A case study.* Unpublished manuscript.

Cohen, R. (1992). *Reframing the launching phase of the life-cycle for families with developmental disabled offspring.* Doctoral dissertation, Texas Women's University at Denton, Order #9300211.

Coles, R. (1990). *The spiritual life of children.* Boston: Houghton Mifflin.

Combrinck-Graham, L. (Ed.). (1986). *Treating young children in family therapy.* Rockville, MD: Aspen.

Combrinck-Graham, L. (Ed.). (1989). *Children in family contexts: Perspectives in treatment.* New York: Guilford.

Combs, G., & Freedman, J. (1990). *Symbol, story & ceremony: Using metaphor in individual and family therapy.* New York: Norton.

Coppersmith, E. (1980a). Expanding uses of the telephone in family therapy. *Family Process*, 19, 411–417.

Coppersmith, E. (1980b). The family floor plan: A tool for training, assessment and intervention in family therapy. *Journal of Marital and Family Therapy*, 6, 141–145.

Crites, S. (1986). Storytime: Recollecting the past and projecting the future. In T. Sarbin (Ed.), *Narrative psychology: The storied nature of human conduct* (pp. 152–173). New York: Praeger.

Davis, J. (1992). *Growing pains: A story about changing stories.* Unpublished manuscript.

Duhl, F., Duhl, B., & Kantor, D. (1973). Learning, space and action in family therapy. In D. Bloch (Ed.), *Techniques of family psychotherapy.* New York: Grune & Stratton.

Erickson, M., Rossi, E., & Rossi, S. (1976). *Hypnotic realities.* New York: Irvington.

Fox, J. (no date). *Dramatized personal story in playback theatre.* Unpublished manuscript.

Fox, J. (1982). Playback theater: The community sees itself. In R. Courtney, & G. Shattner (Eds.), *Drama in therapy: Vol. II.* New York: Drama.

Gale, J., & Newfield, N. (1992). A conversation analysis of a solution-focused marital therapy session. *Journal of Marital and Family Therapy*, 18, 2, 153–165.

Gardner, R. A. (1969). Mutual storytelling as a technique in child psychotherapy. In J. H. Masserman (Ed.), *Science and psychotherapy* (pp. 123–125). New York: Grune & Stratton.

Gardner, R. A. (1971). *Therapeutic communication with children: The mutual storytelling technique.* New York: Jason Aronson.

Gardner, R. A. (1976). *Dr. Gardner's stories about the real world.* New York: Avon.

Goldman, M. (1933, May 30). One idea, and that a bad one. *New York Times Book Review*, pp. 10–11.

Gordon, D. (1982). Ericksonian anecdotal therapy. In J. Zeig (Ed.), *Ericksonian approaches to hypnosis & psychotherapy* (pp. 113–119). New York: Brunner/Mazel.

Griffin, P. (1992). From hiding out to coming out: Empowering lesbian and gay educators. In K. Harbeck (Ed.), *Coming out of the classroom closet: Gay and lesbian students, teachers, & curricula*. New York: Haworth.

Grossman, C. L. (1993, August 3). At museum, crowds vow: "Never again." *USA Today*, pp. 1D, 2D.

Hadas, R. (1990). *Living in time*. New Brunswick, NJ: Rutgers University Press.

Haley, J. (1987). *Problem-solving therapy*. San Francisco: Jossey-Bass.

Heat-Moon, W. L. (1991). *PrairyErth*. Boston: Houghton Mifflin.

Hoffman, E. (1989). *Lost in translation*. New York: Penguin.

Hoffman, L. (1989). *A constructivist training manual*. Unpublished manuscript.

Imber-Black, E. (1988). *Families and larger systems: A family therapist's guide through the labyrinth*. New York: Guilford.

Imber-Black, E. (1989). Idiosyncratic life cycle transitions and therapeutic rituals. In B. Carter, & M. McGoldrick (Eds.), *The changing family life cycle: A framework for family therapy* (pp. 149–163). Boston: Allyn and Bacon.

Imber-Black, E. (Ed.). (1993). *Secrets in families and family therapy*. New York: Norton.

Imber-Black, E., & Roberts, J. (1992). *Rituals for our times: Celebrating, healing, and changing our lives and our relationships*. New York: HarperCollins.

Imber-Black, E., Roberts, J., & Whiting, R. (Eds.). (1988). *Rituals in families and family therapy*. New York: Norton.

Interplay. (1991a, March). [Newsletter of the international playback theatre network. PO Box 1173, New Paltz, NY 12561].

Interplay. (1991b, November). [Newsletter of the international playback theatre network. PO Box 1173, New Paltz, NY 12561].

Interplay. (1992, July). [Newsletter of the international playback theatre network. PO Box 1173, New Paltz, NY 12561].

Irwin, E. C., & Malloy, E. S. (1975). Family puppet interview. *Family Process*, 14(2), 179–191.

Junge, M. B. (1992). The book about daddy dying: A preventive art therapy technique. In J. D. Atwood (Ed.), *Family therapy: A systemic behavioral approach* (pp. 286–297). Chicago: Nelson-Hall.

Kincaid, J. R. (1992, May 3). Who gets to tell their stories? *New York Times Book Review*, pp. 1, 24–29.

Krementz, J. (1982). *How it feels to be adopted*. New York: Knopf.

Laird, J. (1989). Women and stories: Restorying women's self-constructions. In M. McGoldrick, C. M. Anderson, & F. Walsh (Eds.), *Women in families: A framework for family therapy* (pp. 427–450). New York: Norton.

Laird, J. (1993a). Women's secrets—women's silences. In E. Imber-Black (Ed.), *Secrets in families and family therapy* (pp. 243–267). New York: Norton.

Laird, J. (1993b). Lesbian families: A cultural rather than a psychological perspective. Part of a plenary presentation, *Dealing with invisibility*, at AFTA preconference workshop, "Culture, power and the family," Baltimore, MD.

Lankton, C., & Lankton, S. (1989). *Tales of enchantment: Goal oriented metaphors for adults and children in therapy*. New York: Brunner/Mazel.

Lankton, S., & Lankton, C. (1983). *The answer within: A clinical framework of Ericksonian hypnotherapy*. New York: Brunner/Mazel.

Lively, P. (1991). *City of the mind*. New York: HarperCollins.

Loury, G. C. (1993). Free at last? A personal perspective on race and identity in

America. In G. Early (Ed.), *Lure and loathing: Essays on race, identity, and the ambivalence of assimilation* (pp. 1–12). New York: Allen Lane/The Penguin Press.

Lynch, P. (1992, June 18). *Presidential Plenary: Facing death and loss: The unmet challenge for families and family therapy.* Presented at the American Family Therapy Academy Annual Meeting, Amelia Island, Florida.

Martin, J., Feldman, M. S., Hatch, M. J., & Sitkin, S. B. (1983). The uniqueness paradox in organizational stories. *Administrative Science Quarterly, 28,* 438–453.

Metzger, D. (1993, March/April). Writing for your life. *MS.,* 82–83.

Minuchin, S. (Therapist), & Goldner, V. (Ed.). (1982). *Just a house, not a home* [Videotape]. Philadelphia Child Guidance Clinic.

Mitchell, J. H. (1984). *Ceremonial time: Fifteen thousand years on one square mile.* Anchor Press/Doubleday.

Mittrof, I., & Kilmer, R. H. (1975, July). Stories managers tell: A new tool for organizational problem solving. *Management Review, 64,* 18–28.

Myerhoff, B. (1982). Life history among the elderly: Performance, visibility and remembering. In J. Ruby (Ed.), *A crack in the mirror: Reflexive perspectives in anthropology.* Philadelphia: University of Pennsylvania Press.

O'Connor, S. (1990). *Tokens of grace: A novel in stories* (p. ii). Minneapolis: Milkweek Editions.

Olson, M. E. (1990). *Reflecting teams and supervision.* Unpublished manuscript.

Onions, C. T. (Ed.). (1983). *Oxford Dictionary of English Etymology.* Oxford, Great Britain: University Press.

Papp, P. (1976). Family choreography. In P. J. Guerin (Ed.), *Family therapy: Theory and practice.* New York: Gardner.

Papp, P., Silverstein, O., & Carter, E. (1975). Family sculpting in preventive work with "well" families. *Family Process, 14*(2), 197–212.

Penn, P. (1985). Feed–forward: Future questions, future maps. *Family Process, 24,* 299–310.

Rampage, C. (1991). Personal authority and women's self-stories. In T. J. Goodrich (Ed.), *Women and power: Perspectives for family therapy* (pp. 109–122). New York: Norton.

Richard, P. (1993, April 18). Obscene pleasure: Art among the corpses. *The Washington Post,* pp. G1, G6.

Roberts, J. (1982). The development of a team approach in live supervision. *Journal of Strategic and Systemic Therapies, I*(2), 24–35.

Roberts, J. (1983). Two models of live supervision: Collaborative team and supervisor guided. *Journal of Strategic and Systemic Therapies, II*(2), 68–84.

Roberts, J. (1986). An evolving model: Links between the Milan approach and strategic models of family therapy. In D. Efron (Ed.), *Journeys: Expansion of the strategic-systemic therapies* (pp. 150–173). New York: Brunner/Mazel.

Roberts, J. (1988a). Use of ritual in "redocumenting" psychiatric history. In Imber-Black, E., Roberts, J., & Whiting, R. (Eds.), *Rituals in families and family therapy* (pp. 307–330). New York: Norton.

Roberts, J. (1988b). Mythmaking in the land of imperfect specialness: Lions, laundry baskets and cognitive deficits. *Journal of Psychotherapy and the Family, 4,* 81–110.

Roberts, J. (1991). Sugar and spice, toads and mice: Gender issues in family therapy training. *Journal of Marital and Family Therapy, 2,* 121–132.

REFERENCES

Roberts, J., Matthews, W., Bodin, N. A., Cohen, D., Lewandowski, L., Novo, J., & Willis, C. (1989). Training with O (observing) and T (treatment) teams in live supervision: Reflections in the looking glass. *Journal of Marital and Family Therapy, 15*, 397–410.

Roiphe, A. (1992, April 12). Children's books. *New York Times Book Review*, p. 28.

Rosen, S. (Ed.). (1982). *My voice will go with you: The teaching tales of Milton H. Erickson*. New York: Norton.

Rosenwald, G. C., & Ochberg, R. L. (Eds.). (1992). *The cultural politics of self-understanding*. New Haven, CT: Yale University Press.

Sacks, J. M. (1974). The letter. *The Journal of Group Psychotherapy and Psychodrama, 27*, 184–190.

Salas, J. (1983). Culture and community: Playback theatre. *The Drama Review, 27*(2), 15–25.

Sanders, G. (1992, June 19). The love that dares to speak its name: A choice for gay and lesbian families. Presented at the American Family Therapy Academy Annual Meeting, Amelia Island, Florida.

Schneider, P. (1993). *Long way home*. Amherst, MA: Amherst Writers & Writer's Press.

Selvini Palazzoli, M., Boscolo, L., Cecchin, G., & Prata, G. (1977). Family rituals: A powerful tool in family therapy. *Family Process, 16*(4), 445–454.

Shadow of a doubt: Therapists and the false memory debate. (1993, September/October). *Family Therapy Networker*.

Shank, R. C. (1990). *Tell me a story: A new look at real and artificial memory*. New York: Charles Scribner's Sons.

Sherman, R., & Fredman, N. (1986). *Handbook of structured techniques in marriage and family therapy*. New York: Brunner/Mazel.

Shorris, E. (1993, June 12). Diversity within diversity: Latinos in the United States. Keynote Address at the AFTA National Conference, Baltimore, Maryland.

Simon, R. M. (1972). Sculpting the family. *Family Process, 11*, 49–57.

Smiley, J. (1991). *A thousand acres*. New York: Alfred A. Knopf.

Smith, H. (1991). *The new Russians*. New York: Avon.

Smith, L. (1986). *Family linen*. New York: Ballantine.

Stone, E. (1988). *Black sheep and kissing cousins*. New York: Times Books.

Strand, M. (1991, September 15). Slow down for poetry. *New York Times Book Review*, pp. 1, 36–37.

Suyemoto, K. L. (1992). *Roles and rules in three Japanese-American families*. Unpublished manuscript.

Tsempoukis, C. (1968). *Bibliocounseling: Theory and research implications for and applications in counseling and guidance*. Unpublished doctoral dissertation, University of Wisconsin, Madison.

Uchida, Y. (1982). *Desert exile: The uprooting of a Japanese-American family*. Seattle, WA: University of Washington Press.

Voices. (1992, Fall). [A report from The Oral History Center, 186½ Hampshire Street, Cambridge, MA 02139].

Watson, B. (1990, October 24). Interview with John Edgar Wideman. *Amherst Bulletin*, pp. 1, 21.

Weatherford, J. (1988). *Indian givers: How the Indians of the Americas transformed the world*. New York: Ballantine.

Weiner, P. J., & Stein, R. M. (1985). *Adolescents, literature and work with youth*. Hazelton, PA: Haworth.

Weltner, L. (1991, October 4). A life history that's overdue for revisions. *The Boston Globe*, p. 63.

White, M. (1994). *Narrative therapy training with Michael White: One week intensive courses*. (Brochure available from Dulwich Centre, 345 Carrington Street, Adelaide, South Australia 5000.)

White, M., & Epston, D. (1990). *Narrative means to therapeutic ends*. New York: Norton.

Whiting, R. (1988). Guidelines to designing therapeutic rituals. In Imber-Black, E., Roberts, J., & Whiting, R. (Eds.), *Rituals in families and family therapy* (pp. 84–109). New York: Norton.

Wiener, D. (in press). *Rehearsals for growth: Theater improvisation for psychotherapists*. New York: Norton.

Yolen, J. (1986). *Favorite folktales from around the world*. New York: Random House.

Zilbach, J. (1986). *Young children in family therapy*. New York: Brunner/ Mazel.

INDEX

Abuladze, T., 124
adoption, 18–19, 103–4
affirmations, 98, 99, 101
African-American stories, 129, 143–44
Akeret, R., 164, 165*n*
alcoholism, 141–42
Alicia's Story, 104–5
Allen, J., 132–33
Anderson, C., 164
Anderson, H., 25, 26
Anonymous, 199
appreciation notes, 99, 100–101, 102
audiotaping stories, 24, 99

Bass, E., 10
Becker, A. L., 8
Being Adopted (Herbert), 104
Belenky, M. F., 57, 58
Benjamin, W., 11
Berger, J., 71
Billingsley, A., 129
Black Ice (Carey), 2–3, 146
Blount, A., 114
Blythe, R., 8
Boscolo, L., 64
Bowen, M., 199
Bowenian family therapy, 9, 167, 172, 175
Brady, K., 142

cancer, 23
Carey, L., 1, 2–3, 146
Carter, E. A., 106

case examples
  adoption
    Deana, 103–4
    Mark Roberts, 18–19
  cultural stories
    Chieh Li, 152–54
    Chin Savin, 141
    Jamila Sands, 143–44
    Jennifer Iré, 173–74
    Karen Suyemoto, 127–29
    Natasha, 125–27
  death
    Katie, 46–47
    Lorna, 183, 190–91
    Peter Lynch, 198–99
  distinct stories, Stan Fujita, 15
  divorce
    Clara and Connie, 107–8
    Droke family, 93–94
  family
    Amanda and Tanya, 101
    Andrew Oxman, 171, 172–73
    Baldridge family, 113
    Claire, 176–77
    Devereux family, 119–120
    Gloria and Norma, 116–17
    Grant family, 162–63
    Kay Odo, 57–58, 71
    Moscone family, 4–5
    Nelson family, 64–65
    O'Callahan family, 88–89
    Sara and Jean, 137
    Stephen, 147, 148, 174–75, 181–82
    Stern family, 192–93

case examples (*continued*)
  floor plans, Burt, 166
  genograms, Rose Lowenstein, 167, 169
  illness, Amita, 156–57
  intertwined stories, Crooms family, 12
  marriage
    Denzler-Wills family, 47–48
    Mata-Rosario family, 7
    Suong family, 139–140
    Thompson-Nelson family, 45–46
  memory, Gary and Greg, 69
  minimal/interrupted stories, Sarah John-
    son, 16
  organizations
    counseling program, 196–97
    homeless organization, 193–94
    human service institute, 183, 194–
      95
    Thanks Cards, 102
  parenting
    Abramson family, 54–55
    Burdette family, 53–54
    Cohen family, 48–50, 92
    Delano family, 43–45
    Guttman-Sneh family, 138–39
    Jones family, 66–67, 71
    Marissa and Doug, 99–101
    Nielson family, 13–14
    Pineda family, 72–74
    Roy and Greg, 94–95
  photos
    Peter Kearn, 164–65
    Yolonda, 165–66
  remarriage
    Diessner family, 29–30
    Donald Dragon's Divorce Book, 31–
      43
    Guttman-Sneh family, 138–39
    Merker-Hamilton family, 51–53
    Natalya Weinstein-Roberts, 89–90
    Saari-Moriarty family, 204–5
    Schutte family, 210
    Sterling-Isaacson family, 102
  rigid stories
    Leon, 156–57
    Tom, 20
  sexual abuse
    Barbara, 142
    Mercedes Gonzalez, 59–63, 71
    Quinlan family, 76–81, 82–83, 85–86
  sculpting stories
    Giardini family, 118
    Harris-Morgan family, 118
  stories
    Lavinia Lockhart, *xiii–xv*
    Natalya Weinstein-Roberts, 5–7
  therapist
    Greg Hocott, 147–48, 181
    Jocelyn Robinson, 148, 179–181
    Gary Sanders, 198
case reports, 112–15
  and the client's voice, 122
  coauthoring with clients, 84, 112–14
Chasin, R., 119
child abuse stories, 53–55
children
  in family therapy, 59
  sharing adult stories with, 92–93
  as silent in families, 57, 152–53
  theater work with, 207
Children in Family Contexts (Combrinck-
    Graham), 59*n*
children's stories, 24, 94–95, 103
  reading other, 106
  written, 104–6
Chinese cultural stories, 152–53
class, stories about, 173–74
Clifton, D., 159*n*
Cohen, C., 201, 202, 205
Cohen, R., 112
Coles, R., 5
Colman-McGill, H., 32–41
Colman-McGill, J., 32–41, 42
Combrinck-Graham, L., 59*n*
Combs, G., 23–24
community stories, 1, 184, 200–203, 205–
    9, 210
  power differentials in, 202
Coppersmith, E., 96, 166
countertransference, 86–87
couples therapy, 7, *see also* marriage
    therapy
The Courage to Heal (Bass), 10–11,
    103
Crites, S., 4
cultural stories, 123–146
  African-American, 129, 143–44
  of American ethnic minorities, 125,
    127–29, 140, 143–44
  Chinese, 152–54
  danger in telling, 129
  dominant, 27, 125, 129, 132
  family therapy theories and, 145–46
  gay and lesbian, 129
  hidden, 129
  of the Holocaust, 144–45
  of identity, 143–44
  Japanese-American, 127–29, 134
  of migration, 132, 143–44
  personal and, 129–146
  of Russia and the former Soviet Union,
    123–24, 125–27, 129, 135–36

silenced, 127–28
therapy techniques with, 134–35
and time, 130–31
cut-offs in families, 147, 170, 181–82

Davis, J., 108
death, 46–47, 56, 155–56, 165, 166, 190–91, 198–99
depression, 16
Desert Exile (Uchida), 128
directive interventions, 9
divorce and separation, 31–42, 43–45, 89–90, 93–94, 106, 107–8, 162–63
Donald Dragon's Divorce Book, 32–40, 106
doubling, 95–96
drawing stories, 76, 78–80, 81
drug abuse, 64–65
Duhl, F., 117

eating disorders, 190–91
empowering clients, 53–54, 112
enacted stories, 81, 82–83, 84, 115–122, 158–160
accessing emotions through, 115, 120
safety in, 115–16
Erickson, M., 23, 24, 31
"Escape from Bickering" (video), 26
ethnicity, 134, 140, 143–44
exercises
Developing as a Supervisor, 185–190
Different Ways of Working with Stories in Therapy, 157–58
Examining Oral, Written, and Enacted Story Forms, 158–160
Finding the Stories [in organizations], 196–97
Listening and Being Listened To, 151–54
Listening and the Therapy Process, 160–63
for story facilitation, 163–170
Stories, Styles, and Resonance, 154–57
Using Family Photos in Therapy, 164–66
Using Floor Plans in Therapy, 166–67
Using Genograms in Therapy, 167–170

fables and storytelling, 93
fables, unfinished, 84, 94–95
"false memory" syndrome, 70n
families
cut-offs in, 147, 170, 181–82
empowering, 53–54
narrative experiences of, 57

ritual life of, 28–29
silent, 57
and voice, 57
family book, 109–111
descriptive chapter titles in, 110
as holding place for emotions, 110
family choreography, 117
Family Linen (Smith), 19n
family photos, 164–66
family stories, 1, 2–3, 23–43, 48–50
and history, 3
multigenerational, 3
shared by therapist, 51, 52
shifts of meaning in, 2
in social context, 2
of therapist trainees, 148–150
writing, 175–78
family therapy
with children, 59
dual listening in, 153–54
listening in, 9
solution-focused, 9
and stories, 10, 23–27
strategic, 9
structural, 9
theories, 9, 28, 145
see also case examples, family
fantasy, 72–74
in storytelling, 48–50
Father's Day (Brady), 142
feminism and women of color, 132
floor plans, 166–67
Foucault, M., 26
Fox, J., 206, 209
Frank, A., 144–45

Gale, J., 58–59
Gardner, R., 24, 31
gay and lesbian stories, 129, 145, 148, 171, 172–73, 179–181, 198
genograms, 143, 167–170
Ghnaim, F. A., 201
Goldman, M., 127
Goolishian, H., 25, 26
Gordon, D., 23
gossip, 194, 195
Griffin, P., 129
Griots of Roxbury project, 202–3
Grossman, C. L., 132
Guest, J., 173–75

Hadas, R., 68
Haley, A., 144
Haley, J., 175–76, 193
Heat-Moon, W. L., 63
Henne, A., 207–8

Herbert family, 104
historical context of stories, 1–2
Hoffman, E., 143*n*
Hoffman, L., 183–84, 190, 191
Holocaust stories, 49, 131–32, 144–45,
    202, 207
Homes, A. M., 171–73
How It Feels to Be Adopted (Krementz),
    103
Howe, J. W., 2
Hugo, R., 71
hypnotherapy, 23–24

I Miss My Foster Parents (Herbert), 104
illness, 161
    stories about, 156–57
images and symbols in stories, 78, 81, 190,
    191–93
imagination, 67
    and memory, 69
    and time, 71
Imber-Black, E., 19*n*, 28, 30, 54, 62, 98,
    112, 114, 147*n*, 152, 191, 202
indexing experience, using stories as a way
    of, 5
Interplay, 206, 207, 208, 209
Irwin, E. C., 119

Jack (Homes), 171–73
Japanese-American cultural stories, 127–
    29, 134
Junge, M. B., 109–110
"Just a House, Not a Home" (video), 93

Katzenback, M., 205–6
Kincaid, J. R., 125
Krementz, J., 103

Laird, J., 9, 27, 145, 168*n*
language and therapy, 27, 149–150, 155
Lankton, C., 23
lesbian stories, 145, 148, 179–181, *see
    also* gay and lesbian stories
"Let Life Be Yours" (video), 202
letter writing, 106–8
    decisions about sending letter in, 106–7
    and stories, 61–62, 84, 93–94, 99
    as structured storytelling, 106
    verbal, 84, 94
life cycle, 20–21, 65, 164
listening, 89–90, 95, 140–42, 151–54
    in family therapy, 9, 153–54
    levels of, 150, 160–63
    to stories, 43–50, 150–163
    and telling stories, 11
literacy training, 184, 200–201

Lively, P., 63
Lockerman, G., 86*n*
loss, 56
    stories about, 46–47
Lost in Translation (Hoffman), 143*n*
Loury, G., 135
Lynch, P., 198–99

Madanes, C., 175–76
marriage stories, 7–8, 45–46, 47–48, 139–
    140, 177–78
marriage therapy, 7, 45–46, 47–48, 139–140
Martin, J., 196*n*
meaning-making, *see* stories and meaning-
    making
memory, 5, 67–70, 71–75
men's stories, *see* stories, men's
Metzger, D., 21
Milan model of family therapy, 9, 28
Mills, A. M., 130–31
"mini" stories, 99–102
Minuchin, S., 93
mirror stories, 84, 92–93, 96
Mitchell, J. H., 63
Mittrof, I., 196*n*
Mullins, J., 111
museums as storytellers, 130, 131–32,
    144–45
Myerhoff, B., 25

Narrative Means to Therapeutic Ends
    (White), 26, 27
Native American stories, 130–31
normalizing, 134
    through storytelling, 51, 52–53, 84–85,
    96
novels in story work, 103, 213–15
    plays and, 170–75, 205–8, 215–16

O'Connor, S., 71
O'Hanlon, W. H., 58–59
Olson, M. E., 189
one-voice families, 57
one-way mirror, 93, 100
    and structured storytelling, 84, 95–96
Onions, C. T., 185
oral history, 184, 200–205
    and community art forms, 203
    and therapy, 203–5
Oral History Center (Cambridge, MA),
    201, 202, 203
oral vs. written storytelling, 9
Ordinary People (Guest), 173–75
organizational context, personal stories in,
    198–200
    guidelines for sharing, 200

organizational stories, 102, 183, 184,
    193–200, 210
  boundaries in sharing, 199–200
  public vs. private, 193–94
  unspoken, 194
Ortega y Gasset, J., 8

Papp, P., 117
parenting, 92
  stories, 13–14, 43–45, 48–50, 53–54,
    54–55, 66–67, 68–69, 72–74, 92,
    99–101, 137, 138–39
"pass rule" in therapy, 119
Penn, P., 139
personal stories, 22, 123–24, 198–200
  in cultural context, 123–146
  and ethnicity, 134
  in larger context, 133–144
photos in storytelling, 29, 164–66
playback theater, 205–8
Playback Theater, 206–8
polyphonic-voice families, 57
power differential in community stories, 202
power and storytelling, 26
Pozner, V., 123, 124
"The Princess That Liked to Say *No!*", 73–74
private stories, 50–53, 54–55, 193–94
psychodrama, 206, 208–9
public stories, 50, 53–55, 76–81, 112–15,
    193–94
  and museums, 130–32, 144–45
puppets, 116, 119–120
  and stories, 78, 79, 84

racism, 144
Rampage, C., 27
recovering memories, 69
refugee stories, 141, 156
Rehearsals for Growth, 208*n*
Reimer, G., 201–2
remarriage, 102, 192–93
  stories, 29–30, 31–43, 51–53, 89–90,
    138–39, 204–5, 210
"Repentance" (film), 124
restorying, 27, 31, 44, 47–48, 50, 61
  and therapy, 25, 27
  with children, 24
Richard, P., 131
Rittenberg, S., 127
rituals and stories, 28–31
Rituals for Our Times (Imber-Black and
    Roberts), 152*n*
Roberts, J., 28, 49, 50, 54, 112, 114, 170
Roiphe, A., 22
role playing, 116–17, 120
  exchanging roles in, 117

Roots (Haley), 144
Rosen, S., 23, 24
Rosenwald, G. C., 145
Russian cultural stories, 123–24, 125–27,
    129, 135–36

Sacks, J. M., 94
safety issues, 119, 160, 184, 199–200
  in storytelling, 17, 19, 115–16
Salas, J., 206*n*, 207
Sanders, G., 198
Sando, Joe S., 125
Satir, V., 176
Schneider, P., *xvi*
school-family groups, 200–201
sculpting stories, 80, 84, 116, 117–19,
    120, 170
secret stories, 12, 17–19, 64–65, 121,
    126, 127–28, 142, 148
Secrets in Families and Family Therapy
    (Imber-Black), 19*n*
Selvini Palazzoli, M., 28, 31
separation and divorce stories, 43–45, 93–
    94, 107–8, 162–63
sexual abuse, 191
  stories, 10–11, 59–63, 69–70, 76–81,
    82–83, 85–86, 142, 145–46
Shank, R. C., 5, 67
Shevstova, L., 208
Sherman, R., 164
Shorris, E., 136
sibling stories, 69
silence, 9, 11
silent families, 57
Simon, R. M., 117
slavery, African-American, 129, 144
Smiley, J., 69–70
Smith, H., 123, 124
Smith, L., 19*n*
solution–focused therapy, 9, 26, 58–59
Soviet Union, former, *see* Russian cultural
    stories
Sparrow, L., 195
spoken stories, 76–97, 122
Stone, E., *xiii*, 143
stories
  see also separate entries for stories: Afri-
    can–American, child abuse, children,
    community, drawing, enacted, fam-
    ily, gay and lesbian, Holocaust,
    Japanese-American, Native Ameri-
    can, organizational, personal, pri-
    vate, public, refugee, Russian cul-
    tural, sculpting, secret, separation
    and divorce, spoken, written
  adapting for different listeners, 140–42

stories (*continued*)
  audio/videotaping, 24, 99
  case reports as, 112–15
  chaotic, 93
  child psychiatry and, 24
  choosing reading material for working
    with, 103
  about class, 173–74
  cohering, 44, 46–47, 60, 148, 155–56
  connecting indices in, 5–7
  connecting people through, 44–45
  correcting, 112–15
  different interpretations of, 4, 7–8
  distinct/separated, 12, 15–16, 64
  double-sided, 123–27
  emotional distance provided by reading,
    103
  emotional state of teller of, 11
  Erickson's use of, 23, 24
  evolving, 12, 20–21, 64
  and family therapy, 10, 23–27
  giving back, 84, 89–91, 96
  hidden, 60, 129
  historical context of, 1–2
  hypnotherapy in, 23–24
  and identity, 143–44
  about illness, 156
  and information-processing, 5–7
  interrupted, 12, 16–17, 64
  intertwined, 12–15, 64, 66–67
    and time, 14
  interweaving, 209–211
  invented, 43, 44, 48–50
  joining with clients through, 43
  and letter writing, 61–62, 93–94, 99,
    106–8
  and life-cycle stages, 20–21, 65
  listeners and tellers of, 11
  listening to, 43–50, 150–163
  about loss, 46–47
  and meaning-making, 4, 5, 6, 14, 25,
    26, 56, 71–72, 74–75, 83, 134
  and memory, 5, 67–70
  men's private, 133
  men's public, 132–33
  of migration, 132, 143–44
  "mini," 84, 99–102
  minimal/interrupted, 12, 16–17, 64
  mirror, 84, 92–93, 96
  mutation of, 2
  normalizing function of, 51, 52–53, 84–
    85, 96
  puppets and, 78, 79, 84
  reading other people's, 84, 102–6
  reauthoring, 25
  resurrecting/building, 16, 17

  rewriting, 68–69
  rigid, 12, 19–20, 64, 121, 156
  rituals and, 28–31
  separated, 12, 15–16, 64
  sharing, 6–7, 199–200
    outside therapy, 183–211
    painful, 61
  silenced/secret, 12, 17–19, 25, 64–65,
    121, 126, 127–28, 142, 148
  in social and historical context, 1–2, 25,
    27, 136–42
  and supervision, 185–193
  symbols in, 78, 81, 190, 191–93
  and theater work, 184, 200, 205–9
  therapist's voice in, 26–27
  in therapy, 7, 21–22, 112–15
    flexibility of, 22
    see also case examples
  and time, 3–4, 5, 14, 15, 19, 20–21, 43,
    63–67, 136
    in cultural and social context, 130–31,
    138–139
  and "truth," 48, 69
  unspoken, 48, 59–62, 194
  untold, 177
  using novels and plays in, 103, 170–75,
    205–8, 213–16
story
  and audience, 9, 10
  cohering a, 44
  domains, 50–55, *see also* private stories;
    public stories
  facilitation exercises, 163–170
  writing one's, 84, 109–111
story form
  choosing a, 83, 121–22, 158–160
  enacted, 81, 82–83, 84, 115–122, 158–
    160
  meaning-making and, 83
  spoken, 81, 82–83
  written, 81, 82, 83
story frames, extended, 170–181
story-go-rounds, 84, 87–89, 96
story styles, 11–21, 22, 154–57
  table of, 13
story techniques, appropriate use of, 134–
  35
storytelling
  changing the listener in, 140–42
  doubling in, 95–96
  fables and, 93, 94–95
  fantasy and, 48–50
  interactive nature of, 140
  museums and, 130, 131–32, 144–45
  normalizing through, 51, 52–53, 84–85,
    96

"pass rule" in therapeutic, 119
photos in, 29, 164–66
and power, 26
safety in, 17, 19, 115–16
silence in, 9
in social and historical context, 1–2, 25,
    27, 136–142
structured, 84, 93–96, 106
time in, 64, 65
story work
    flexibility of, *xv*
    in therapy, *xv*
    with novels and plays, 170–75
Strand, M., 56
structured storytelling, 84, 93–96
    letter writing as, 106
    one-way mirror and, 95–96
suicide, 109–110, 169–170
supervision, 159, 185–193
    fit of, 193
supervisor as "expert," 185
Suyemoto, Karen, 127–29
symbols in storytelling, 78, 81, 190, 191–93

"teaching tales" in family therapy, 23, 24
thank you cards, 99, 102
theater stories, 184, 200, 205–9
theme stories, 44, 45–46, 50, 66
"therapeutic conversations," 25
therapeutic questions for
    choosing a story form, 121, 158
    evolving stories, 21
    intertwined stories, 14
    listening, 152, 154, 161
    minimal/interrupted stories, 17
    organizations, 197
    restorying, 27
    rigid stories, 20
    separated stories, 15
    silenced/secret stories, 19
    a solution–focus, 26
    story environment, 154–55
    supervision, 159, 186, 188
    taking a family history, 57, 168
    time, 65
therapist
    as "expert," 58–59, 112, 149
    in relation to client stories, 7–8
    training, 147–182
        exercise in listening in, 150–163
        feedback in, 159–160
        sharing stories in, 148–150
therapist-client relationship, *xv*, 30, 59,
    84, 134–35
    and trainees, 150
therapists and power, 58–59

therapists' personal stories, 23–25, 84–86,
    178–181
    sharing with clients
        countertransference in, 86–87
        as normalizing, 84–85
therapists' professional stories, 85, 148,
    170–71
    of lesbian therapists, 148, 179–181
    other professionals as a resource for,
        178–181
therapy
    with cultural stories, 134–35
    and language, 27, 149–150, 155
    narrative, 24–25
    and oral history, 203–5
    "pass rule" in, 119
    and politics, 25, 26
    and restorying, 25, 27
    solution-focused, 9, 26, 58–59
    stories, 7, 21–22, 112–15, *see also* case
        examples
    and story work, *xv*, 157–58
    strategic, 9
    structural, 9
    and theater, 184, 200, 205–9
    witnessing in, 9
A Thousand Acres (Smiley), 69–70
time
    and cultural stories, 130–31
    and evolving stories, 64
    and future-oriented questions, 139
    and imagination, 71
    and the life cycle, 65
    and memory, 69
    as a perspective in storytelling, 64, 65
    and stories, 3–4, 5, 14, 19, 20–21, 43,
        63–67, 130–31, 136, 138–39
time line, historical, 135–36
    personalizing, 136
    Russian, 135, 136
trainee feedback, 159–160
*Treating Young Children in Family Ther-
    apy* (Combrinck-Graham), 59*n*
"truth" in stories, 48, 69
Tsempoukis, C., 102

Uchida, Y., 128

violence, 190–91, 202–3
    in relationship, 47–48
The Visit (Herbert), 104
voice, 1, 10, 26–27, 56–63, 115, 122
    and memory, 69, 71–75
voices, women's, 57–58
Voices, 202, 203
volunteer literacy, 184, 200–201

Watson, B., 125
Weatherford, J., 130
Weiner, P. J., 102–3
Weinstein-Roberts, N., 5–7, 31–41, 42, 89–90
Weltner, L., 68–69
White, M., 25, 26–27, 190
Whiting, R., 66, 98
Wideman, J. E., 125
Wiener, D., 208*n*
Wilkerson, C., 192–93
women's stories, 27, 111, 136, 139–140, 202

women's voices, 57–58
written stories, 9, 31–43, 81, 82, 83, 84, 98–115, 122, 175–78
    flexibility of, 98, 109
    presenting, 106
    reflective distance in, 115
    using computer for, 98–99

Yolen, J., 1
Young Children in Family Therapy (Zilbach), 59*n*

Zilbach, J., 59*n*